AILA Review

World Applied Linguistics

A Celebration of 40 years of AILA

VOLUME 17 2004

Guest Editors Susan M. Gass
Michigan State University

Sinfree Makoni
Pennsylvania State University

Editors Jasone Cenoz
University of the Basque Country

Jean-Marc Dewaele
University of London

Editorial Board Kees de Bot
University of Groningen

Marilda C. Cavalcante
State University of Campinas

Ulrike H. Meinhof
University of Southampton

Dieter Wolff
University of Essen

John Benjamins Publishing Company
Amsterdam/Philadelphia

Table of contents

Introduction

Susan Gass and Sinfree Makoni

Michigan State University / Pennsylvania State University

This volume celebrates the 40th anniversary of the International Association of Applied Linguistics/ Association Internationale de Linguistique Appliquée (AILA).

Applied Linguistics is a diverse discipline with many scholarly areas incorporated into the mainstream. To commemorate this anniversary, we invited contributors from around the globe to present their perspectives of Applied Linguistics and to represent a sampling of ideas from the geographical area in which they conduct research. This is, of course, from the outset an impossible task and one on which we tread lightly and with some trepidation.

When the idea for this volume was raised at an AILA Executive Board meeting, objections were brought forward relating to the impossibility of thorough coverage. Comments such as "what about research in X, where will that be covered?" For us that missed the point of what we aim to accomplish with this collection of papers. We hope that the issues raised will acquaint the reader with a wide-range of perspectives and will allow the reader to understand how researchers from across the globe approach some of the same applied linguistic problems but from different vantage points.

But perhaps it is just as easy to say what this volume is not as it is to say what it is. It is not intended to represent all areas of Applied Linguistics; nor is it intended to cover all geographical areas/countries of the world. This would be akin to acquainting people with all the culinary tastes of the world, another impossible task. What we hope it does do is present a snapshot of applied linguistic research from as many directions and traditions that are possible in a small volume of this sort and in this sense to celebrate the diversity that is applied linguistics. We also intend that this volume will be of some relevance historically in giving a sense of the different directions applied linguistics is taking in various parts of the world. Given the diversity of the geographical contexts in which applied linguistics has emerged there are multiple histories of applied linguistics which differ depending on the geographical location. We therefore hope this may provide opportunities to reflect on what applied linguistics looked like 40 years ago and what its current 'complexion' is.

We begin the volume with a paper Albert Valdman that gives a brief history of AILA. The paper is not a history of Applied Linguistics as a discipline, but focuses on AILA as an organization. This is followed by a paper by Martin Bygate that addresses issues of concern to applied linguists regardless of location — that of applied linguistics as an emerging discipline and of the responsibility of applied linguistics to a lay and an academic public. The remainder of the papers in this issue are written about research in various locations of the world, including, Europe, Asia, Africa, Latin America (Brazilian focus), North America, and Australia/New Zealand. The collection concludes with a paper by Chris Brumfit who was tasked with the responsibility of examining whether there was any underlying conceptual unity in all the diversity that has become Applied Linguistics.

We would like to thank Jasone Cenoz and Jean-Marc Dewaele for their constant support and assistance. We also greatly appreciate the reviewers of this volume who went to great lengths to give fast and thoughtful comments to the papers that appear here and we are grateful to Kerry Ard for het editorial assistance. Finally, we thank Kees Vaes of John Benjamins for his patience throughout the process. We are grateful to all of these individuals.

AILA Review 17 (2004), 1–1.

ISSN 1461–0213 / E-ISSN 1570–5595 ©John Benjamins Publishing Company

Réflexions sur l'histoire de l'AILA

Albert Valdman
Indiana University

Albert Valdman traces the history of AILA through his memories of its origins in the early 1960s in France to its place today as the umbrella organization of over 30 national associations from all over the world. He begins with a discussion of AILA's early days — centered in Western Europe and focused on language learning — and follows its expansion in North America and the rest of the world and to other domains of applied linguistics. Along the way, he cites significant meetings, resulting publications, research groups, the question of language use within the organization and many linguists who have contributed to the evolution of AILA.

Mots clés : Applied linguistics, history of the AILA organization

J'ai le plaisir de répondre à l'aimable invitation de Susan Gass de livrer quelques réflexions sur l'AILA. Certes, il serait trop ambitieux de tenter une sorte d'historique de l'Association, surtout qu'à ma connaissance il n'existe guère d'archives centrales. Aussi, je me contenterai de faire état d'événements que je considère comme marquants. Evidemment, je ne pourrais me libérer totalement de tout subjectivisme et mes remarques seront teintées de mon expérience personnelle en tant que membre du Bureau Exécutif (BE) durant une période que j'estime déterminante pour l'évolution de l'AILA.

Rédiger cette note sur certains moments clé de l'AILA en français s'imposait puisque c'est en France qu'a été fondée l'Association. Sa création a été due aux efforts conjugués de linguistes français sous l'impulsion d'Antoine Culioli, professeur à la Sorbonne et initiateur de la linguistique de l'énonciation, et de Guy Capelle, didacticien de langues étrangères et linguiste appliqué, créateur et directeur du BEL (Bureau d'étude et de liaison pour l'enseignement du français dans le monde, créé en 1959), organisme destiné à promouvoir la recherche et la documentation sur l'enseignement du français langue étrangère (FLE) dans une optique internationale, en particulier grâce à la publication de la revue *Le Français dans le monde*.

A cette époque, le BEL, le British Council et le Center for Applied Lingiuistics (CAL) de Washington tenaient des réunions annuelles de coordination. Charles Ferguson, directeur du CAL avait invité Guy Capelle à visiter les centres universitaires (Indiana University, Bloomington, UCLA et the University of Michigan, Ann Arbor entre autres) où fonctionnaient des programmes de linguistique appliquée. A l'issue de ces visites, Guy Capelle avait organisé en décembre 1962, au Centre d'Etudes internationales pédagogiques (CIEP) de Sèvres, une réunion à laquelle avaient assisté les principaux linguistes français. C'est alors que fut lancée l'idée d'une association française de linguistique appliquée, l'AFLA. Dès l'été 1963, le BEL organisa, au nom de la nouvelle association, un premier séminaire d'été, présidé par Antoine Culioli, à La Bouloie, dans le cadre de l'université de Besançon. En novembre 1963, un groupe de linguistes français (Culioli, Bernard Pottier, Denis Girard, Capelle) rencontrèrent Max Gorosh à Stockholm et c'est là que fut décidée la création de l'Association Internationale de Linguistique Appliquée (AILA).

En juillet 1964, un second congrès international fut organisé avec un succès grandissant à Nancy, sans la présence de Capelle, invité au même moment à participer au célèbre Summer Institute de Bloomington organisé sous l'égide de la Linguistic Society of America.

Pendant les dix premières années de sa création l'AILA demeura une institution ancrée en Europe occidentale. En témoigne le lieu des cinq premiers congrès: Besançon, Nancy, Cambridge, Copenhague et Stuttgart. Parmi les personnalités qui marquèrent cette période fondatrice figurent, en plus des Français déjà cités, le Suédois Max Gorosch, le Canadien Guy Rondeau, le Britannique JohnTrim et l'Allemand Gerhardt Nickel — les services inestimables que rendirent ces deux derniers furent reconnus par l'insigne honneur de leur élection au rang de membres honoraires de l'Association. Non seulement ces linguistes appliqués organisèrent des congrès internationaux, mais ils furent les fers de lance de la fondation des associations nationales qui formèrent les assises de l'AILA et en assurèrent les ressources financières. En effet, le rôle des premiers présidents et secrétaires-généraux de l'AILA était bien autre que celui d'assurer la bonne marche des réunions du BE et du Comité International (CI). Il leur incombait de négocier auprès des instances universitaires et scientifiques de leur pays l'obtention des moyens pour l'organisation des réunions annuelles et des congrès et d'étendre l'influence de la discipline par la création d'associations au delà du petit cercle initial de l'Europe de l'ouest et de la Scandinavie.

Un grand tournant dans l'histoire de l'AILA fut l'organisation du congrès de 1978 à l'Université de Montréal. Non seulement cette manifestation représentait-elle la première extension de l'influence de l'AILA et, partant, une certaine structuration de la discipline, dans les terres fertiles de l'Amérique du Nord où, en fait, elle s'était développée et où elle pouvait recevoir l'appui d'un nombre important de chercheurs et d'organismes tels que le CAL. Mais surtout, elle marquait l'élargissement des domaines de la linguistique appliquée au delà de la didactique de l'apprentissage des langues secondes et étrangères. Avec l'avènement de la Révolution Tranquille dans les années soixante s'amorçait au Québec une politique linguistique qui conduisit à la promulgation de la Loi 101 qui instaurait le français comme unique langue officielle. Pour appuyer l'extension de la langue aux domaines commerciaux et administratif, anciens fiefs de l'anglais, furent créés en 1961 l'Office de langue française et, en 1968, la Commission Gendron pour enquêter sur la situation de la langue. A la même période, la Confédération canadienne s'engageait sur la voie du biculturalisme anglais-français et consacrait l'égalité des deux langues sur tout le territoire. En 1968 le Congrès des Etats-Unis adoptait le projet de loi sur l'éducation bilingue. Le site de Montréal se révélait ainsi propice à des communications portant sur les diverses problématiques associées à ces initiatives politiques et sociales: aménagement linguistique, aspects psychologique et psycho-social du bilinguisme, contact linguistique et (autre) sociolinguistique. C'est aussi lors de ce congrès que l'on instaura les commissions scientifiques, réseaux de chercheurs et de professionnels œuvrant dans les divers champs de la linguistique appliquée redéfinie non plus comme discipline tampon entre la linguistique descriptive et la didactique mais comme une discipline carrefour qui promouvait le tissage de liens entre les diverses sciences du langage.

Outre les activités inter-congrès des commissions scientifiques, émergèrent des initiatives collaboratrices regroupant des chercheurs de différents pays pour lesquelles les congrès avaient servi de catalyseurs. C'est le cas exemplaire des colloques de Neuchâtel organisés en Suisse par Pit S. Corder et Eddy Roulet, suite à une rencontre au congrès de Stuttgart. D'abord lieu de discussions stimulantes entre linguistes appliqués européens (Henry Widdowson, Chris Candlin, Jürgen Meisel, Daniel Coste, pour ne mentionner qu'eux), ces colloques attirèrent plus tard des Nord-Américains. L'on comprendra que sous la co-présidence de Corder les colloques de Neuchâtel eurent une influence certaine dans la diffusion de la notion des systèmes approximatifs et des points de vue sur l'acquisition de la langue seconde qui prirent le relais de l'analyse contrastive des années soixante. Je me permets d'inclure ici une note tant soit peu personnelle. Me trouvant en Europe en 1976, j'eus l'honneur de pouvoir me joindre à mes collègues européens et j'introduisis la problématique de la créolisation aux discussions. Se posa, après plusieurs colloques, le problème de la diffusion des actes, disséminés dans diverses publications relativement fugitives qui s'avéraient difficilement accessibles. C'est pour réunir ces actes qu'émergea l'idée de la création d'une revue qui devint *Studies in Second Language Acquisition*.

Un autre résultat direct du congrès de Montréal fut la création de l'American Association for Applied Linguistics grâce aux efforts déployés par Bernard Spolsky, à l'époque doyen à l'University of New Mexico. Ce développement tardif peut surprendre eu égard au poids qu'exerçait la linguistique appliquée américaine dans le domaine théorique et au nombre de centres de recherche et de formation. Cela s'explique par le fait que l'existence du CAL servait à la promotion et à l'articulation d'initiatives dans une large gamme de domaines. Mais ce centre, en tant qu'institution autonome et donc non représentative, ne pouvait être habilité à représenter la totalité des enseignants-chercheurs américains au sein de l'AILA. On peut affirmer qu'à partir de 1981 et du congrès de Lund en Suède l'AILA atteignit sa vitesse de croisière. Le nombre d'associations nationales affiliées augmenta considérablement et leur répartition géographique s'étendit pour inclure l'Amérique Latine, l'Australie, le Japon, Israël, la Côte d'Ivoire et la Tunisie ainsi que les Balkans et quelques pays situés derrière le Rideau de Fer, malgré des procédures et des critères d'admission plus rigoureux pour assurer la représentativité des groupes candidats dans les pays respectifs. Le prestige grandissant de l'AILA se traduisait par une compétition serrée entre associations nationales pour l'organisation des congrès, ce qui en assurait un haut niveau de qualité et créait pour l'Association un source de revenus complétant la modeste cotisation au prorata du nombre d'adhérents imposée aux affiliées. Un BE plus performant élargissait la recherches de ressources financières et de soutien moral auprès d'organismes internationaux tels que l'UNESCO et l'AUPELF (Association des universités entièrement ou partiellement de langue française). Chaque réunion annuelle conjointe du Bureau et du CI s'accompagnait d'un colloque axé sur une problématique scientifique particulière. Par ailleurs ces réunions servaient à familiariser les membres de l'exécutif et du CI avec les conditions logistiques des sites des congrès retenus. Ici, il convient de rendre hommage au dévouement et à l'efficacité de mon prédécesseur aux postes de secrétariat-général et de la présidence, le feu Jos Nivette, membre du bureau de 1975 à 1987, auquel on doit la mise en place d'un grand nombre des ces innovations et améliorations administratives.

C'est aussi cette période qui vit la parution du bulletin de liaison, *Nouvelles de l'AILA* et de la *Revue de l'AILA* et de la signature de conventions avec les revues dans le domaine de la linguistique appliquée qui acceptèrent d'offrir aux membres individuels des affiliées nationales des abonnements à tarif réduit. Rédacteur de la *Revue* et, par surcroît trésorier, Johan Matter, grâce à des efforts personnels, arrivait à produire les milliers d'exemplaires de la Revue à un coût réduit imbattable. La présence de plusieurs des rédacteurs des principales revues de la discipline, dont Alex (Shony) Guiora rédacteur-en-chef de la vénérable *Language Learning*, assurait la haute qualité scientifique de la *Revue*. Il régnait alors au sein du BE un esprit remarquable de dévouement désintéressé qui, par exemple, grâce à la mise à la disposition de l'AILA des ressources des universités où enseignaient les membres du noyau central du BE réduisait les frais de fonctionnement. C'est entre 1987 et 1993 que, grâce aux économies ainsi réalisées, fut lancé le programme de solidarité dont l'objet était de permettre à des chercheurs des pays en voie de développement d'assister aux congrès et de réduire les frais d'adhésion des affiliées de ces pays. On ne peut quitter le volet des publications sans mentionner la *Revue Française de Linguistique Appliquée*, qui relaya le *Bulletin de l'AFLA*, et qui, tout en recevant le soutien de cette Association, jouit aujourd'hui d'une complète indépendance éditoriale. Actuellement placée sous la responsabilité scientifique de Hélène Huot qui, durant de nombreuses années, représenta l'association fondatrice de l'AILA au CI, la *Revue Française de Linguistique Appliquée*, qui a opté pour un regroupement thématique, atteint aujourd'hui, par l'excellente tenue de ses articles, le même niveau de qualité que ses homologues internationaux. La dominance croissante de l'anglais comme lingua franca internationale qui accompagne la mondialisation des échanges culturels et économiques pose le problème de la communication au sein des organismes à vocation internationale.

Comme l'AILA fut fondée en France, il s'ensuivit que ses statuts furent rédigés en français (leur dépôt juridique se fit en Belgique, pays officiellement trilingue). La politique linguistique énoncée dès la formation de l'Association était que les communications aux congrès pouvaient se faire dans l'une ou l'autre des deux langues reconnues comme officielles, l'anglais et le français, ainsi que dans la langue officielle du pays hôte. A ma connaissance, cette dernière option ne fut exercée seulement peut-être qu'en Allemagne puisqu'il n'est pas dans l'intérêt des intervenants de présenter leur recherche dans une langue incompréhensible au public. Le seul cas litigieux fut la proposition d'une communication en macédonien — langue ou dialecte slave selon les diverses opinions à ce sujet en République macédonienne, Bulgarie et Grèce — lors du congrès de 1990 à Halkidiki (Thessalonique), proposition de toute évidence provocatrice vu le contentieux historique qui existe encore concernant la province grecque de la Macédoine. Grâce au bon sens diplomatique des organisateurs grecs le conflit potentiel fut rapidement désamorcé et la communication, portant sur la konéisation d'un dialecte macédonien en Australie, fut présentée en anglais. Durant ma participation aux réunions du BE et du CI des circonstances fortuites firent que le bilinguisme franco-anglais animait les discussions. Outre la présence de Hélène Huot (France), de Jacques Girard (Canada), Jos Nivette et Marc Spoelders (Belgique) et de Georges Lüdi (Suisse), représentants de pays où le français est la langue officielle ou l'une des langues officielles, participaient des spécialistes de l 'enseignement du français langue étrangère comme Ross Steele (Australie et organisateur du congrès de Sydney), David Singleton (Irlande), Johan Matter (Pays-Bas) auxquels se joignaient régulièrement la psycholinguiste roumaine Tatiana Slama-Cazacu et, cela pourrait surprendre, Andrew Cohen. On ignore généralement que cet éminent didacticien de l'anglais langue seconde et étrangère fût « French major » durant ses études universitaires à Harvard. Par ailleurs, Cohen a le mérite d'être le linguiste appliqué dont l'association au BE s'étend sur presque trois décennies, y compris le plus long mandat comme secrétaire-général.

En guise de conclusion, c'est avec une grande satisfaction que je constate l'élargissement de l'AILA qui coiffe actuellement plus de trente associations nationales réparties sur tous les continents. Aussi, au vu des titres des conférences plénières annoncées pour le prochain congrès de Madison, cette manifestation périodique consacrera l'extension des problématiques que traitent les enseignants-chercheurs qui servent de truchement entre les domaines théoriques des sciences du langages (et non plus seulement de la linguistique) et les problèmes pratiques auxquels sont confrontés, du moins dans le monde occidental, des sociétés de plus en plus multiethniques qui doivent gérer l'attribution des domaines d'utilisation aux langues et aux variétés langagières en contact de manière a harmoniser les pulsions identitaires et l'universalisme du Siècle des Lumières dont ces sociétés sont les héritières. Cela démontre clairement que l'AILA, en évoluant au delà d'un groupement de spécialistes appliquant les théories de la linguistique structurale à des problématiques didactiques, épouse bien le 21e siècle.

Résumé

A travers ses souvenirs, Albert Valdman retrace l'historique de l'AILA de ses origines en France au début des années 60 à nos jours, en soulignant son importance comme organisme reliant plus de 30 associations nationales à travers le monde. Il débute en parlant de la naissance de l'AILA en Europe occidentale, et de son premier centre d'intérêt, l'apprentissage du langage; il suit son expansion géographique qui passe par l'Amérique du Nord pour s'étendre au monde, ainsi que celle de ses centres d'intérêts qui recouvre, de nos jours, une large variété de domaines en linguistique appliquée. Ce faisant, il évoque les réunions les plus significatives, les publications, les groupes de recherches, la question de la langue au sein de l'organisation et plusieurs linguistes qui contribuèrent à l'évolution de l'AILA.

Some current trends in applied linguistics

Towards a generic view[*]

Martin Bygate
Lancaster University

This paper argues that the most significant trend in applied linguistics is the emergence of the field as a generic discipline, involving several subareas, all characterised by the aim of developing theoretical and empirical studies of language as a key element in real world problems. Various subsidiary trends are apparent including numerous methodological and theoretical developments. The paper argues that so far these trends respond only inconsistently to two major challenges in the relationship between the academy and the lay community: (1) identifying and studying issues held to be problems by those outside the academy; and (2) clarifying the nature of the contributions of research to those real world problems. Three themes are considered: the relationship between surface data and theory development; the problem of the specific and the general; and the importance of problematicity. The paper concludes that applied linguistics needs to be accountable to two communities, the academy and the lay communities it aims to work with.

Keywords: Applied Linguistics, a generic view

Introduction

Applied linguistics is well known for its close early associations with the teaching of foreign languages, and in particular English (see for instance Davies 1999:6; Grabe & Kaplan 1992:1; Howatt 1984:265; Cook 2003:69). As Cook (2003) (for instance Chapters 1–7), and Davies (1999:1–2) make clear, however, the discipline now extends well beyond foreign language instruction, reaching into 'language practices' (Brumfit 1997:90, cited in Davies 1999). This evolution can be seen as reflecting a generalisation of the parameters of the discipline. However in the early years, the initial concerns were largely with understanding the needs of language learners; the problems and development of language learners; how learners' needs might be met; how their development assisted; and how their achievements assessed.

From this starting point, it gradually became apparent that our initial educational preoccupations raised significant and non-trivial methodological questions, many of them concerning the relationship between the academy, research and the world which the academy was studying. These were questions such as, what procedures can be used to validly document learners' genuine needs? What methods can be employed to accurately document and understand their problems and their development? How can research into language teaching and learning be used to inform the design and use of materials and programmes? How can it address problems of learners' development? How can appropriate tests be designed and implemented?

These apparently simple questions concealed matters of complexity and sensitivity, which on closer scrutiny raise more general issues, which also characterise the broader field of applied linguistics. These more general issues engage at least five main problems:

First of all, are researchers correct in their identification of potential problems for research, or in the way they conceptualise them? And if so, are they investigating them at the appropriate level of specificity or generality? For instance, are educational problems that are perceived as pedagogical in fact best studied at the level of the classroom activity, or in terms of the individual learner, or of the

AILA Review 17 (2004), 6–22.
ISSN 1461–0213 / E-ISSN 1570–5595 © John Benjamins Publishing Company

class as a whole, or of the teacher and class, or of the institution, or more widely in terms of the broader social and cultural context? That is, is a second language problem, which is manifested as a classroom problem, perhaps rather a problem of regional or national language policy? Associated with problems such as this is the question of which are the most appropriate or productive categories of analysis — both linguistic (such as discoursal or other), and non-linguistic (such as professional, social, cognitive or other). In other words, how to locate and to conceptualise the problem?

Secondly, given that observation and prescription are inadequate to understand the needs, learning problems and progress of learners, and that stakeholders' (such as teachers' and learners') own accounts of these phenomena need to be tapped, how can this be done in such a way that the data are not an artefact of the researchers' own assumptions, and are reflective of the learners' actual experiences? Furthermore, assuming trustworthiness within the data, how can the academy achieve trustworthy interpretations of it?

Thirdly, given that the overall purpose of research is not simply to enable understanding on the part of researchers, but to promote effective classroom learning, how far should research itself be a joint enterprise between members of the academy and relevant lay parties?

Fourthly, given that understanding of research whether on the part of professionals or researchers does not itself point to practical implications, how can researched understandings most effectively be translated into educational action — that is, how can they best be shared with teachers and learners, and how can appropriate action responses be negotiated and implemented, so as to be subsequently evaluated and improved?

Finally, since of course not all applied research can directly serve practical needs, the question arises, what overall is the place of theory in relation to data collection and interpretation, and in relation to subsequent action? That is, how far is applied linguistic theory independent of — and/or indifferent to — the concern for responsive action?

Issues such as these raise fundamental questions about the involvement of lay members of the community in research; and about the nature of different types of research outcomes and their relationship to potential real world action. These matters are not purely linguistic; nor for that matter are they purely educational: they go beyond these domains into issues of the relationship between the scholarly apparatus of the academy and the social reality which is under scrutiny.

The problems I am outlining are not of course specific to the area of language education. Indeed the issues raised in language education itself contain the seeds of a less specific, more generic identity. In particular, exploring specific aspects of language education (such as the development of oral or written skills) or types of language education (such as language education for specific needs) engages broader more generic issues. For instance teaching and testing of language in the context of specific needs such as those of non-native speaker professionals within the health service, so as to ensure say their functionality as doctors, quickly leads into concerns about the relationship between language, clinical ability and professional capacity. Similarly, teaching and testing the language proficiency of asylum seekers and immigrants leads to concerns about the relationship between language and language provision and the democratic rights of learners, in terms of their freedoms both as asylum seekers, and as asylum beneficiaries. The teaching and testing of language in the workplace draws us into concerns not only about the nature of language proficiency of employees, but of language practices of employers: an eye to potential areas of worksite conflict rapidly raises the stakes not only in terms of the language to be taught, but also in terms of the language use of line managers and employers. In similar vein, language proficiency becomes a potential problem and matter of scholarly interest in ever widening contexts: for instance, in exploring how far problems of attainment across the curriculum are a reflection of issues of language practice; in asking how far the delivery of justice in courts of law is influenced by the language practices of the various parties and their counsel; in investigating the extent to which employment and promotion opportunities are a function of language skills; in exploring how far the interests and well-being of the community, commerce and the consumer hinge on the language practices of the respective parties. Likewise we might ask in what ways language practices affect the effectiveness of public education institutions such as museums, libraries, theatres, cinemas, and art galleries, or the exercise of political and democratic rights. Crystal (2003) enumerates further areas of applied investigation such as language issues in the context of music or the internet. In each of these contexts, we find ourselves asking the same kinds of general questions as those we have seen emerging in the area of second/foreign language education:

1. Where is the real world problem and how is it defined?
2. What are the stakeholders' views?
3. How far can the research be a joint enterprise between scholars and lay stakeholders?
4. How can research be designed to help find effective responses to stakeholders' concerns?
5. What different kinds of applied research are needed to enable effective responses?

Against this backdrop, a broad denotation of the field is useful, and I find helpful to adopt Brumfit's (2001) definition of the field as 'the theoretical and empirical study of real world problems in which language plays a central role'. In the following sections in order to reflect current developments within the field, I briefly consider the range of areas of specialism and content focus, and some current trends in applied linguistics methodology. Although this is written from the perspective of a specialist in language education, my concern is to attempt to map the generic features of the field. In order to do this I then turn to three thematic concerns which seem shared across the subareas of the field: a concern to work from the surface of applied language phenomena; the issue of relating the specificities of the insider to the generalisations needed for outsiders' understanding; and finally the concern to find responses to real world problems. My main argument is that these thematic concerns point interesting directions for the overall development of the field as a generic specialism.

The domains of applied linguistics

Main domains
To reflect on current directions in applied linguistics, one basic question is where is the focus of applied linguistic research? To help to answer this question, as an outgoing editor of *Applied Linguistics* journal (*ALJ*), it makes sense for me to refer where possible, though not exclusively, to recent publications in this journal.

It is probably true to say that the areas of work published in *ALJ* over the past few years have been principally oriented towards language education and the description of discourse, with some representation of research into language and the law, the study of language in its social context, language planning and the language expertise of non-language professionals. It will be very clear to members of AILA, which has long had a commitment to the development of a wide range of sub-areas through its various scientific commissions, that this is a small proportion of the range of work which could — and to varying degrees is — being undertaken. Other areas include fields that have been actively researched for decades, such as child language acquisition, language pathology, language loss, language and the media, language across the curriculum, as well as some that are less widely known, such as language and professional development, language and the family, language and the public services, language and health, language and human rights, and language and international development.

However, apart from these areas of research, the field can also be described in terms of research focus, in terms of the kinds of issues studied, and in terms of research methodology, the heuristic procedures used to access, analyse and interpret data.

Research focus

There are three main types of research focus: language categories; language processes; and language users.

Language categories. In terms of the categories of language being researched, a wide range of options are available. Studies in corpus linguistics for instance explore parameters of collocation, the relationship between words and grammar, and the distributional properties of different genres. Work in this area has potentially far-reaching implications for the study of child language, second language learning, and classroom data, is central to work in forensic linguistics, and has exciting applications in historical linguistics and stylistics. Research into vocabulary explores the properties associated with vocabulary size and lexical frequency, as well as the nature of types of lexical syntagmatic relationships. Metaphor studies highlight the semantic structuring of discourse. Work in the area of genre has focussed on the definitional nature of genre, on the rhetorical structures of specific genres, and on selected moves, and the ways they are expressed (such as questionnaires), as well as the circumstances of its teaching (such as the language of literature). Research into pragmatics explores the existence of pragmatic patterns in discourse, and the nature of appropriate methodologies for its research.

Language processes. Attrition research is looking for patterns of language loss, and exploring methodologies for its study. Transfer studies have been examining ways in which transfer can be charted across distinct levels of language use from L1 to L2 or L3, and the development of the study of bi-directional transfer, in which L2 or L3 features are imported back into the L1, suggests that transfer studies can be closely related to studies of language loss. A concern with language processing is also evident in studies of the language of tasks, and explorations into a particular mode of language use (such as listening), and in work aiming to elucidate categories and models of language processing. A major branch of variationist study is that represented by research into English as a Lingua Franca (e.g., Jenkins 2002). Current developments in conversation analysis for second language acquisition constitute a particular attempt to study the relationship between micro-phenomena of learner language interaction and language learning. Within *ALJ* studies of language in the workplace are principally represented by papers on classroom discourse (Zuengler & Mori (eds) 2002), and by papers on the discourse of workplace practice (Sarangi & Candlin (eds) 2003).

Language users. A further major area of work focuses on the people behind the language, that is the histories, perceptions and approaches of people in relation to language. Those focusing on the experience behind the language are represented by research into language learning memoirs (Pavlenko 2001), into the styles and strategies of learners (Littlemore 2001), and into their attitudes and motivation. In addition, a number of papers continue to explore the principles of language teaching, whether working from theory to practice (e.g., G. Cook 2001 and V. Cook 2002), from research to practice (e.g., Lightbown 2000; Mitchell 2000) or from practice to theory (e.g., Breen et al. 2001, Hird et al. 2000). Studies of the discourse of workplace practice (Sarangi & Candlin eds 2003) shift the focus to the ways in which workplace practice is itself discussed by language specialists and non-language specialist professionals.

Finally a small number of papers represent the continuing concern for the development of a meta-theory of applied linguistics, with a particular interest in the exploration of complexity theory as a potential macro-theory for conceptualising applied linguistic research (Larsen-Freeman 1997).

To summarise, research explores categories at all levels of analysis, from phoneme, through lexico-grammar, discourse genre, language norm and language variety, to the people behind the language, whether ordinary users and learners, or professionals. It is in this latter focus that principles of professional intervention come into play. As can be seen, the range of potential focus for the discipline is rich.

Research methodology

Apart from a repertoire of categories of analysis and areas for analytical focus, a discipline requires a methodology for the collection and treatment of data. Here too there is a richness in the range of scholarly methods. In this paper I will limit discussion to two broad approaches — quantitative, and qualitative.

Statistical techniques have long been applied to experimental or pseudo-experimental studies, and to acquisition studies. However, the use of statistics is changing in interesting ways, particularly through work carried out in sub-areas such as corpus linguistics (e.g., Biber et al. 1994; Hunston & Francis 2000; Stubbs 2001) and vocabulary studies (Adolphs & Schmitt 2003; Meara forthcoming; Wang & Nation 2004). Corpus studies use the frequency of words, or strings of words, co-occurring in existing corpora as a basis either for assessing characteristics of the discourse type (Biber et al. 1994), or to study the identity and patterning of individual lexical and grammatical items (Hunston & Francis 2000; Stubbs 2001). This kind of research provides considerable potential for assessing the language exposure available to speakers (e.g., Meara, Lightbown & Halter 1997), whether native or non-native; for assessing the distinctiveness of patterns of occurrence in difference dialects, discourses, genres or idiolects (e.g., Altenberg & Granger 2001), and potentially tracking changes across time, either of individuals, or of groups, or of communities. Such analyses can provide a basis for making predictions about the likelihood of any particular pattern occurring in a given context. This is a technological development which suggests the possibility of tracking patterning in linguistic data in ways which might enable us to monitor — and indeed simulate — the linguistic learning experiences typical of a wide range of real world users. This has the potential of enabling the application of quantitative techniques to quite sensitive linguistic patterning, suggesting a possible quantitative pathway towards qualitative phenomena.

However, quantitative approaches of this kind carry with them various well known in-built limitations. In particular they do not provide the user perspective on the data, or on the language events from which it was gathered. Rather the focus is observable linguistic phenomena, charted as Stubbs suggests (2001: 154), rather the way a geologist might record the contour lines, water courses, rock and soil types, fault lines and coast lines across the surface of the globe, carefully sifting them for systematic patterning. This enables the analyst to provide comprehensive pictures of dialects — of individuals or communities, across or within discourses — and their changes. A key aspect of what can be known about language is what can be observed. What people do with language is different from what they think they do, and this fundamental insight about the status of observable language has provided the empirical base for the development of linguistic studies throughout the 20th century. As has been frequently pointed out, corpora provide a basis for investigation of what people do and have done with language on a truly massive scale, both in its ability to handle tiny details of a language, and in its ability to provide information about macro-patterns. Within applied linguistics, this facilitates the empirical study of all language data in problem situations, such as learner data, classroom data, legal data, pathological data, and various kinds of institutional language data.

It also provides the possibility of exploring the interaction of different aspects of language. For instance it can help knowledge of grammar to be studied in relation to use of lexis; metaphorical competence to be apprehended through the surface features of language; language acquisition and change to be explored through the analysis of the fluctuating co-occurrences of linguistic chunks; that is, 'competence' to be grasped in the careful analysis of 'performance'. In addition modelling performance through computer simulations can be used to explore the kinds of variations which are the source of development or attrition (Meara 2004). This reliance on surface evidence places a huge emphasis on attested data, and on the care with which it is analysed. This of course is not to deny the importance of theory. Data do not describe or explain themselves: this too is the applied linguists' role. However, from a corpus perspective, explanations are seen as following the data closely. That is, the surface of discourse is a primary source of our understanding, and basis for cross-checking our intuitions.

Yet it has been noted that the objectivity this kind of approach can claim through the use of substantial corpora of attested use nonetheless has to be mediated by the subjectivity of the analyst's own focus and interpretation (Widdowson 2000). Furthermore, the very nature of large scale quantitative studies, particularly those aggregating findings across large numbers of language users in myriad ranges of different contexts carries with it the major flaw that at best it can reflect an approximate mean, much of which might fit poorly the language experiences, and even less the language output, of any particular speaker. Ironically the surface of discourse viewed from this perspective carries with it the danger of becoming an abstract and idealised phenomenon. Concerns of this kind raise questions about the nature of the relationship between a corpus and the knowledge and language use of any given speaker. Clearly it is bound to be complex, whether in terms of the relationship between a corpus and a given speaker's active and passive vocabulary, or in terms of a speaker's range of types and registers of language use. Work in forensic linguistics (Solan & Tiersma forthcoming) shows ways in which the relationship between the language of individuals and broader corpora can be used as a basis for assessing likely authorship of given texts. Similar techniques are used in the analysis of plagiarism (Coulthard, 2003). However until the relationship between individual data bases and community data bases has been teased apart, the unprecedented opportunity corpora provide for the identification of patterning in problem language data needs to be read against the possibility of their being fairly blunt instruments until complemented by significant banks of data for individual users.

A key counterpoint to developments in the use of quantitative techniques is the substantial growth in the use of qualitative methods. Qualitative methods in current applied linguistics seem to respond to at least three major concerns: a concern for research to highlight the personal and particular; an acknowledgement of the importance of gathering data on users' interpretations of language and language events; and a belief that a holistic account of phenomena is only achievable through the analysis of specific cases, a position often described as anti-reductionist.

Qualitative approaches embrace at least two major types of research: one focusing on the collection and analysis of surface data (e.g., Swain & Lapkin 2000, Schegloff 2000; Wong 2000) and the other studying various types of self report data (e.g., Block 1998; Pavlenko 2001). In both cases, qualitative approaches sanction the researcher to act as analyst and interpreter of the data. And rather like quantitative analysis, researchers from a socio-constructivist angle can be willing to read into the surface of the language data the underlying processes (such as learning of new language) which they believe are occurring (e.g., Swain & Lapkin 2000).

Both see the personal and particular as significant because these dimensions often promise the most detailed level of analysis: patterns of language use, however pervasive, are all driven by unique people's meaning intentions in specific places on particular occasions. Qualitative studies, such as those undertaken from a socio-cultural perspective, can uncover these intentions. In counterpoint to the large scale basis of corpus studies, qualitative researchers have been concerned to carry out micro-analyses in case study mode. In doing this their tacit — though not always articulated — assumption is that generalisations can be drawn from the range of cases analysed. This can be seen as a kind of bottom-up approach to data-gathering and theory building — from individual case to subsequent generalisation. It is this which leads qualitative studies to be most closely associated with claims of anti-reductionism — and with the criticism that quantitative paradigms are more ready to accept an element of reductionism. In considering this issue, it is worth noting that there is both a strong and weak form of anti-reductionism. The strong version would abhor all loss of information in any data set through the process of analysis. To adopt this position, however, is to set an impossible albeit understandable ideal, since in fact no data set can possibly be analysed, or even reported, without the loss of some information: the contrary would imply the possibility of what Byrne (1998) calls an 'isomorphic theory' — that is, a theory which describes and explains all aspects of an event, both in general and in detail. Since research is incapable of gathering all possible data, and since what original data it does succeed in capturing has to be transformed into different semiotic modes, such as transcriptions, analyses, descriptions and commentaries, it is clear that information loss is inevitable. This appears uncontroversial.

However a weaker form of anti-reductionism might argue that working with individual cases offers a safety precaution against mistaken overgeneralisation. It also proposes that the pooling of data can generate patterns which do not correspond to those of any individual user, but rather emerge as artefacts of the very procedure of pooling. The response to this would be to explore the potential for the careful accumulation of case studies, each one with its qualitative but also its statistical analysis, enabling the analyst to ensure that any categories that arise are all the property of the contributory cases, and not a methodological fiction. One example of work of this sort is that by Lynch & Maclean (2000) in which the authors seek similarities across a series of seperate dyadic interactions. From this perspective, anti-reductionism is not incompatible with the use of quantitative methods.

I have suggested that both quantitative and qualitative researchers can find themselves in danger of generating analyst-based accounts and interpretations of the data which are uncorroborated by the language user-participants in the research. It has been argued for some time (e.g., Roberts et al. 1992) that triangulation is needed, as a way of cross checking the analyst's independent findings. Various types of informants can fulfil this role. For instance learners or teachers can comment on the classroom interaction that has been analysed; learners can comment on the strategies which have been identified by the researcher; lawyers and legal experts can assess the likely impact on courts of particular interaction patterns or formulations of witnesses evidence; employees and employers, or interviewees and interviewers can contribute their perspectives to the analysts' account. Although the use of triangulation has been frequently endorsed, and the growth in the popularity of the use of stimulated recall as expounded for instance by Mackey & Gass (2000) is one example of this, it is striking that triangulation is not pervasively drawn on. More radically, approaches such as personal construct theory, which have been available for over half a century, and which make an absolute requirement to gather data using only the working vocabulary spontaneously chosen by the participants themselves, have been very rarely used (an exception is in the work reported by J. Roberts 1999). There is here a challenge which researchers from all paradigms might need to confront: to what extent can and should their account of the data be exposed to the potentially disconfirming view of the users? And more importantly, how can potentially disconfirming accounts be effectively gathered?

The term 'potentially disconfirming view' raises some teasing questions. For how can we as researchers crosscheck our analyses? One central issue here is the extent to which the views of researchers can be reliably confronted with those of others — and how this can best be done. One approach of many — particularly those working from a qualitative position — is to propose that the analysis, the interpretation, and the resulting theory are somehow independent of the analyst. There are in the work of researchers working from this perspective some interesting turns of phrase. The data 'tell' the analyst things; patterns, findings, or theories 'emerge' from the data. From this perspective, the data and the participants are primarily conceptualised as the major informing agents, with the researcher being cast in the role of the neutral and unbiased observer. Yet the data have to be noticed and interpreted as significant by the researcher. So that the question always arises: why are particular aspects of the data noticed and interpreted by the researcher as significant? What external evidence independent of the researcher can the researcher draw upon for these choices? There is a tension here then that revolves around the checks and balances that provide the assurance that the data and participants do have a genuinely independent influence on the research, and are not simply invoked as a covert way of justifying the analyst's own beliefs and intended conclusions.

Although, as I have said above, much of the work is very largely oriented towards educational issues, the methods, focuses and issues discussed here could apply to any of a wide range of other contexts.

The challenge: Towards a generic conception of AL

As pointed out in the introduction to this paper, applied linguistics has been most closely associated with language education. Yet, as argued earlier, the study of language education has itself involved the gradual uncovering of complex issues which reach well beyond language classrooms. These include issues such as the nature of second language processing and its development, the psycho-sociology and politics of second language use, the relationship between language use and language development, the relationship between language learning and social context, and the relationships between discourse functions, discourse, and the structural elements which constitute it. Understanding these phenomena takes applied linguistics beyond the classroom into the community and its wide range of individual and socio-cultural contexts. That is, educational concerns lead to a broader conceptualisation of applied linguistics, resulting from the increase in the number of interfaces between language and other aspects of the real world which researchers have come to recognise as important. And at the same time, as we have also seen, applied linguists have developed other areas of specialism. As a result, it can be argued that applied linguistics is evolving a more generic identity, capable of conceptualising a wide range of language-real world interfaces, and able to mobilise a growing repertoire of research methods.

An implication of this is the possibility that particular areas of applied linguistics might review the approaches to research which, for contingent historical or institutional reasons each has tended to prefer. This could lead to our methodologies renewing themselves by drawing on paradigms developed in other areas of the field. For instance what are the methods of forensic linguistics, and how far are they relevant to fields such as speech and language therapy, or language teaching? Are there aspects of task design in language teaching which relate to the study of language in the workplace? Are the negotiations of understanding found in the public debates over GM policies related in any way to the negotiations of meaning found in classrooms, and if so, in what ways? Language teaching, language testing, and speech and language therapy are intimately concerned with issues of intervention, evaluation, and impact assessment: in what ways do these concerns relate to the practices of forensic linguists, of those studying language in the workplace, or those advising institutions on the conduct of public consultations? The probability is that there are such potential connections between subareas of the field and that articulating them could enrich the different areas in producitive ways.

Hence, although language acquisition has for many been the single most intellectually stimulating applied linguistic problem to address, refusing to take language development for granted, maybe language acquisition is no more than an instance of a general problem. Rather, perhaps the question now is whether we can take for granted the success of communication between service providers or professionals on the one hand, and clients, lay people and members of the public on the other. Indeed, if we take *real world problems* as our focus of attention, communication and the learning of communication might replace acquisition as the key focus of concern in language teaching; but perhaps more severe and urgent real world language problems are not in acquisition, per se, but elsewhere.

In what follows, I briefly explore three themes of a generic nature, which all seem to encapsulate significant issues for the field. The first concerns the nature of the relationship between surface data and theory, and in particular the importance of the development of practical theories. The second theme concerns the relationship between the particular or specific on the one hand, and the need for generalisation on the other, with particular reference to the insider-outsider problem. And the third theme concerns the relationship between applied linguistic research and real world problems, and in particular the relationship between the academy and those whose problems it seeks to address.

Working from the surface

In *The Blind Watchmaker*, Richard Dawkins (1986) asks the reader to answer the following two evolutionary questions about the human eye:

1. Could the human eye have arisen directly from no eye at all, in a single step?
2. Could the human eye have arisen directly from something slightly different from itself, something that we may call X?

He continues:

> [the] answer to Question 1 is clearly a decisive *no*. The odds against a 'yes' answer for questions like Question 1 are many billions of times greater than the number of atoms in the universe. It would need a gigantic and vanishingly improbable leap across genetic hyperspace. The answer to Question 2 is equally clearly *yes*, provided only that the difference between the modern eye and its immediate predecessor X is sufficiently small. Provided, in other words, that they are sufficiently close to one another in the space of all possible structures. [...]
>
> 3. Is there a continuous series of Xs connecting the modern human eye to a state with no eye at all? (1986: 77–8)

To question 3), Dawkins again concludes that the answer must be 'yes'.

The issue which Dawkins is concentrating on here concerns the nature of the developmental steps which would be needed to account for the existence of complex structures. The ultimate surface structure — that is, the physiology of the eye — can be accounted for through progressive alterations in the structure at any one time. That is, a complex physical structure — along with its accompanying complex of neurological and cognitive processing capacities — can come into existence through a series of small, simple physical developmental steps.

There is an interesting similarity between this position, and current conceptualisations of the processes of language learning. From the perspective of Ellis (1996, 2001), the acquisition of the complexities of language, and the complex human skills which underpin it, can be largely explained by the simple memorisation, one-step-at-a-time, of numerous linguistic strings, together with their context of occurrence and indexed for meaning. This can then be followed by the learner analysing memorised strings and regularly occurring sub-strings, on the basis of significant patterning. That is, complex linguistic structures and the ability to process them can be acquired by step-by-step accretion and analysis. Just as it may not be necessary to hypothesise a one-step creation of the eye, it may not be necessary to think of the acquisition of grammatical structures as occurring through a one-step process. If we consider the abstract mental recognition and storage of structures as emerging through the gradual development of structures on the surface, then the underlying deep structures may not be that far below the surface.

The surface is significant in the work of numerous other applied linguists. Collocations for instance are fundamentally a surface phenomenon, and connotative values of words are detectable through their surface co-occurrences (e.g., Stubbs 2001). Scholars see grammatical structures as largely emergent surface phenomena (Hunston & Francis 2000). The selection and patterning of metaphors is essentially traceable across the surface of language (Cameron & Low 1999). Discourse structures and genres are tracked through their surface realisations (Hoey 1983, 1993; Swales 1990), and characterised in terms of the surface level clustering of linguistic features (Biber et al. 1998), though in a recent article Askehave & Swales (2001) acknowledge the need for aspects of genre analysis to extend to 'prolonged fieldwork'. The surface is also important in other types of research. For example socio-constructivist studies identify scaffolding in terms of the overt interactional formulations and moves of the adult which interlock at the surface level with the moves of the learner (Jarvis & Robinson 1997). Teacher behaviour and teacher cognition are studied on the basis of the individual mix of actions and words used by particular teachers. That is, the surface reveals the underlying structure, and is scrutinised for patterning which our theories may not have dreamt of.

However there are problems with surface-driven approaches. The reasons for the co-occurrences of features are not necessarily directly accessible to the observer, and nor are they necessarily motivated by a single explanation. Close to my laptop there may be a number of objects: a phone, a jar of pencils and pens, a coffee cup, a copy of *Applied Linguistics* 21/3, a copy of *The Blind Watchmaker*, a screwdriver, a book of crossword puzzles, a map of France. The explanations for their proximity cannot be inferred with any certainty simply by inspection, and no single explanation will be sufficient to account for all of them, other than for rather uninteresting reasons, such as that they were all put there by one or more people who between them used them all. That is, the various juxtaposition are each likely to need to appeal to a number of sometimes unrelated reasons (for example, the proximity of the phone and the laptop is for reasons which have little to do with the proximity of the screwdriver, which itself is only connected to the book of puzzles by the multiply useful location of the table that they are both on). The point is that while the surface is a key reference point, we need a series of theoretical explanations for what is happening on the surface, along with a repertoire of procedures for detecting them. From this we might anticipate research attending cyclically to the surface of data, and to the explanatory theories and procedures used to attempt to understand them.

It could be argued that it is in response to the heterogeneous nature of surface phenomena that AL researchers orientate themselves most strongly. Some, such as corpus linguists, restrict themselves largely to using frequency of occurrence and co-occurrence of features as a tool in identifying and inferring the nature of patterning within their corpora. Others stressing the human dimension of applied linguistic phenomena (such as Breen et al. 2001; Pavlenko 2001) tend rather to elicit personal narrative accounts of participants (for example through the use of stimulated recall (Gass & Mackey 2000)) to shed light on the data. Those working with a more context-specific focus, such as those researching tasks (Bygate 2000; Robinson 2001; Samuda 2001; Skehan & Foster 1999; Yuan & Ellis 2003) or classrooms (Lightbown 2000; Mitchell & Martin 1997) often take relatively untheorised but naturally occurring contexts, such as classroom events or activities as the starting point for their work. That is, the surface professional relevance of the event is deemed sufficient justification for their choice of data

Three observations arise from this, however. Firstly, although the surface data are unilinear, the theorisations that can be generated around it are susceptible to successive increases in depth and complexification. Hence for example the complex of the hallidayan constructs of ideational, interpersonal and textual functions can be woven around the simplest of linguistic samples, as for instance in the analysis of a child's utterance such as 'dog Mummy'. And analysis of such a data sample need not stop there, but can easily run into a series of analyses at the phonological, grammatical, lexical and socio-linguistic levels. The surface of language can be multiply theorised.

Secondly, within applied linguistics, data itself are insufficient. This is because the discipline is concerned not so much with generating descriptions of language, but rather with understanding language in relation to problematic aspects of its use (particularly its relation to human cognition, and to the social context within which it is used). Given this focus, the surface of data is never in fact enough. Other factors need to be brought into the picture — the user, the user's cognitive processes, the social functions of the language used.

The third point is that in any case there is a sense in which data on its own are inert. The interest for the discipline lies in the ways in which the data are *effectively* theorised. That is, the focus of a discipline is the value of the theoretical accounts which are generated around the available raw material. There is debate over the relative merits of alternative theories. But rather than focus on the issue of the adequacy of proposed theoretical accounts, following Rorty (1999) I would like to argue that a productive focus might very well be the extent to which the proposed theories are useful. That is, applied linguistics is not particularly interested in simply accounting for data, but rather in providing useful accounts of it. Hence while theory generation is crucial, this is not for its own sake, so much as for its capacity to help us solve problems. The key issues then become not: which theorisation is correct, but how do they function, and as Rorty would ask, which are the most useful?

One area for urgent consideration within the field might then be the ways in which research relates its theories to the surface of data, and to considerations of what might constitute usefulness. The reader might object that what constitutes usefulness in one part of the field (such as genre analysis) may be no help to another part (such as language pathology). I would argue however that to be able to distinguish between theoretical accounts in this way may be useful for the discipline.

The specific and the general

My second generic theme concerns the question of whether to focus on the specific or the general. This is a recurrent issue in any field of research. Disciplines depend on terms and concepts which, once identified, are used to group similar cases, and distinguish them from those cases which differ from them at least on that feature. In making statements about the prototypicality of the meanings or uses of particular words and phrases, about the linguistic structures in which they are used, or about the contextual circumstances in which they occur and change, linguists and applied linguists find themselves making generalisations about the data or instances that they describe. Concordances cannot function without aggregating observations. The phenomena being described are fundamentally norm-referenced. The identification, by specialists, of deviance and abnormality also depends upon generalisation.

And mirroring the applied linguist, language users, and those who linguists investigate, themselves also generalise constantly. The spread of ad hoc deviance into slang requires the users to spot the deviance, and then to adopt it; by which means, the deviance itself becomes a norm. Similarly learners have to make generalisations about the samples of new language they encounter; teachers have to make generalisations from samples of learner language about the speed and quality of progress of their learners; expert witnesses in court have to make estimates of the relative typicality of samples of language; translators need to judge the comparability of expressions in different languages, in a given context; grammars, dictionaries, and the people who use them, generalise the typical meanings and patterns of use of the expressions they explain. Users, whether expert or lay, need to generalise.

Indeed one could argue that generalisation is the substance of elements of language and of their use, along with the definition of boundaries between one and another. Yet applied linguistics is not only concerned with recurring elements of language and their use. It is also concerned with the experiences of specific individuals and groups. Generalisations by language users take place in combinations of contextual circumstances and socio-cognitive processes, perceptions and values which cannot be entirely predicted by a general theory. Generalisation is bound to miss at least a part of the picture. Hence an emphasis in much applied linguistics on the unique, the context-specific, and the local. However just as there are problems with a commitment to generalisation, so there are also problems with a commitment to the unique. Those attempting to tell the individual story need to consider the limits on accuracy. In his stories of life in a French village in which he lived, John Berger starts by examining the difficulty of being both an outsider and part of the community he was writing about: 'A reader may ask: What is the writer's relationship with the place and the people he writes about?' He recounts an experience of haymaking.

> Forking hay, turning it, lifting it, can be like playing, but on that heavy, treacherous, wasp-filled afternoon forking the hay down was like trying to carry a split sack. I cursed the heat. The heat was no longer a condition, it had become a punishment. And I cursed the punisher. I cursed the slope and the work which still had to be done. If I could have struck the sun and its heat I would have done so. I looked down on to the tiles of the farmhouse below and I swore at the sky. Half an hour later, long before we had got the hay in, it began to rain and thunder. And then I cursed the rain, even though welcoming its freshness. My anger that afternoon joined me to the field, the slope, the hay. At other times my relationship to the place and the people who live here is less simple. I am not

a peasant. I am a writer: my writing is both a link and a barrier. [...] My writing about peasants separates me from then and brings me close to them. I am not, however, only a writer. I am also the father of a small child, a pair of working hands when needed, the *subject* of stories, a guest, a host. (Berger 1979: 5–7)

How can an applied linguist get any closer to overcoming that separation?

Of course, s/he can't. And there are three good reasons for this. One is that the outsider's account cannot by definition be the insider's account. But what's more the insider's account would not be accessible to the outsider-reader. The account needs to be comprehensible to others: for it to work, it cannot be purely an insider's account (though it is essential to have the insider's account as the data source). But more than this, the emphasis on the integrity of the insider's account is in any case mistaken: the insider's account even if superficially comprehensible would of itself not be reliably interpretable within the broader context of the field. That is, to signify within the field of discourse it needs to be related whether coherently or incoherently to the assumptions of others. Hence, the specific is a relevant starting point. But starting from the specific requires a pathway to be built to the bigger picture. In other words, it has to be negotiated with the outside community. This does not only involve negotiating with the academy: it can also involve negotiations with other interested communities, lay, or professional.

The building of pathways is therefore a necessity whether we approach our field of study from a generalising or a particularising perspective. For those committed to a generalising perspective it is important for the generalisations to be linked ontologically to specific experiences or to specific instances. This is true whether we are concerned with language acquisition — the process whereby learners establish general patterns from a series of specific encounters — or with the study of other kinds of normal or problematic language use — that is, those studies which make claims about (ab)normality on the basis of the aggregation of numerous individually produced instances. For both kinds of work, the relationship between the particular and the general is central.

However it is one thing to be concerned, with Berger, to generate valid accounts of his subject. This though leaves two issues untouched: one is the question of whether the resulting account is accessible to different discourse communities. A second is that in the case of applied linguistics we are dealing not only with a discipline devoted to accurate documentation: its applied vocation goes further, which leads to the issue of problematicity. This is the topic of the next section.

Problematicity

Ever since applied linguistics has emerged as a distinct academic field, applied linguists have quite properly been concerned with defining it both through the development of the research to which they aspired, and through meta reflection on its definition and methods. The notion of 'application' came to be defined in terms of studying language in relation to problems of the real world. Through the phrase 'real world' the problems are crucially defined not simply in terms of the academy, but with reference to the understanding of non-applied linguist members of the community. This includes language related problems experienced for instance by medical patients, by members of the public in contact with the justice system, in relation to human rights, or in the education system; language related problems in the context of job applications, of asylum seekers, or of unemployment; or problems of parenting, of language support for child language development, multilingual development, of democratic representation, of management and personnel development. Applied linguistics is a field broad in scope, and very rich in potential. And by this definition, its focus is partly rooted within the society.

From this a number of issues quickly follow. For instance, what if the problem being studied is not seen as being of any interest by people in the real world? What if the data are not recognised as authentic by people in the real world? And what if the analysis, or the interpretation, and the conclusions, are not accepted by people in the real world? Clearly, while on the one hand it must be possible for specialist applied linguists to define the focus, terms and methodology of their work, it would fall short of the disciplinary definition for them to develop their agendas without reference to the priorities, concerns and interpretations of people in the real world. In these circumstances the field would develop a trajectory simply in terms of what resonates within the academy: 'applied' in terms of what it focuses on, but without a commitment to the external endorsement of the problems it explores. For this reason the field needs to ask a range of safety-first questions, such as: who has identified the problem? How have the data been collected, by whom, under what circumstances, and for what purposes? Who analyses the data? Who interprets the data? Who evaluates the overall findings? And what happens with the results?

These are concerns which many applied linguists are clearly very sensitive to. Mitchell (2000) offers a particularly forceful presentation of this view in relation to the role of the applied linguistic community within the context of government-led educational reform. And there is of course work which aims to address real world problems from across the full range of the field. For instance, Low (1999) studies the very genuine real world problems of comprehension posed by the wording of questionnaires, and the threats these pose to the validity of questionnaires as a source of information. Gibbons (2001) explains the procedures used to provide advice to the police in dealing with second language users of English; the research reported in Towell & Tomlinson (1999) aims to inform the development of their graduate modern languages programme; Kiely (2001) explores the function of course evaluation within teacher development; Lindstromberg (2001) aims to address problems associated with preposition entries in dictionaries. Thompson's (2001) study provides a usable framework which can inform the teaching and learning of academic writing skills in a second language. Lightbown (2000) examines in detail the potential contributions of applied linguistic research to language pedagogy. Borg (2001) explicitly proposes the research journal as functional in promoting researcher development. Yet in spite of the original contributions of these studies, they are generally not explicitly located in problems perceived by the lay communities, and even when they are (e.g., Matras 1999: 483–488, and arguably Bogaards 2000), it is even rarer for them to discuss submitting their responses back to those communities.

The main problem with ignoring these issues is that by so doing we run the risk of defining applied linguistics as a solely theoretical discipline. That is, even if the problems studied are potentially of real world interest, at least in the eyes of the academy, the research is not conceptualised in terms of having a real world role. So that, while the nature of the problems of study are defined in terms of the real world, the function of the research remains academic. Yet for many applied linguists, the academy also has an applied *function*. As Byrne (1998) says this is risky: 'applied is dodgy always' (1998: 161). But for applied social sciences in general, the purpose is not merely to study, but to intervene, and to propose directions for *change* — to 'inform social action' (1998: 167). From this perspective, it is not sufficient to collect and chart and interpret information: the research needs also to respond to the real world problems it studies through some form of potential action. That is, applied linguistics is doubly applied — in terms both of the nature of the problems studied, and the potential uses to which the research can be put. This second level of application raises additional significant issues. For it isn't sufficient to generate conclusions for direct application to real world problems. Potential solutions then need to be tried out and evaluated. This means trying them out with real world participants, and engaging those same participants in evaluating them.

Problematicity of the language of real world issues then has two points of connection to research: firstly as the stimulus for research; and secondly as the target for potential research-generated responses. Maybe we need to keep an eye on these connections.

Of course the kind of account of applied linguistics which I have briefly outlined here has been available in the literature for some considerable time — and stated rather more finely and fully then here (Cameron et al. 1992, and Roberts et al. 1992 are two distinguished examples). However, if these criteria are applied to much of the applied linguistic research published in the major journals over the past five years, the record is at best patchy. With some notable exceptions, the field is still to acknowledge regularly through its publications the non-academic community whose problem-issues it aims to address, both in the focus and outcomes of its work.

Conclusion

This discussion leads me to the conclusion that to distinguish themselves from other disciplines, applied linguists need to be doubly accountable, in ways which non-applied academics need not be. I take it as axiomatic that in so far as they are academics, they need to be accountable in their choice and use of theories and methods to the rigours and informed criticisms of their academy, and from related academies from which they may need to borrow and adapt the tools necessary for their work. It is from this disciplinary specialism that they can work with authority to the highest academic levels of their societies. However, applied linguists also owe accountability to the lay communities which they also claim to serve. This they cannot convincingly do without attending beyond the discourses of those communities to their perceived needs. This raises the question of how learned publications can articulate with these two types of accountability, a question to which various answers are possible. Some might argue that scholarly publications should themselves be bi-discoursal, enabling access by both communities of reference. It is not obvious however that scholarly publications need to address the matter in such a way. An alternative would be to work with two sets of texts, scholarly and lay, each mutually informing and supporting the other. Cross-referencing would link them, so that the different communities can find the points of connection, and access the corresponding texts as necessary.

Berger reminds us that we cannot be at one and the same time both outsider and insider. He identifies the things he has in common, and the ways in which he differs from the people he is writing about (such as mother tongue, religion, economic prospects, landed patrimony, lifetime in one place, kinship connections). He concludes that although much is shared, the things they share and those they don't are 'unequal':

> We remain strangers who have chosen to live here. We are exempt from those necessities which have determined most lives in the village. To be able to choose or select was already a privilege. Yet the way we chose to live within the work and life of the community, and not in seclusion, immediately revealed, also, disadvantage, even a lack of privilege in local terms. This disadvantage was our relative ignorance, both practical and social. Everyone from schoolchildren to grandparents knew more than we did about certain aspects of life here. Everyone was in a position, if she or he so chose, to be our teacher, to offer information, aid, protection. And many did. (1979: 7)

If we are doomed to be outsiders, perhaps the next best thing would be for us as outsiders to be *validated* by our lay community of reference. This after all is what already happens in much of the work we are engaged in — whether in forensic linguistics, or language pathology, language planning and for a proportion of the work in language education.

This is what appears to have happened for Berger in the way he shared his writing project with his neighbours. I quote this at length because it is suggestive:

> The fact that a stranger does not belong to this centre [of the peasants' world] means that he is bound to remain a stranger. Yet provided the stranger's interests do not conflict with those of his neighbour — and such a conflict is likely immediately he buys land or builds — and provided he can recognise the portrait already in existence — and this involves more than recognising names or faces — he too may contribute to it, modestly but in a way that is unique to him or her. And one must remember that the making of this continuous communal portrait is not a vanity or a pastime: it is an organic part of the life of a village. Should it cease, the village would disintegrate. The stranger's contribution is small, but it is to something essential.
>
> Thus, in our double role as novices and independent witnesses, a certain reciprocity has been established. Often the lesson given to me as a novice was also a request for the recognition and

comment of myself as witness. "Have you ever met T...? No? Then come. I'll introduce you. And perhaps one day you'll write a story with him in it." (1979:11)

The validation of the applied linguist's work in this kind of way would imply that a major pragmatic function of applied linguistics would be through its dialogue with the lay community.

Research in an applied linguistics of this type would of course have to be based on relevant enabling conceptual work, not all of it meeting this criterion (papers by for instance Foster et al. 2000, Meara 2004, and Wray 2000 are examples). And clearly significant proportions of research successfully generate findings which have clear applications (not least Flowerdew & Dudley Evans 2002 study of the letters from editors of applied linguistic journals to authors of papers). But unless the lay community becomes a central reference point of our field, both for the generation and reception of our research, another applied language discipline will need to be constructed to fill the gap which ours may be neglecting.

Note

* I am very grateful to Gin Samuda for comments on draft versions of this paper. Any omissions and weaknesses in the argument are my own.

References

Adolphs, S. and N. Schmitt. (2003). Lexical coverage of spoken discourse. *Applied Linguistics* 24(4): 425–438.

Altenberg, B. and S. Granger. (2001). The grammatical and lexical patterning of MAKE in native and non-native student writing. *Applied Linguistics* 22(2): 173–194.

Ashkehave, I. and J. Swales (2001). Genre identification and communicative purpose: A problem and a possible solution. *Applied Linguistics* 22(2): 195–212.

Berger, J. (1979). *Pig Earth*. London: Writers and Readers Publishers' Cooperative.

Biber, D., S. Conrad and R. Reppen (1994). Corpus-based approaches to issues in applied linguistics. *Applied Linguistics* 15(2): 169–189.

Block, D. (1998). Tale of a language learner. *Language Teaching Research* 2(2): 148–176.

Bogaards, P. (2000). Testing L2 vocabulary knowledge at a high level: the case of the *Euralex French Tests*. *Applied Linguistics* 21(4): 490–516.

Borg, S. (2001). The research journal: a tool for promoting and understanding researcher development. *Language Teaching Research* 5(2): 156–177.

Breen, M., B. Hird, M. Milton, R. Oliver and A. Thwaite. (2001). Making sense of language teaching: teachers' principles and classroom practices. *Applied Linguistics* 22(4): 470–501.

Brumfit, C. J. (1997). How Applied Linguistics is the same as any other science. *International Journal of Applied Linguistics,* 7(1): 86–94.

Brumfit, C. J. (2001). *Individual freedom in language teaching*. Oxford: Oxford University Press.

Bygate, M. (2000). Introduction. *Special Issue: Tasks in Language Pedagogy. Language Teaching Research*. 4/3: 185–192.

Byrne, D. (1998). *Complexity theory and the social sciences*. London: Routledge.

Cameron, D., E. Fraser, P. Harvey, B. Rampton and K. Richardson. (1992). *Researching language: issues of power and method*. London: Routledge.

Cameron, L. & G. Low (eds) (1999). *Researching and applying metaphor*. Cambridge: Cambridge University Press.

Cook, G. (2001) 'The philospher pulled the lower jaw of the hen.' Ludicrous invented sentences in language teaching. *Applied Linguistics* 22(3): 366–387.

Cook, G. (2003). *Applied linguistics*. Oxford Introductions to Language Study. Oxford: Oxford University Press.

Cook, V. (2002). The functions of invented sentences: A reply to Guy Cook. *Applied Linguistics* 23(2): 262–269.

Coulthard, R. M. (2003). *Norm and creativity in language use — at what point does linguistic similarity suggest plagiarism?* Talk given to the Language Research Network, University of Leeds, May (2003).

Crystal, D. (2003). Final frontiers in applied linguistics. In Srikant Sarangi, S & T. van Leeuwen (eds), *Applied Linguistics & Communities of Practice.* British Studies in Applied Linguistics. Volume 18. London: Continuum.

Davies, A. (1999). *An introduction to applied linguistics.* Edinburgh: Edinburgh University Press.

Dawkins, R. (1986). *The Blind Watchmaker.* Harmondsworth: Penguin.

Ellis, N. (1996). Sequencing in SLA: Phonological memory, chunking and points of order. *Studies in Second Language Acquisition* 18: 91–126.

Ellis, N.C. 2001. Memory for language. In P. Robinson (ed). Cognition and Second language instruction. Cambridge: CUP. 33–68.

Flowerdew, J. and T. Dudley-Evans (2002). Genre analysis of editorial letters to international journal contributors. *Applied Linguistics* 23(4): 463–489.

Foster, P., A. Tonkyn and G. Wigglesworth (2000). Measuring spoken language: A unit for all reasons. *Applied Lingustics* 21(3): 354–375.

Gass, S.M. & A. Mackey (2000). *Stimulated recall methodology in second language research.* Lawrence Erlbaum Associates.

Gibbons, J. (2001). Revising the language of New South Wales police procedures: Applied Linguistics in Action. *Applied Linguistics* 22 (4): 439–469.

Grabe, W. & R. Kaplan (eds) (1992). *Introduction to applied linguistics.* Reading, Mass; Addison-Wesley Publishing Company.

Hird, B., A. Thwaite, M. Breen, M. Milton and R. Oliver. (2000). Teaching English as a second language to children and adults: variations in practices. *Language Teaching Research* 4(1): 3–32.

Hoey, M. (1983). *On the surface of discourse.* London: George Allen & Unwin.

Hoey, M. (1993). The case for the exchange complex. In M. Hoey (ed.), *Data, description, discourse. Papers on the English Language in honour of John McH Sinclair.* London: Harper Collins.

Howatt, A.P.R. (1984). *A history of English language teaching.* Oxford: Oxford University Press.

Hunston, S. & G. Francis. (2000). *Pattern grammar.* Amsterdam: John Benjamins.

Jarvis, I. and M. Robinson (1997). Analysing educational discourse: An exploratory study of teacher response and support to pupils' learning. *Applied Linguistics* 18(2): 212–228.

Jenkins, J. (2002). A sociolinguistically based, empirically researched pronunciation syllabus for English as an international language. *Applied Linguistics* 23(1): 83–103.

Kiely, R. (2001). Classroom evaluation — values, interests and teacher development. *Language Teaching Research* 5(3): 241–262.

Larsen-Freeman, D. (1997). Chaos/complexity science and second language acquisition. *Applied Linguistics* 18(2): 141–165.

Lightbown, P.M. (2000). Classroom SLA research and second language teaching. *Applied Linguistics* 21(3): 431–462.

Lindstromberg, S. (2001). Preposition entries in UK monolingual learners' dictionaries: Problems and possible solutions. *Applied Linguistics* 22(1): 79–103.

Littlemore, J. (2001). An empirical study of the relationship between cognitive style and the use of communication strategy. *Applied Linguistics* 22(2): 241–265.

Low, G. (1999). What respondents do with questionnaires: Accounting for incongruity and fluidity. *Applied Linguistics.* 20(4): 503–533.

Lynch, T. and J. Maclean. (2000). Exploring the benefits of task repetition and recycling for classroom learning. *Language Teaching Research Special Issue: Tasks in Language Pedagogy* 4(3):251–274.

Matras, Y. (1999). The pragmatics of codification in a stateless language. *Applied Linguistics* 20(4): 481–502.

Meara, P. (2004). Modeling vocabulary loss. *Applied Linguistics* 25(2): 137–155.

Meara, P. forthcoming. Lexical frequency profiles: a Monte Carlo analysis. *Applied Linguistics.*

Meara, P., P.M. Lightbown and R.H. Halter. (1997). Classrooms as lexical environments. *Language Teaching Research* 1(1): 28–47.

Mitchell, R. (2000). Applied linguistics and evidence-based classroom practice: the case of foreign language grammar pedagogy. *Applied Linguistics* 21(3): 281–303.

Mitchell, R. and C. Martin. (1997). Rote learning, creativity and 'understanding' in classroom foreign language teaching. *Language Teaching Research* 1(1):1–27.

Pavlenko, A. (2001). Language learning memoirs as a gendered narrative. *Applied Linguistics* 22(2): 213–240.

Roberts, C., E. Davies and T. Jupp. (1992). *Language and discrimination.* Harlow: Longman.

Roberts, J. (1999). Personal Construct Psychology as a framework for research into teacher and learner thinking. *Language Teaching Research* 3(2): 117–145.

Robinson, P. (2001). Task complexity, task difficulty, and task production: Exploring interactions in a componential framework. *Applied Linguistics* 22(1): 27–57.

Rorty, R. (1999). *Philosophy and social hope.* Harmondsworth: Penguin.

Samuda, V. (2001). Guiding relationship between form and meaning during task performance: the role of the teacher. In M. Bygate, P. Skehan and M. Swain (eds) *Researching pedagogical tasks: second language learning, teaching and testing.* Harlow: Longman.

Sarangi, S. & C. N. Candlin (eds) (2003). *Special Issue. Researching the discourse of workplace practice. Applied Linguistics* 24(3).

Schegloff, E. A. (2000). When 'others' initiate repair. *Applied Linguistics* 21(2): 205–243.

Skehan, P. & P. Foster. (1999). Task type and task processing conditions as influences on foreign language performance. *Language Learning* 49(1): 93–120.

Solan, L. M. & P. M. Tiersma (forthcoming) Author Identification in American Courts. *Applied Linguistics.*

Stubbs, M. (2001). Texts, corpora, and problems of interpretation: a response to Widdowson. *Applied Linguistics* 22(2): 149–172.

Swain, M. and S. Lapkin. (2000). Task-based second language learning: the uses of the first language. *Language Teaching Research Special Issue: Tasks in Language Pedagogy* 4(3): 251–274.

Swales, J. (1990). *Genre Analysis.* Cambridge: Cambridge University Press.

Thompson, G. (2001). Interaction in academic writing: learning to argue with the reader. *Applied Linguistics* 22(1): 58–78.

Towell, R. and P. Tomlinson. (1999). Language curriculum development research at university level. *Language Teaching Research* 3(1): 1–32.

Wang, K. and P. Nation (2004). Word Meaning in Academic English: Homography in the Academic Word List. *Applied Linguistics* 25(3).

Widdowson, H. (2000). On the limitations of linguistics applied. *Applied Linguistics* 21(1): 3–25.

Wong, J. (2000). Delayed next turn repair initiation in native/non-native speaker English conversation. *Applied Linguistics* 21(2): 244–267.

Wray, A. (2000). Formulaic sequences in second language teaching: Principle and practice. *Applied Linguistics* 21(4): 463–489.

Yuan, F. and R. Ellis. (2003). The effectgs of pre-task planning and on-line planning on fluency, complexity and accuracy in L2 monologic oral production. *Applied Linguistics* 24(1): 1–27.

Zuengler, J. and J. Mori (eds) (2002). *Special Issue: Microanalyses of classroom discourse. Applied Linguistics.* 23(3).

Résumé

L'article propose que l'évolution récente la plus significative en linguistique appliquée c'est l'épanouissement du champ en discipline générique. Elle y arrive principalement à travers ses nombreux domaines de spécialisation distincts, chacun d'entre eux ayant pour but de promouvoir — à ses propres fins — l'étude théorique et empirique de la langue en tant qu'élément constitutif de problèmes du monde réel. A partir de cette perspective générique, de nombreuses innovations ont déjà vu le jour, autant méthodologiques que théoriques. Cependent, l'article propose que jusqu'ici les diverses spécialisations de notre discipline ne se sont adressée que rarement à deux défis-clés que nous pose le rapport entre la communauté public et l'académie: premièrement celui d'identifier et d'étudier des questions qui constituent aux yeux du public lui-même des problèmes du monde réel; et deuxièmement celui de s'interroger sur la contribution de ses propres recherches à la résolution des problèmes visés. En rapport avec ce problématique, nous relevons en particulier trois thèmes de la recherche en linguistique appliquée: premièrement celui du rapport entre les données de surface et l'élaboration de la théorie; deuxième- ment celui du rapport entre le cas spécifique et la généralisation; et troisièmement celui du rôle de la problémati- cité en général en linguistique appliquée. L'article en conclut que la linguistique appliquée a besoin de répondre de ses recherches devant deux communautés de référence: devant sa propre communauté académique, mais tout aussi bien devant les divers publics du monde quotidien avec lesquels la discipline elle-même cherche à travailler.

Applied Linguistics

Brazilian perspectives

Marilda C. Cavalcanti
State University of Campinas

The aim of this paper is to present perspectives in Applied Linguistics (AL) against the background of a historical overview of the field in Brazil. I take the stance of looking at AL as a field of knowledge and as a professional area of research. This point of view directs my reflections towards research-based Applied Linguistics carried out from within in places where it is continuously[1] developed, that is, in universities. Having done this, I locate the Brazilian experience within Latin America.

Keywords: Applied Linguistics, historical overview, Brazil, Latin America

Introduction

The development of an area of knowledge is both political and academic. Applied Linguistics, as well as other areas of knowledge, certainly shows different faces in different countries. These differences are a consequence of several factors including the way segmentation of knowledge is politically decided in universities and in funding bodies. Some areas are born in "a room of their own" (Woolf 2002) and others, and here I include Applied Linguistics, have to conquer a room (See Cavalcanti 1998). The history of Applied Linguistics in Brazil is intermingled with the history of Linguistics.[2] AL was seen as part of Linguistics and until today there are traces of this link, as for example, in research funding bodies where AL is still presented as a subarea of Linguistics. However, at the end of the first half of the first decade of the new millenium, when Applied Linguistics is approaching its fortieth anniversary in Brazil, what I want to focus on is the history of consolidation of AL as an area of knowledge of its own. In this paper, I briefly present a historical overview as a way to pave the way towards a reflection on future perspectives.

Historical overview

The 60's and the 70's

Applied Linguistics has been in Brazil since the mid sixties[3] according to Gomes de Matos (1976). However, in those days few scholars called themselves applied linguists. Among those who did were F. Gomes de Matos who at the time had already established contact with AILA, and M. A. A. Celani who founded the first postgraduate programme in Applied Linguistics at Pontifical Catholic University of Sao Paulo (PUC-SP) in 1971. It should be pointed out that, besides being the first, this was also the only AL programme in the country for fifteen years.

As in other places of the world, Applied Linguistics in Brazil was a synonym for matters related to the teaching of English as a Foreign Language (EFL) when it first started, although the PUC-SP programme also focused on Portuguese L1. At that time, the current view of AL as application of linguistic theories to classroom questions was well shown in the titles of the M.Sc. dissertations produced. These titles were related to themes such as how to understand a grammatical point to be able to teach it, or emphasis was given to the drawing of suggestions about materials production. In the case of Portuguese L1, the focus of research was mainly the description of Brazilian Portuguese.

AILA Review 17 (2004), 23–30.
ISSN 1461–0213 / E-ISSN 1570–5595 © John Benjamins Publishing Company

The 80's — The b(l)oom of AL
The eighties saw a unique moment in the country for the boom/bloom of Applied Linguistics. On the one hand, there was a group of very active applied linguists in several Brazilian universities. In one of these universities, an Applied Linguistics department was started. On the other hand, this group was joined by several new Ph.D.s who had studied abroad (mainly in the UK and in the US). The group became very active and visible as they participated in several conferences, mainly related to EFL teaching and learning, which were taking place at the time. Many of the returning scholars had focused their Ph.D. research on reading or writing in English as a Second Language (ESL) and EFL. Part of this Ph.D. group of scholars who were full of ideas and ideals, I experienced situations where assertive actions in the area of Applied Linguistics were called for in face of researchers who continuously repeated that they did not know what AL was whenever they saw themselves as invited speakers at AL conferences. To call oneself an applied linguist was the usual reaction of the group who was in search of establishing an association of applied linguists in Brazil. Another assertive action was related to epistemological discussions about Applied Linguistics which resulted in a forum that the AL working group created in the National Association of Research and Postgraduate Programmes in Literature and Linguistics (ANPOLL). Some of these discussions came out in writing as, for example, Almeida Filho (1987, 1991), Cavalcanti (1986, undated ms., 1990), Schmitz (1987), Bohn (1988). It was within this working group that the Brazilian Association of Applied Linguistics (ALAB) was contemplated. However, it took some time for it to surface as an official association.

The eighties also witnessed the beginning of two refereed journals in AL: *Trabalhos em Lingüística Aplicada* [Works in Applied Linguistics] (1983) and Documentation of Studies in Theoretical and Applied Linguistics (D.E.L.T.A.) (1985). The latter started with a stronger focus on Linguistics. Nowadays the focus is balanced between Linguistics and Applied Linguistics. These two journals were the only ones to have AL in their titles until the late nineties when *Revista de Lingüística Aplicada* [Journal of Applied Linguistics] came out as an ALAB publication. Although these were the only three specific AL publications, today there are about seven journals which publish papers reporting AL research. Only one[4] of these has AL in its title.

In 1986, the second postgraduate programme of Applied Linguistics was started at State University of Campinas (UNICAMP). As part of the activities of the new programme, that same year, the first Brazilian Congress of Applied Linguistics (CBLA) took place. The CBLA, now a conference of the Brazilian AL Association (see below), is the main applied linguistic conference in Brazil. With its 6th edition scheduled for October 2004, this conference has always attracted scholars from Brazil and from South America, mainly from Uruguay and Argentina.

Besides the CBLA, the late eighties also saw two other new AL conferences: the SimPLA (Symposium of Applied Linguistics — now discontinued) at UFRJ (Federal University of Rio de Janeiro) and the InPLA (Interchange of Research in Applied Linguistics which had its 15th annual edition in 2004) at PUC-SP. The latter was the first one to make room for postgraduate and undergraduate students' paper presentations.

The 90's — En route to consolidation
The decade began with the foundation of ALAB (the Brazilian Applied Linguistics Association). Brazil, which had first become an affiliate of AILA through the Brazilian Linguistics Association, was for some time at a limbo in relation to the AL international association. It was only after the foundation of ALAB in 1990 that the link was re-established.

The nineties showed the publication of another group of papers on epistemological issues in doing Applied Linguistics: Serrani (1990), Kleiman (1991, 1992), Schmitz (1991, 1992), Celani (1992), Moita Lopes (1991, 1994a, 1994b), Cavalcanti (1998), and the publication of books whose titles highlighted Applied Linguistics as Paschoal and Celani (1992), Moita Lopes (1996) and Signorini and Cavalcanti (1998).

In the early nineties, the insertion[5] (sometimes a rebirth) of Applied Linguistics into undergraduate language teacher education courses was started.[6] The nineties also witnessed the birth of new[7] postgraduate programmes in AL, the growth of research and a diversification of subareas in Applied Linguistics including language in the workplace, language and media, language and gender, language and technology; and also a diversification of subareas in AL in its interface with education including distance education, teacher education and linguistic minorities, and bi/multilingual education.

In the late nineties, several interinstitutional research groups in AL were formed. Applied Linguistics as an area of knowledge of its own was then consolidated in the country. The view of AL as a discipline and area of knowledge production searching for inter/multi/crossdisciplinarity was established and favoured against the view of application of linguistic theories.

As part of the work of postgraduate programmes there was a growth of research in the area of AL followed by a growth in the participation of scholars and postgraduate students in conferences and seminars in the country. This was also reflected in some of the AILA world congresses of the decade where Brazil held its position as having the participation of the fifth[8] largest contingent of scholars.

The nineties saw the beginning of a new national and some regional conferences. The national conference, which also attracted an international[9] audience, was the Encontro Nacional sobre Política de Ensino de Línguas Estrangeiras (National Meeting on Foreign Language Teaching Policy) started in 1996. It had a second edition in 2000. As to the regional conferences, they were started in postgraduate programmes and geared towards students' presentations of their ongoing research work. In my view, these regional conferences indicated the great movement in the area developed by new Ph.D.s who had joined the staff of these programmes.

Focus of research in AL throughout the years
With the historical overview in mind, I shall turn my attention to the development of research in AL. According to Kleiman (1992:28), the first moments (the seventies) of AL in Brazil focused on contrastive analysis, later (the eighties) the emphasis was on reading. In the early nineties, both Kleiman (1992) and Moita Lopes(1994a) agree that the subarea of FL research was well developed in AL in Brazil. Both authors also agree that the subarea of mother tongue research was still left behend and Kleiman (1992) refers to it as "a less productive route". Throughout the decade, however, there was a change in the *status quo* of mother tongue research. The interest in the subarea increased mainly in relation to literacy studies, writing and teacher education and to that end several studies were carried out. Other subareas of AL had already been established in postgraduate programmes, such as translation studies (nowadays in three universities) and bilingual education (in one). Besides, language and gender, language and new technologies, discourse and identities found their way in AL research. Regarding discourse, it should be added that the French current of Discourse Analysis has many followers in the country and the area of applied studies in Discourse Analysis (which does not necessarily see itself as Applied Linguistics) has had a great deal research input since the early nineties. The results are shown in several publications and theses.

Although very much geared towards the educational context, research in the nineties, began to show signs of diversification towards other contexts, for example, with projects on language and the workplace carried out at PUC-SP and Pontifical Catholic University of Rio de Janeiro (PUC-RJ).

As indicated above, the late nineties show a consolidation of applied linguistics as an area of knowledge of its own. This is reflected in the growth of research (see Leffa 2000), publications and in the presentation of results in national conferences, in the recognition of the area by funding bodies, and in the evaluation from within the area which came out in papers (Kleiman 1992; Moita Lopes 1994a; Signorini 1998). Undoubtedly a consequence of the growth of human resources formed in the postgraduate programmes in the area, the growth of research was also shown in the submission of proposals to the national funding bodies and in the participation of scholars in academic forums. This created a demand for AL representatives and *ad hoc* reviewers from the area of AL in funding bodies. Until the eighties, AL research proposals were reviewed by peers from theoretical linguistics.

One of the characteristics of this consolidation phase is the diversification of research methodologies in applied research. If research was mostly experimental and quasi-experimental in the past, in the late nineties, there was a tendency towards qualitative methodologies ranging from school ethnography, action research, collaborative research, narrative studies, life stories to introspective studies as can be seen in conference programmes (see Signorini 1998; Kleiman 1992; Moita Lopes 1994a, 1994b). As to be expected, this diversification of methodologies within the interpretive paradigm (see Guba & Lincoln 1998; Erickson 1986) live together with research developed within the quantitative paradigm.

The state of the art in the new millennium: Future perspectives

In my view the key words for Brazilian Applied Linguistics in the new millennium are 'recognition' and 'challenge'. As to 'recognition', I mentioned it above in relation to the consolidation of this research area. I see 'challenge' as a natural consequence to the follow up of the recognition of the area and as such related to future perspectives. Before looking forward, I will focus on the present moment.

This new moment is characterized by an issue discussed in the previous decade, that is, inter/multi/crossdisciplinarity (See Serrani 1990; Paschoal and Celani 1992; Moita Lopes 1994a, 1995, 1998; Signorini 1998, Signorini and Cavalcanti 1998). Behind this issue is a tendency in AL towards establishing itself as a locus of interface with other areas of knowledge. This is shown in research works where theorizing in Applied Linguistics means establishing a dialogue with other areas of knowledge be they in Linguistics & beyond (Interactional Sociolinguistics, Discourse Analysis, Pragmatics, etc) or in the Social Sciences (Anthropology, Sociology, Social Psychology, Cultural Studies, etc).

As another piece of evidence of AL as a locus of interface with other areas of knowledge there are two conferences which took place in the beginning of the millennium: a) *Simpósio Nacional Discurso, Identidade e Sociedade* [National Conference on Discourse, Identity and Society] jointly organized by the AL Postgraduate Programme at Federal University of Rio de Janeiro (UFRJ) and by the Language and Literature Studies at PUC-RJ in 2001. The publication (See Moita Lopes and Bastos 2002) that followed the event lists chapters by specialists from eleven areas related to the Social Sciences, including AL and b) *Metáfora na Linguagem e no Pensamento* [Metaphor in Language and Thought] organized by the Postgraduate Programme of Applied Linguistics and Language Studies at PUC-SP in 2002 which has a new edition planned for the early future. This event has planned a publication (Zanotto, Cameron and Cavalcanti in preparation) which places Applied Linguistics in dialogue with Cognitive Linguistics, Cognitive Psychology, Pragmatics, and Social Psychology, besides bringing research methodologies to the centre of debate.

I agree with Moita Lopes (1995: 2) that some of the research developed in AL today "shares the same principles that base other areas of investigation in the Social Sciences". I actually include myself among those who see AL as being closer to the Social Sciences than to Linguistics itself although it shares the focus on language (in use) with Linguistics.

Any consolidated area has to show its development and present its tendencies. To reflect on this development I now turn to Moita Lopes (1994a: 75–6) who ten years ago indicated seven aspects which he thought would direct the development of AL in the country. In a summarized way, these aspects were related to the development of human resources (researchers and teachers) and the development of research action and dissemination of results for classroom use. The author claimed the following "prospective tasks":

1. an investment in the formation of human resources, mainly Ph.D.'s, creating opportunities for the beginning of new postgraduate programmes in AL and consolidating the existing ones;
2. the development of the area of mother tongue research. His concern was mainly related to researchers who were also teacher educators;

3. an encouragement for FL researchers to act also in mother tongue research;
4. an enhancement of opportunities for classroom research results to get their way to classroom practice through interventionist classroom research proposals and research which focus on teacher education;
5. the widening of focus of researcher action to language use contexts other than the classroom in an attempt to change "discursive practices which usurp/take away workers', patients'", minority peoples' "power, voices";
6. the route towards a more inter or crossdisciplinary research in AL; and
7. an increase in the number AL specialized journals and in the publications specially written for classroom practitioners.

Looking back, Moita Lopes' prospective tasks[10] were all accounted for, some being more emphasized than others. The development of human resources has gone a long way with the consolidation of existing postgraduate programmes and the creation of new ones. These programmes are important partners and would benefit greatly from a more aggressive interchange policy among themselves both in relation to the education of researchers and to teacher education.

Regarding research action, interaction among researchers working in different subareas has started, but it is not enough. The implication is that it is important to look within Applied Linguistics as well as outside towards other areas of knowledge (as discussed above). Dialogue opportunities even within the same subarea, for example, minority bilingual education, are needed since the contexts are so different among themselves.

It should also be noted that AL as an applied area has a social contribution to make. This is an issue in some of the subareas but not in others. Each subarea will thus need to evaluate what type of contribution it can make. This is particularly relevant in a country where social problems are abundant. It is important to add to the discussion on social contribution a continuous debate about ethics and power issues to do away with neocolonization in postcolonial times.

Besides, and this links development of human resources with research action, a plan of action should be discussed with minority groups now opening themselves to do research. What I have in mind are, for example, linguistic/ideological minority movements (in native people's, afrodescendants' and deaf people's contexts) started under the sign of activism with the aim to devise short and long term solutions to urgent social, political problems. In my opinion, what should be encouraged in these cases is research from within (See Tuhiwaii Smith 1999), that is, developed by scholars from these particular contexts. This will place the researched as the researcher and perhaps the outside researcher as part of the researched (see Cavalcanti 2001).

As to dissemination of research results, a more concerted plan has to be developed and this has to be done in a language which is available to lay people and not in academy-like writing.

What is the future of AL in Brazil? From the portrait depicted so far, I would say the area has potential to have a still greater influence in professional development including teacher education. It also has potential to contribute to the ethical debate in research. Although the ethical issue has been a theme in conferences in Brazil, such as the National Association of Research and Postgraduate Programmes in Literature and Linguistics and the Brazilian Congress of Applied Linguistics, it is yet a point to be more addressed in publications as does Kleiman (in press.). Besides there is potential for a contribution to the debate on research/researched/researcher and the issue of power and empowerment drawing inspiration from Paulo Freire.

How does the Brazilian experience fit into Latin America?

The Brazilian AL experience is perhaps only comparable to the Mexican experience in Latin America. Actually, it should be pointed out that Mexico has been in AILA much longer than Brazil has. A landmark in the Mexican AL history, the journal *Estudios de Linguistica Aplicada*, a well known publication, first came out in 1983, the same year the first Brazilian AL journal was published. Another landmark is the MA programme in Applied Linguistics in the Centro de Enseñanza de Lenguas Extranjeras/Universidad Nacional Autónoma de México.

To my knowledge so far, from the publications I have seen and from the contacts I have established throughout the years with people from Latin America, other countries with some movement in AL (or with a shorter and sometimes discontinued history) are Argentina, Uruguay and Colombia. However, as it sometimes happens/happened in Brazil, it may as well be that AL work in Latin America is carried out but not publicized.

The subareas of Applied Linguistics which seem to call for interaction between Brazilian applied linguists and scholars from other LA countries are: Portuguese and Spanish as foreign languages and indigenous bilingual education (the latter specifically with Mexico, Peru, Colombia and Bolivia). Another potential field would be choice (elite) bilingual education since there is a proliferation of bilingual schools in Latin America, much more so than in Brazil.

Being the only Portuguese speaking country in Latin America and having Portuguese as its language of publication, Brazil is distanced from its nearby neighbours and also from the more distant Spanish speaking countries or has done so for a number of years. The exception again is related to Mexico, since, in the late eighties, some applied linguists in both countries started a long term relationship. In Mexico, Universidad Nacional Autónoma Metropolitana was the focus, in Brazil, several universities were involved in this dialogue which proved fruitful and involved an exchange of research students and also of visiting scholars.

More recently among the Mercosul countries, more systematic contacts have been established. As I mentioned before, this interaction is more with Argentina and Uruguay. Beyond the Mercosul, there have also been sporadic contacts with Colombia, Peru and Bolivia also with exchange of scholars in academic events.

There is much more that could be done and perhaps now that AL is consolidated in Brazil, it is time to make a more concerted effort to establish stronger links within Latin America. A Latin American AL academic event could be a call for Latin American countries to get together and find their points of commonality and difference in doing AL, including discussions on views of Applied Linguistics. It could also be an opportunity to make more contacts and think about joint research projects in the future. Undoubtedly, there is also room for exploiting other subareas of AL in these contacts to be.

Notes

1. From time to time there is news about a research movement as part of teacher education programmes in big private language schools. This is usually done by hiring a foreign professional to work with the teacher (practitioner research). The movement usually lasts while there is contact with the professional. Sometimes it is abruptly discontinued as research is not a priority in these schools. Sometimes it is individually continued by language teachers who decide to carry out a degree course either abroad or in the country.

2. Applied Linguistics is usually embedded in Linguistics departments. To my knowledge there is only one Applied Linguistics department in the country.

3. There is also another history of AL related to private language schools in the country. This history is not part of the scope of this paper because, as stated in the abstract, the focus is on research based AL and not on research done sporadically. I do acknowledge though the fact that AL was a label of importance for some of these language schools. As expected, their focus has been foreign language teaching.

4. The reference is to *Novos Horizontes em Lingüística Aplicada* [New Horizons in Applied Linguistics] published at the Universidade de Brasília [University of Brasília].

5. In the past when Linguistics was introduced in undergraduate courses, sometimes Applied Linguistics also found a place of its own within a view of application of theory to the teaching of foreign languages.

6. It should be pointed out, however, that AL, within the view of application of linguistic theories, had already been in some undergraduate courses.

7. Nowadays there are six programmes with Applied Linguistics in their names and seven postgraduate programmes in *letras* [language education and literature] or in linguistics which focus AL in their areas of study. (Source: CAPES/Ministry of Education — http://www.capes.gov.br)

8. The beginning of the new millennium showed a decrease in the number of scholars present at the AILA conferences due to fear of traveling because of international terrorism, difficulties in visa issuing and also due to an economic recession in the country. This scenario may have reflections in the next AILA conference.

9. Mainly from the *Mercosul* countries, that is., Argentina, Uruguay and Paraguay.

10. Numbers 1 and 2 have received a great deal of attention. Number 6 is a tendency. Number 5 is yet shyly coming out. Number 4 seems to be coming out in publications and publications in preparation.

References

Almeida Filho, J. C. (1991). Maneiras de compreender a Lingüística Aplicada [Ways of understanding Applied Linguistics]. *Revista Letras* [Journal of Letters/Brazil], 2: 7–18.

Almeida Filho, J. C. (1987). Lingüística Aplicada, aplicação de Lingüística e ensino de línguas [Applied Linguistics, application of linguistic theories and language teaching]. Anais do 3o Encontro de Letras e Lingüística [Proceedings of the 3rd Meeting of Letters and Linguistics]. Porto Alegre: PUC-RS.

Bohn, H. (1988). Lingüística Aplicada. In H. Bohn and P. Vandresen (eds), *Tópicos em Lingüística Aplicada* [Topics in Applied Linguistics], pp. 11–38. Florianópolis: Editora da Universidade Federal de Santa Catarina.

Cavalcanti, M. C. (1986). A propósito de Lingüística Aplicada [On Applied Linguistics]. *Trabalhos em Lingüística Aplicada* 7: 5–12.

Cavalcanti, M. C. (undated ms). Visões de Lingüística Aplicada [Views of Applied Linguistics].

Cavalcanti, M. C. (1990). Lingüística Aplicada: Revendo o texto de 1986. [Applied Linguistics: Revisiting the 1986 paper]. Paper presented at the II Simpla [II Conference in Applied Linguistics], UFRJ, 08–09/11/1990.

Cavalcanti, M. C. (1998). AILA 1996 e um estado da arte em miscrocosmo da Lingüística Aplicada [AILA 1996 and a miscocosmic state of the art of Applied Linguistics]. In I. Signorini and M. C. Cavalcanti (eds), *Lingüística Aplicada e Transdisciplinaridade: questões e perspectivas* [Applied Linguistics and Crossdisciplinarity: issues and perspectives] Campinas: Mercado de Letras, Brazil.

Cavalcanti, M. C. (2001). A pesquisa do professor como parte da educação continuada em curso de magistério indigena no Acre [Teacher research as part of in-service indigenous teacher education in Acre]. In A. B. Kleiman (ed.) *A Formação do Professor: Perspectivas da Lingüística Aplicada* [Teacher Education: Applied Linguistics Perspectives]. Campinas: Mercado de Letras.

Celani, M. A. A.(1992). Afinal, o que é Lingüística Aplicada? [What then is Applied Linguistics?]. In M. S. Z. Paschoal and M. A. A. Celani (eds), *Lingüística Aplicada: da aplicação da lingüística à lingüística transdisciplinar* [Applied Linguistics: from application of linguistic theories to transdisciplinary linguistics]. São Paulo: EDUC.

Erickson, F. (1986). Qualitative methods in research on teaching. In M. Wittrock (ed.), *Handbook of Research on Teaching*. New York: MacMillan.

Gomes de Matos, F. (1976).1965–1975: Dez Anos de Lingüística Aplicada no Brasil [Ten years of Applied Linguistics in Brazil]. *Revista de Cultura Vozes*, 1: 49–58.

Gomes de Matos, F. (1985). Mais dez anos de Lingüística Aplicada no Brasil: 1975–1985 [Another ten years of Applied Linguistics in Brazil: 1975–1985]. *Revista de Cultura Vozes*, June-July: 60–65.

Guba, E. G. and Lincoln, Y. S. (1998). Competing paradigms in qualitative research in D. K. Denzin and Y. S. Lincoln (eds), *The Landscape of Qualitative Research — Theories and Issues*, pp. 195–220. Thousand Oaks: Sage.

Kleiman, A. B. (1991). Afinal o que é Lingüística Aplicada [What is then Applied Linguistics?]. *Intercâmbio* [Interchange], São Paulo: PUC-SP:1–12.

Kleiman, A. B. (1992). O ensino de línguas no Brasil in M. S. Z. Paschoal and M. A. A. Celani (eds) *Lingüística Aplicada: da aplicação da lingüística à lingüística transdisciplinar* [Applied Linguistics: from application of linguistic theories to transdisciplinary linguistics]. São Paulo: EDUC.

Kleiman, A.B. (in press). A interface de questões éticas e metodológicas na pesquisa em Lingüística Aplicada [The interface of ethical and methodological issues in Applied Linguistics research]. *Cadernos de Linguagem e Sociedade* [Language and Society Notebooks]. Brasília: Thesaurus.

Leffa, V. (ed.) (2000). TELA — Textos em Lingüística Aplicada. [Texts in Applied Linguistics]. Digital data. Editora da Universidade Católica de Pelotas, Brazil.

Moita Lopes, L.P. (1991). Applied Linguistics in Brazil: Perspective. *The British Association for Applied Linguistics Newsletter,* 39: 27–30.

Moita Lopes, L.P. (1994a). Lingüística Aplicada no Brasil: um olhar retrospectivo e prospectivo [Applied Linguistics in Brazil: a retrospective and a prospective look]. *Boletim Informativo da ANPOLL,* 21: 66–77.

Moita Lopes, L.P. (1994b). A pesquisa interpretativista em Lingüística Aplicada: A linguagem como condição e solução [Interpretive research in Applied Linguistics: Language as condition and solution] *D.E.L.T.A.,* 10(2): 329–338.

Moita Lopes, L.P. (1995). Contextos institucionais em Lingüística Aplicada: Novos Rumos [Institutional contexts in Applied Linguistics: New Directions. Paper presented at the 5th InPLA [Interchange of Research in Applied Linguistics]. PUC-SP [Pontifical University of São Paulo].

Moita Lopes, L.P. (1996). *Oficina de Lingüística Aplicada.* [Applied Linguistics Workshop]. Campinas: Mercado de Letras, Brazil.

Moita Lopes, L.P. (1998). A transdisciplinaridade é possível em Lingüística Aplicada? [Is crossdisciplinarity possible in Applied Linguistics?] In I. Signorini and M.C. Cavalcanti (eds), *Lingüística Aplicada e Transdisciplinaridade: questões e perspectivas* [Applied Linguistics and Crossdisciplinarity: issues and perspectives], pp. 113–128. Campinas: Mercado de Letras, Brazil.

Moita Lopes, L.P. and Bastos, L.C. (eds) (2002). *Identidades — Recortes Multi e Interdisciplinares* [Identities — Multi- and Interdisciplinary Cuttings]. Campinas: Mercado de Letras/CNPq.

Paschoal, M.S. and Celani, M.A.A. (eds) (1992). *Lingüística Aplicada: Da Aplicação da Lingüística à Lingüística Transdisciplinar* [Applied Linguistics: From Application of Linguistics to Crossdisciplinary Linguistics]. São Paulo: EDUC.

Schmitz, J.R. (1987). Rumos e tendências da Lingüística Aplicada [Ways and tendencies of Applied Linguistics] *Trabalhos em Lingüística Aplicada,* 10: 71–85.

Schmitz, J.R. (1991). Lingüística Aplicada e o ensino de português como língua materna no Brasil [Applied Linguistics and the teaching of Portuguese as mother tongue in Brazil]. *Revista Internacional de Língua Portuguesa* [International Journal of Portuguese Language], 4: 35–42.

Schmitz, J.R. (1992). Lingüística Aplicada e o ensino de línguas estrangeiras no Brasil [Applied Linguistics and the teaching of foreign languages in Brazil], *ALFA* 36: 213–236.

Serrani, S.M. (1990). Transdisciplinaridade e Discurso em Lingüística Aplicada. [Crossdisciplinarity and Discourse in Applied Linguistics] *Trabalhos em Lingüística Aplicada,* 16: 39–45.

Signorini, I. (1998). CBLA 1995: Uma amostragem da pesquisa no Brasil [CBLA 1995: A sample of Brazilian research]. In Signorini and Cavalcanti (eds), *Lingüística Aplicada e Transdisciplinaridade: questões e perspectivas* [Applied Linguistics and Crossdisciplinarity: issues and perspectives], pp. 171–184. Campinas: Mercado de Letras, Brazil.

Tuhiwaii-Smith, L. (1999), *Decolonizing Methodologies: Research and Indigenous Peoples.* Zed Books (UK) and University of Otago Press (New Zealand).

Woolf, V. (2002). *A Room of One's Own.* London: Penguin (First published in 1929).

Zanotto, M.S., Cameron, L.J. and Cavalcanti, M.C. (eds) (in preparation) *Confronting Metaphor in Use: An Applied Linguistic Approach.*

Résumé

Le but de cet article est de présenter des perspectives en Linguistique Appliquée (LA) en relation avec les sources d'une vue d'ensemble historique de ce domaine au Brésil. Je prends le parti de traiter la Linguistique Appliquée comme un champ de connaissances et comme un domaine professionnel de recherches. Ce point de vue oriente ma réflexion vers une Linguistique Appliquée basée sur des recherches effectuées de l'intérieur, dans des endroits où elle se développe continuellement, autrement dit, dans les universités. Ayant fait cela, je situe l'expérience brésilienne à l'intérieur de L'Amérique Latine.

Australia and New Zealand applied linguistics (ANZAL)

Taking stock

Robert C. Kleinsasser
University of Queensland

This paper reviews some emerging trends in applied linguistics in both Australia and New Zealand. It sketches the current scene of (selected) postgraduate applied linguistics programs in higher education and considers how various university programs define applied linguistics through the classes (titles) they have postgraduate students complete to be awarded a degree. Evidence of program requirements and topics reveal not only what applied linguistics generally entails, but offers insights into how applied linguistics is defined and practiced. Additionally, some of the salient research topics (titles) being published in the journals from the two countries' applied linguistics associations are sketched.

Keywords: Applied Linguistics in Australia/NZ, post-graduate courses

Introduction

This paper reviews some emerging trends in applied linguistics in both Australia and New Zealand.[1] Any such review must be selective and this one sketches the current scene of (selected) postgraduate applied linguistics programs in higher education, since to understand what is emerging in applied linguistics it is relevant to consider the manner in which students are inducted into the discipline. McNamara (2001) has reviewed the history of Australian applied linguistics and notes the influential personalities and trends in the nineteen-seventies. Now that applied linguistics has become an accepted discipline, it seems appropriate to consider how various university programs define applied linguistics through the classes (titles) they have postgraduate students complete to be awarded a (coursework) Master's degree. Selected postgraduate applied linguistics programs within Australia and New Zealand provide evidence of program requirements and topics revealing not only what applied linguistics generally entails, but offering insights into how applied linguistics is defined and practiced in various postgraduate programs in these two nations.[2] Following this review, some of the salient research topics (titles) being published in the journals from the two countries' applied linguistics associations will be sketched.

Background

Arguing that historical factors play a crucial role in debating the fundamental character of applied linguistics, McNamara (2001) defined "the historical character of applied linguistics in Australia, using data from interviews with three of its most influential figures: Terry Quinn, Michael Clyne and Michael Halliday" (p. 13). The paper, which reflected these three persons' academic careers and interests led McNamara to suggest

> Australian Applied Linguistics originated in the applied linguistics of modern languages, and the languages of immigrants, rather than of English. The Australian tradition shows a surprisingly strong influence of continental Europe and of the United States rather than of Britain, which is surprising given the powerful general influence of British educational traditions in Australia right up until this day. (p. 13)

AILA Review 17 (2004), 31–56.
ISSN 1461–0213 / E-ISSN 1570–5595 © John Benjamins Publishing Company

McNamara noted that linguistics has played a crucial role in applied linguistics especially with the work of Clyne and Halliday, but Quinn was more of an applied linguist with a focus on language teaching and contended that "[t]he complex and paradoxical relation between the two disciplinary areas [linguistics and applied linguistics] is still being played out in the Australian context" (pp. 27–28).

Yet, since that early period applied linguistics has grown dramatically outside the specific universities where the three worked. Research (especially in languages other than English) has been boosted by funding of projects through Language Australia (The National Language and Literacy Institute of Australia) in the early and mid 1990s, and (over the last two decades) for ESL by research from the National Centre for English Language Teaching and Research (NCELTR). This growth of research activity has lead to the development of programs offering postgraduate degrees in applied linguistics. Such programs offer some evidence of the character of the emerging scene of applied linguistics in both Australia and New Zealand. Their growth, especially in the past decade to cater for the needs of an increasing overseas student population working toward higher degrees, would seem to signal that a current definition of applied linguistics based on practice could be sought by reviewing program requirements and classes that prepare postgraduate students to become (professional) applied linguists. In fact, Davies (1999) — who worked extensively in Australia — writes, "Training courses, especially vocational training courses, such as the MA in Applied Linguistics, are ways of defining the subject. In all cultures, the training of the young provides a *rite de passage*, a ritualised entry into senior status by the provision of the necessary keys to that culture" (p. 14, italics original). This advice suggests it would be prudent to review the documentation of university programs (courses) in both Australia and New Zealand to begin sketching an understanding of how programs define and represent applied linguistics.

The perusal of program documentation also can serve as evidence of not only an emerging applied linguistics profession but an evolving, if not fully defined field of study. Atkinson & Coffey (1997) argue documentary materials need to be given due weight and proper analytic attention because they "often enshrine a distinctively documentary version of social reality. They have their own conventions that inform their production and circulation. They are associated with distinct social occasions and organized activities" (pp. 47–48). Hodder (2000) further contends that "Such texts are of importance for qualitative research because, in general terms, access can be easy and low cost, because the information provided may differ from and may not be available in spoken form, and because texts endure and thus give historical insight" (p. 704). With this in mind the web pages of (selected) university programs in Australia and New Zealand were reviewed to develop a perspective of the social reality and historical character of applied linguistics and to further add to the description of applied linguistics in this particular part of the southern hemisphere. (University websites were accessed during April, May, and June 2004.[3])

Selected university programs

Given the need to limit the focus of this review, applied linguistics postgraduate (Master level) programs in nine universities, eight of which comprise the Group of Eight (Go8) (2004) in Australia are examined. This particular group was chosen because of these Universities acknowledged status and reputation. According to their website the Go8, among other things, "[r]eceive over 70% of national competitive research grants and conduct over 60% of all Australian university research", "[p]roduce over 60% of Australian university research publications and two-thirds patents", "[g]enerate over 80% of the most highly cited Australian university publications", and "[a]ttract nearly 60% of competitive international Postgraduate Research Scholarships". Together, these eight universities receive 71% of the Australian Research Council Discovery Grants and 83% of the National Health and Medical Research Council Grants and Research Fellowships. These eight universities include the University of Adelaide (ADE), the Australian National University (ANU), the

University of Melbourne (MEL), Monash University (MON), the University of New South Wales (NSW), the University of Queensland (QLD), the University of Sydney (SYD), and the University of Western Australia (WA). To these eight, Macquarie University (MAC) is added because of its historic relationship to Adult Migrant Education via the Commonwealth of Australia's NCELTR, it having the largest linguistics department of its kind in Australia, and it having a Doctor of Applied Linguistics degree (Macquarie University Linguistics, 2004).

In these universities applied linguistics programs are variously located in different faculties (e.g., Humanities, Arts, Arts and Social Sciences), colleges (e.g., Science and Technology), schools (e.g., Language Studies; Languages Cultures, and Linguistics; English Media Studies, and Art History, Languages and Comparative Cultural Studies, Education), divisions (e.g., Division of Linguistics and Psychology), departments (e.g., Linguistics and Applied Linguistics, Linguistics), and a centre (e.g., Centre for European Studies and General Linguistics) (see Table 1).

A list of New Zealand programs was accessed from the Applied Linguistics Association of New Zealand, Inc. (2004). These universities include the University of Auckland (AUC), Auckland University of Technology (AUT), Massey University (MAS), the University of Otago (OTA), Victoria University of Wellington (VUW), and the University of Waikato (WAI). Massey University and the University of Otago have (post)graduate diplomas in second language teaching but do not appear to have coursework MA level degrees in either second language teaching or applied linguistics. Nonetheless, MA degrees by research are offered, so students could complete a research degree in these particular academic areas.

In these universities, applied linguistics are variously located in different faculties (e.g., Arts, Arts and Social Sciences, Education), schools (e.g., Languages, Language Studies, Linguistics and Language Studies), and departments or programs (e.g., Applied Language Studies and Linguistics, Arts and Language Education, General and Applied Linguistics, Linguistics, Second Language Teaching) (see Table 2).

The majority of programs require two semesters of study, with the exceptions of Macquarie University which takes 2–3 semesters, the University of Queensland which takes 3 semesters, Victoria University of Wellington which takes 3 trimesters, Auckland University of Technology which takes 4 semesters, and the University of Auckland's MA in Language Teaching and Learning which takes 4 semesters. Coursework programs were perused for compulsory and elective classes at each university. Although various universities identify classes as courses, papers, units, points, credits etc., all have been identified in this review as the more inclusive term classes as it allows for more general cross comparisons to be made. In the main, the number of courses, papers, units, points, or credits was easily translated to classes to represent the number of classes required to complete the degree in the amount of time (usually 2 semesters) set forth in each program. Similarly, the term compulsory was used for required or core classes to allow for consistency in this discussion. Also, most programs offer a Master's degree by research. As research degrees in both Australia and New Zealand focus specifically on a research project, thesis, or dissertation, with little to no coursework as part of the research degree, they were not included in this review. Therefore, the focus of this review is on master level coursework involving the field of applied linguistics.

Limitations

This review was limited by several factors. First, it was necessary to limit the review within Australia for practical reasons and representative universities were chosen for their status and their focus on research. There are of course applied linguistics programs in many of the other Australian universities. Second, the Master's coursework degree was used as the level for comparisons, although graduate certificate and postgraduate diploma degrees, along with one doctor of applied linguistics degree (MAC) could also have been reviewed (and many classes within these awards may serve as classes within the varying Master degrees). There are also some Bachelor degrees offered by

Table 1. Faculties, schools, departments, etc. in Australia

	ADE	ANU	MAC	MEL	MON	NSW	QLD	SYD	WA
Faculty of Humanities and Social Sciences	Centre for European Studies and General Linguistics								
Faculty of Arts		School of Language Studies Linguistics and Applied Linguistics Program		Department of Linguistics and Applied Linguistics	School of Languages, Cultures, and Linguistics		School of Languages and Comparative Cultural Studies[a]	School of Society, Culture and Performance, Linguistics Department	
College of Science and Technology			Division of Linguistics and Psychology Department of Linguistics Programs in Applied Linguistics						
Faculty of Arts and Social Sciences						School of Linguistics and School of Education			
Faculty of Education				Master of TESOL	MEd (TESOL) and MEd (TESOL — International)			MEd TESOL/ Languages	
Graduate School of Education									MEd AL

[a]MA in TESOL Studies is a joint programme between the School of Languages and Comparative Cultural Studies and the School of English, Media Studies, and Art History in the Faculty of Arts and the School of Education in the Faculty of Social and Behahavioural Sciences

Table 2. Faculties, schools, departments, etc. in New Zealand

	AUC	AUT	MAS	OTA	VUW	WAI
Faculty of Arts	Department of Applied Language Studies and Linguistics	School of Languages				General and Applied Linguistics
Faculty of Arts and Social Sciences						
College of Education			Department of Arts and Language Education			
Humanities and Social Sciences			School of Language Studies (Thesis only)		School of Linguistics and Applied Language Studies	
Humanities				School of Language, Literature and Performing Arts, English Department, Linguistics Programme		

universities, but such programs are few. Third, the entry requirements also could have been more closely examined to see what qualifications are expected of students enrolling in the Master programs but that would have moved the focus away from what the profession expected. Finally, program websites offer varying amounts of information concerning applied linguistics (and linguistics) in general; some websites offer a paragraph or two about each class while others provide class syllabi. Yet, these sites are so varied in what information is offered that it would have been difficult to compare and contrast such information across sites at the present time. (As accountability begins to grow within Australian universities, websites may become more comprehensive with detailed materials available for viewer consumption). Despite these limitations, use of the title of classes as data offers some insights as to the themes and areas of study involved in the selected programs that make up ritualised entry to applied linguists (Davies 1999). Moreover, examining the data in this way offers the opportunity for readers to review the evidence for themselves, thereby vicariously participating in the creation of text and understandings about applied linguistics MA level programs (Eisner 1991). Presenting the data in tabular form also follows Wolcott's (1990) admonishment to (qualitative) researchers not to be tempted to make too many judgments, but to allow readers to make their own.

Applied linguistics in Australia
Coursework degree programs from the nine selected Australian universities offer nine Master level degrees, in general, in the areas of applied linguistics and include the Master of Arts in Applied Linguistics (MA AL), Master of Applied Linguistics (MAL), Master of Applied Linguistics for Language Teachers (MA AL LT), Master of Education in Applied Linguistics (MEd AL), Master of TESOL (MTESOL), Master of Education (TESOL) (MEd TESOL), Master of Education (International TESOL), Master of Arts in TESOL (MA TESOL), and Master of Arts in TESOL Studies (MA TESOL Studies) (see Table 3).

Applied linguistics compulsory classes
A typical program structure includes compulsory and elective courses (Table 4 outlines information concerning length of study and total number of courses for the degree in the headings for each university. The compulsory table presents the number of compulsory classes and the remaining number of classes would then be the number of electives needed for the degree to be awarded). For instance the MA AL at Sydney requires a total of eight classes, four compulsory and four electives. The compulsory courses include: *Language analysis, Sociolinguistics, Additional language learning, Additional language teaching.*[4] The electives are selected from: *Register and genre in English, Semantics and pragmatics, Language for specific purposes, Bilingualism, Language and culture, Language testing, Media discourse (analysing language in mass media), Pragmatic grammar of English, Cross-cultural communication, Translation, Educational linguistics, Language and identity, Essay, Dissertation Part 1* and *Part 2,* and *MLitt treatise.* In general the number of compulsory classes for the MA AL degrees in the four universities offering this program consist of none at the University of New South Wales, one at the University of Adelaide (*Language and meaning*), four at the University of Sydney, to seven at the University of Queensland (see Table 4).

The canvassing of the compulsory classes in all applied linguistics degrees (see Table 4) reveals that eight universities require a type of linguistics, language analysis, or grammar class, six universities require a type of research methods class, six universities require a type of language teaching and/or curriculum and materials development class, and five require second language acquisition with one requiring a class in language learning. Variations of sociolinguistics are required in four universities or could be selected as one of the requirements instead of something else identified in the program compulsory classes. Assessment/Testing/Evaluation is required in three universities. In the main, these requirements partially develop applied linguists' awareness expressly in four of the nine fields identified by the International TESOL Organisation to support the development of teacher

Table 3. Applied Linguistics Degrees in Australia

	ADE	ANU	MAC	MEL	MON	NSW	QLD	SYD	WA
MA in AL	X							X	
MAL		X	X[c]	X[d]	X[e]	X[a]	X[b]		
MA AL LT					X				
MEd AL						X			X
MTESOL				X[f]					
MEd TESOL					X			X	
MEd International TESOL					X				
MA TESOL						X			
MA TESOL Studies							X		

[a] NSW also has MA in Korean Applied Linguistics and MA in Japanese Applied Linguistics
[b] Three streams including AL, AL Second Language Learning and Teaching, AL CALL
[c] Four streams including AL, AL TESOL, AL Literacy, AL Language Program Management
[d] Four streams including TESOL, CALL, Language Testing, English Language
[e] Monash also has Master of Applied Japanese Linguistics
[f] Four streams depending (two thesis oriented streams and two coursework streams)

Table 4. Australian Applied Linguistics (Compulsory Classes)

	ADE	NSW	QLD	SYD	ANU	MAC	MEL	MON	MON	NSW	WA
	MA AL	MA AL	MA AL	MA AL	MAL	MAL	MAL	MAL	MAL IT	MEd AL	MEd AL
	2 sem	2 sem	3 sem	2 sem	2 sem	2–3 sem	2 sem	2 sem	2 sem	2 sem	2 sem
	6 classes	6 classes	12 classes[e]	8 classes	8 classes[a]	10 classes or 8 and dissertation[b]	8 classes or 6 and thesis[c]	6 classes	6 classes[d]	6 classes	8 classes
		No compulsory									
Linguistics/Structure of Language			X X X		X	X - - -		X			
Language Analysis				X							
Language and Meaning	X										
Grammar Meaning & Discourse						X - X -					
Grammar & Discourse: Applied Linguistics							X[f] - X				
Context and Use and Analysis of English Language						- X - -					
Applied Linguistics			X X X								
Children's LA											
SLA			X X X	X X	X[k]	- X - -	X - X -		X X		
Lang Learning				X	X[k]						
Sociolinguistics				X							X
Language in Society						/h - - -		X			
Lang & Cult in Contact							- - - /g				
World Englishes											
TESOL in Context						- X - X	- - - /g				
Lang in Thinking & Learning											X
Pragmatics						/h - - -					
(Second) Language Teaching			X X X	X	X[k]	/h - - -	X[f] - X			X	
(Issues) Curric & Materials Development			- X -			- X X X					
Literacy Development						- - X -					X

Table 4. (continued)

Theory & Practice of TESOL	- X
Reading Dev & Disorders	- - X -
Assess/Eval/Test	- X - - X - - - X - -
Lang & Cog	X - - -
CALL (Intro)	X X X X X X X X X X X X X X[i]
Res Meth	X X X X - - X X X X
Concepts in Managing Lang Prog	- - X
Leading and Managing Lang Prog	- - - X
Port & Synthesis/Major Paper (2 classes)	X X X X
Quant Methods	- - X - X -
Teaching Asian Languages	
Student Autonomy	- - [j]
Technology Design	- - [j]
Electronic Networking	- - [j]
Lang Skills and Computer	- - [j]

Note: Most of the class titles fit under these names or categories; there are variations, but they are slight and do not affect the general compulsory requirement.

[a] Three options: (1) 6 classes and thesis (15,000 words), (2) 5 classes and thesis (20,000 words), (3) 4 classes and thesis (25,000 words)

[b] Four streams: Applied Linguistics, AL (TESOL), AL (Literacy), AL (LPM)

[c] Four streams: TESOL, CALL, Language Testing, English Language

[d] Two streams: TESOL, CALL, Teaching Asian Languages, Teaching English as a Second/Foreign Language

[e] Three streams: AL, AL Second Language Learning and Teaching, AL CALL

[f] Select one or the other

[g] Select one or the other

[h] Select one or the other

[i] Two classes: Introduction to CALL and CALL and Language Program

[j] Select three of the four

[k] At least two must be selected

quality (TESOL 2003). These include linguistics, second language acquisition, sociolinguistics, and language pedagogy and methodology. To a lesser extent curriculum and materials development, literacy development, and assessment are covered by some programs. In the main, cross-cultural communication and applied linguistics are not specifically represented.

Bardovi-Harlig & Hartford (1997) consider ten elements in their idea of language education that include psycholinguistics, second language acquisition, phonology, syntax, sociolinguistics, pragmatics, world languages, reading, writing, and assessment. When canvassing the compulsory requirements for the applied linguistics degrees, it can be seen that sociolinguistics and second language acquisition receive attention in these programs with world languages, literacy (e.g., reading and writing), and assessment also represented by a few programs. Although other features could be scattered throughout various classes (either compulsory or electives) little direct emphasis is given to psycholinguistics, pragmatics, phonology, and syntax (although the grammar classes may cover these), per se. Additionally, Kaplan (2002) suggests,

> With respect to the training of incipient applied linguists, a curriculum grounded in linguistics and its various hyphenated subcomponents should be considered basic. Beyond that, perhaps a wide variety of academic minors ought to be available, or, alternatively, joint degrees in applied linguistics and any of the fields mentioned ought to be possible, assuming that bureaucratic obstacles can be overcome. (p. ix)

The review of these (selected) applied linguistics degree programs in Australia challenges Kaplan's idea of curriculum grounded in linguistics, but certainly entertains his ideas of (varying and various) subcomponents (see also elective classes below). It is also clear that applied linguistics in these programs concern language teaching, language acquisition, and language learning.

TESOL compulsory classes

A typical TESOL type of degree consists of a few more compulsory courses than many of the AL degrees. The MA in TESOL at the University of New South Wales, for instance, requires three compulsory classes that include *Language teaching methodology, Testing and evaluation,* and *Syllabus design* and three electives selected from: *The structure of English, Functional grammar, Functional discourse analysis, Adult language learning and teaching, Language for specific purposes,* and *Special project in TESOL.*

The canvassing of the compulsory classes in all the TESOL degrees (see Table 5) reveals that three universities require a type of linguistics, grammar, or language and language acquisition class, four universities require a type of language teaching, methods, and/or curriculum design class (the fifth university requires just Teaching Oral English), and two universities require some type of practicum teaching experience. Variations of sociolinguistics are required in two universities. Assessment/Testing/Evaluation is required in two of the five universities. In the main, these requirements partially develop TESOL teachers' awareness expressly in four of the nine fields identified by the International TESOL Organisation to support the development of teacher quality (TESOL 2003). These include linguistics, sociolinguistics, language pedagogy and methodology, and curriculum and materials development. To a lesser extent assessment and second language acquisition is covered by some programs. In the main, cross-cultural communication, applied linguistics, and literacy are not specifically represented in compulsory classes.

Again considering Bardovi-Harlig & Hartford's (1997) ten elements of language education, it can be seen that sociolinguistics receives attention in these programs with assessment also represented by a few programs. Although other features could be scattered throughout various classes (either compulsory or electives) little direct emphasis is given to psycholinguistics, phonology, syntax (although the grammar classes may cover these), reading, writing, world languages, second language acquisition, and pragmatics, per se.

Table 5. Australian TESOL (Compulsory Classes)

	MEL[a] (M TESOL)	MON[b] 2 sem 6 classes	SYD (MEd TESOL) 2 sem 8 classes (Select 4 or the following 5)	NSW (MA TESOL) 2 sem 8 classes	QLD (MA TESOL Studies) 3 sem 12 classes
Linguistics					X[c]
Grammar: Text & Context			X		
Lang & Lang Acq	- - X X				
Perspectives on Lang Development			X		
Lang as Social Prac			X		
Language Society and Cultural Difference		1a, 1b, 1c; 2a, 2b, 2c; 3a, 3b, 3c			
Language Teaching/Methods				X	X
Curriculum Design				X	
TESOL Methods & Curriculum	- - X X				X
Theory and Practice of TESOL		1a, 1b, 1c; 2a, 2b, 2c; 3a, 3b, 3c			
Curric & Assessment		1a, 1b, -; 2a, 2b, -; 3a, 3b, 3c			
Teaching Oral English			X		
Assessment/Testing/Evaluation	E[d] X - X			X	
(TESOL) Prof Prac/Advance Prac	- - X X	1a, 1b, 1c; 2a, 2b, 2c			
Literacy			X		
Innovation and Change in L Ed	E[d] X X X				
Critical Perspectives on TESOL					X
Intro to CALL					X
Interpreting Research		1a, 1b; 2a, 2b; 3a, 3b			
Embarking on Research		1c; 2c; 3c			
Thesis/Professional Project‡		-, 1b, 1c; -, 2b, 2c; -, 3b, 3c			

[a]Four streams: 100A (selects 1 elective), 100B, 150A, 150B
[b]3 degress: (1) MEd TESOL, (2) MEd TESOL — International (without teaching qualifications or experience), (3) MEd TESOL — International (with teaching qualifications and higher scores on standardised English tests; note there are three options in each degree program (a, b, c)
[c]Two classes: Foundations of Syntax & Semantics and Foundations of Morphology and Phonology
[d]Select one of these, or others from elective list (see web page)

Elective classes
The electives range is quite eclectic across all programs and additionally quite numerous for others. For example, in New South Wales (a Faculty of Arts and Social Sciences) the electives for the MA AL degree include: *Special project in applied linguistics, second language acquisition, Language teaching methodology, Testing and evaluation, Syllabus and design, The structure of English, Bilingualism, Translation (theory and practice), First language acquisition, Functional grammar, Language and mind, Functional discourse analysis, Professional communication, Adult language learning and teaching, Language for specific purposes,* and *Analysing spoken discourse.* In the Linguistics Department at Macquarie the electives for the MAL degrees variously include: *Grammar, meaning and discourse, Phonetics and phonology, Language and cognition, Languages and culture in contact, Pragmatics, Language testing and evaluation, Stylistics and the teaching of literature, Language planning and policy, Second language acquisition, Literacy, Lexicography, Concept in managing language programs, First language acquisition, Language for specific purposes, Reading development and disorders, Bilingualism, Context, use and analysis of the English language (a global perspective), TESOL in context, Curriculum innovation in language teaching, Special study in applied linguistics, Leading and managing language program,* and *Discourse in professional and organisational contexts.* Queensland's MA TESOL Studies degree offers classes across three schools. The electives from the School of Education includes classes titled *Teaching for literacy and multi-literacies, Productive pedagogies productive schools, Rousing minds to life, Professional development, Globalising education,* and *Special topics in education.* The School of English, Media Studies, and Art History offers electives titled *English (history, change, and variation), Special topics in linguistics A, Educational linguistics, Grammar in texts, Sociolingustic perspectives on communication,* and *Thesis.* The School of Languages and Comparative Cultures offers *Second language acquisition, Research methods, Language in Australia, Issues in language program development, The lexicon and second language learning, Language testing and assessment, Electronic networking, Elective course A, Language and intercultural communication,* and *Portfolio and synthesis.*

Applied linguistics in New Zealand
Coursework degree programs from the five New Zealand universities offer seven Master level coursework degrees in the areas of applied linguistics and include the Master of Arts in Applied Linguistics (MA AL), Master of Arts in Applied Language Studies (MA ALS), Master of Arts in Language Teaching and Learning (MA LTL), Master of Arts TESOL (MA TESOL), Master of TESOL (MTESOL), Master of Professional Studies (MPS), and Master of Education (MEd) (see Table 6).

MA Applied Linguistics/Applied Language Studies/Language Teaching Compulsory Classes
A typical program structure includes compulsory and elective courses as found in Australian programs. For the two MA AL degrees, one program takes three trimesters to complete while the other takes two semesters to complete. Both programs require two compulsory classes. The program at the University of Waikato requires one class in *Research methods in applied linguistics* and another in *Current issues in applied linguistics.* At the Victoria University of Wellington, the compulsory classes include *Evaluating research in AL* and *Research methodology.* The program for MA ALS at AUT requires *Language analysis, Language culture and communication, Discourse Analysis, Approaches to research,* and two from *Language and Society, Qualitative Research Methods,* and *Quantitative Methods.* The University of Auckland's MA LTL requires the majority of its courses; however, if a dissertation, thesis, or research portfolio is included, the requirements for classes decreases (see Table 7's footnote).

The canvassing of the compulsory classes in all applied linguistics degrees (see Table 5) reveals three universities require approaches or methods of research, with one (Waikato) where research and current issues classes are specific to applied linguistics. Language analysis and variations of sociolinguistics are required in two universities. Assessment/Testing/Evaluation is required in one university. Variously, the compulsory requirements, along with electives partially develop applied

Table 6. Applied Linguistics Degrees in New Zealand

	AUC	AUT	MAS	OTA	VUW	WAI
MA AL					X	X
MA ALS[a]		X				
MA LTL[b]	X					
MA TESOL					X	
MTESOL	X					
MPS[c]	X					
MEd			X			
MA			(Thesis Only)	(Thesis Only)		

[a]Applied Language Studies
[b]Master of Arts in Language Teaching and Learning
[c]Professional Studies

Table 7. New Zealand Applied Linguistics (Compulsory Classes)

	AUC	AUT	VUW	WAI
	4 semesters	4 semesters	3 trimesters	2 semesters
	14 classes[a]	16 classes (8 dissertation)	12 classes	4 classes
Language Analysis		X		
Language Culture and Communication		X		
Language and Society		/[b]		
Discourse Analysis		X		
Evaluating Research in AL			X	
Approaches to Research/Research Methods		X	X	
Qualitative Methods		/[b]		
Quantitative Methods		/[b]		
Research Methods in AL				X
Current Issues in AL				X
Specialty Paper		X (2 classes)		
Language Assessment	X			
Teaching English as an International Language	X			
Grammar for Teachers	X			
Task-based Language Teaching and Learning	X			
Corpus Linguistics	X			
Sociolinguistics and Language Teaching	X			
Developing Academic Literacy	X			
Language Analysis for Teachers	X			
Discourse Analysis for Teachers	X			
Learner Language	X			
Theories of Language Learning	X			
Curriculum Development for Language Teaching	X			
Linguistic Research	X			
Linguistic Research in Linguistics	X			

[a]Or 12 classes and 2 classes worth of dissertation, 9 classes and 5 classes worth of dissertation, 7 classes and 7 classes and 5 classes worth of thesis, 7 classes and 7 classes of thesis, 7 classes and 7 classes worth Research portfolio
[b]Select two of three

linguists' awareness expressly when revisiting the nine fields identified by the International TESOL Organisation to support the development of teacher quality (TESOL 2003). Depending of course on the program, these include linguistics, assessment, applied linguistics, second language acquisition, sociolinguistics, language pedagogy and methodology, curriculum and materials development, literacy development, and cross-cultural communication.

Considering Bardovi-Harlig & Hartford' (1997) ten elements when canvassing the compulsory requirements for the Applied Linguistics degrees in New Zealand, it can be seen that sociolinguistics receives attention in these programs. Although the remaining features could be scattered throughout various classes (either compulsory or electives) little direct emphasis is given to the remaining features, per se. Additionally, the review of these New Zealand (selected) applied linguistics degree programs challenges Kaplan's (2002) idea of curriculum grounded in linguistics, but certainly, as in Australian programs, entertains his ideas of (varying and various) subcomponents.

New Zealand TESOL Compulsory Classes
Two universities offer TESOL oriented programs, Victoria University of Wellington and three different programs at the University of Auckland (see Table 8). In the main, these various classes (compulsory and electives) could variously touch upon the nine TESOL fields and ten features by Bardovi-Harlig & Hartford (1997). Yet, the emphasis is on teaching and involving applied linguistics issues to the teaching of English. The Master of Education degree at Massey University includes one specific class for the degree: "At postgraduate level, students can study the Teaching of Non-English Speaking Background (NESB) Students in a Regular Classroom. This paper [class] (207.769) is offered as part of the MEd programme, and is aimed at teachers in the mainstream setting (particularly early years and primary)."

Elective classes
The electives range, as in Australia, is quite eclectic across various programs. At the Victoria University of Wellington the electives for both degrees include variously *Methodology 1, Methodology 2, Description of English 1, Description of English 2, Second language acquisition, Language curriculum design, Special topic, Studies in second language development, Language for specific purposes, Teaching and learning vocabulary, Language assessment, Language testing, Sociocultural theories of language teaching and learning, Languages in the workplace, Discourse analysis, Syntactic analysis, Phonetics and phonology, Sociolinguistics, Research paper, Research project, Research dissertation.* The University of Waikato' electives include *Educational linguistics, Discourse analysis, CALL for language teaching, Language policy and planning, Special topic. Directed study, Dissertation (one, two, or three papers).* At the University of Auckland electives for the MTESOL degree include, *Second language classroom research, Material development and evaluation, Individual learner differences and second language learning, Bilingualism and bilingual education, Sociolinguistics and language teaching, Language planning and policy, Special topic in TESOL,* and *dissertation.* For the MPS degree the electives include *Teaching English as an international language, Task-based language teaching and learning, Corpus linguistics,* and *Developing academic literacy.*

Discussion
One of the things that becomes clear from the class titles of various programs dealing with applied linguistics in both Australia and New Zealand is that the area of study (field) has expanded well beyond the linguistic focused discipline of the 1970s described by McNamara (2001). In fact, it would be right to suggest that applied linguistics in these two countries is much more than linguistics applied (see Davies 1999, pp. 12–14). There also seems to be a proliferation in having both applied linguistics and TESOL classes that focus mainly on the teaching of second languages. Many of these programs might/seem to cater for the developing overseas student clientele who are seeking higher

Table 8. New Zealand TESOL (Compulsory Classes)

	AUC[a]	VUW 3 trimesters 12 classes
Methodology 1		X
Methodology 2		X
Description of English 1		X
Description of English 2		X
Language and Learning Processes		X
Language Curriculum Design		X
Second Language Course Design and Methodology	X - -	
Language Assessment and Evaluation	X X -	
Second Language Acquisition	X X -	
Discourse Analysis	X X -	
Language Assessment	- - X	
Language Analysis for Teachers	- - X	
Curriculum Development for Language Teaching	- - X	
Discourse Analysis for Teachers OR	- /[b]	
Sociolinguistics and Language Teaching	- /[b]	
Learner Language OR	- - /[c]	
Theories of Language Learning	- - /[c]	

[a] Master of TESOL-without DipTESOL or equivalent (2 semesters, 7 classes), Master of TESOL-with DipTESOL or equivalent (2 semesters, 7 classes), Master of TESOL or equivalent (2 semesters, 7 classes), Master of Professional Studies (2 semesters, 7 classes)
[b] Select one
[c] Select one

education degrees and produce additional funding within institutions struggling for financial capital due to tight budgetary constraints.[5] For example, in Queensland, it was recently reported that the "seven public universities reaped $313 million in fees from overseas students last year" (Odgers 2004, p. 4). This is a 15% increase from the previous year. Many programs host students from the particular Asian region; however other students from other countries in various parts of the world are also increasing. In a recent second language teaching class at the University of Queensland, there were sixty-six students working toward either their applied linguistics or TESOL studies degrees representing 17 countries (including Australia, China, Czech Republic, Germany, Hong Kong, Indonesia, Japan, Oman, Papua New Guinea, Philippines, Saudi Arabia, Singapore, South Korea, Taiwan, Thailand, USA, Vietnam). In order to tap this rich experience, programs may attempt to meet the needs and wishes of their clientele providing some compulsory classes while also allowing for numerous electives that cater for individual needs and/or contexts. At this time this is purely conjecture, but might be well worth further investigating and documenting to more completely capture the historical context of applied linguistics development near the beginning of the twenty-first century.

What is most clear in the data is that the central focus of many of these programs rest on what Cook (2003) categorises as language and education (including first and additional language education, language testing, and clinical linguistics) and the way in which Grabe (2002) suggests that applied linguists deal with various issues concerning language learning problems, language teaching problems, language assessment problems, and literacy problems. To be sure, some of the programs (and their class titles) touch upon other issues such as language, work, and law (workplace communication, language planning, and forensic linguistics) and language, information, and effect (literary stylistics, critical discourse analysis, translation and interpretation, information design, and lexicography) (see Cook 2003) and problems concerning language contact, language inequality, language policy and planning, language use, language and technology, and language pathology (see Grabe 2002); however, the major emphasis (compulsory and elective classes) in the vast majority of Master degree programs included in this review deal with language and language education issues. Grabe (2002) defines "applied linguistics as a practice-driven discipline that addresses language-based problems in real-world contexts" (p. 10). It would seem that the majority of the programs analysed in this paper would probably consider the definition of applied linguistics as a practice-driven discipline that addresses language-based problems in second language teaching and learning environments.

The melange of elective classes within most degree programs makes it extremely difficult to pinpoint just what type of language-based problems in second language teaching and learning environments applied linguists completing such coursework are indeed interested. The wide array of topics allows for a myriad of directions that any one person could take within each program; thus, making it difficult to define the scope of applied linguistics within these selected programs in Australia and New Zealand. The arduous task of defining applied linguistics remains perplexing. Even Kaplan (2002) admits "Applied linguistics is a difficult notion to define" (p. vii) and laments the handbook he edits probably does not provide a definitive definition of the field; nor can the selected programs reviewed here provide a definitive definition of the field. Nonetheless, such a review offers initial glimpses of the types of classes available in applied linguistics programs and how those entering the field may view their discipline upon completing both compulsory and elective classes.

With such a focus on second language teaching and learning in most applied linguistics programs it is not surprising to find a burgeoning literature codifying research that is uncovering teacher perceptions, beliefs, and actions in second language teaching and learning environments in Australia, New Zealand, as well as the Asia-Pacific region. There is growing interest investigating learning environment (school) cultures (McKay 2002; Savignon 1991, 2003). For instance, Kleinsasser and his doctoral students at the University of Queensland are investigating school technical cultures both in Australia and neighbouring regional countries (e.g., Hongboontri 2003, Kleinsasser 1993; Liu, forthcoming; Sato 2002; Sato & Kleinsasser 1999a, 1999b, forthcoming; Zulaiha, forthcoming). An important factor in uncovering technical cultures (a term used by Lortie [1975]) is to examine teachers' beliefs and practices. As Thompson (1967) noted, the technical culture of education "rests on abstract systems of belief about relationships among teachers, teaching materials, and pupils; but learning theories assume the presence of these variables and proceed from that point" (p. 19). Sato & Kleinsasser (1999a, 1999b) examine Australian teachers of Japanese and consider the extent to which communicative language teaching is understood by the participants. They also consider the use of triangulation and discuss the relevance of having more than one particular data source when investigating teacher beliefs and actions. Zulaiha examines the various perspectives of shareholders concerning Indonesian language teaching and learning in an independent college in Australia. She includes perceptions of not only teachers, but administrators, students, parents, and ancillary staff also. Such a complex picture is rarely seen in the second language teaching and learning literature. Kleinsasser & Crouch (2000) discuss a review of the Spanish program at an independent primary school using interview and survey data from LOTE teachers, regular primary teachers, students, and parents. Hongboontri considers the beliefs of university English teachers in a Thai university context, Liu investigates the induction of two student teachers in a Taiwan high school, and Sato (2002) and Sato & Kleinsasser (forthcoming) examine teachers in a (private) Japanese high school English department dealing with government guidelines to implement CLT.

Other researchers within Australia and New Zealand further direct their attention toward teachers in their language teaching and learning cultures. In Western Australia, Breen, Hird, Milton, Oliver, & Thwaite (2001) investigate 18 experienced teachers of ESL in both primary and high schools, uncovering the complex relationships "between thinking and action in the work of experienced language teachers" and how these relationships have "implications for curriculum innovation, teacher education, and for language classroom research" (p. 470). Mangubhai, Marland, Dashwood, & Son (2004) at the University of Southern Queensland document a teacher's personal practical theory of communicative language teaching (CLT). They conclude that the teacher's understanding of CLT "incorporates many of the commonly listed features of CLT, other features of CLT not usually listed and many features of her general approach to teaching. In other words, Doreen has integrated many features of general teaching into her practical theory of CLT" (p. 308). Burn's (1999) work at Macquarie University in Sydney concerning English language teaching practitioners also helps give insights into some of the cultural dimensions of classroom learning and teaching. More recently in New Zealand Crabbe (2003) outlines issues salient to the quality of language learning opportunities and "proposes three domains of enquiry: theoretical, cultural, and management, and puts forward arguments in favour of learning opportunity standards as the basis for institutional dialogue about quality in language education" (p. 9). Barsturkmen, Loewen, & Ellis (2004) offer a case study of New Zealand language teachers into "the relationship between three teachers' stated beliefs about and practices of focus on form in intermediate level ESL communicative lessons" (p. 243). Barkhuizen (1998a, 1998b, 2002) at the University of Auckland is also offering valuable insights using language learners' perceptions. Such investigations further expand the research within second language teaching and learning cultures. It would appear that the potential to further and more deeply research second language teaching and learning cultures is alive and well with many applied linguistics programs focusing on second language teaching and learning. How to integrate the various findings, completing reviews and meta-analyses, might eventually prove fruitful to unify the various practical and theoretical perspectives offered in the literature within the two countries.

Applied linguistics publications

Obviously there are other research areas being developed and extended. Both countries have vital applied linguistics associations. The Applied Linguistics Association of Australia offers a newsletter, conferences (this year entitled, Applying Applied Linguistics), jointly sponsors the Australian Linguistics Institute with the Australian Linguistic Society, hosts an on-line discussion group APPLIX, and publishes the *Australian Review of Applied Linguistics* (twice a year), among other services (Applied Linguistics Association of Australia, 2004). The Applied Linguistics Association of New Zealand offers a newsletter, an ELIST, and publishes the *New Zealand Studies in Applied Linguistics* (twice a year), among other services (Applied Linguistics Association New Zealand, 2004).

Australia

Topics published more recently in the *Australian Review of Applied Linguistics* include studies focusing on Japanese that investigate learning strategies for learning words in Kanji (Kubota & Toyoda 2001), perceptions of kanji learning strategies (Gamage 2003), searching for the semantic boundaries of the Japanese coulour term "AO" (Conlon 2003), and the effects of individual Japanese and Korean individual learner factors and task type on negotiations (Bitchener 2003). In the area of the Chinese language topics include placement of important ides in lengthy Chinese text (Ramsay 2001) and the cultural significance of coda in Chinese narratives (Ho 2001). There are articles concerning language teaching issues including Indonesian teaching (Hassall 2001; Sneddon 2001), Swiss themes in three "pluricentric" German language textbooks (Boss 2003), and influences on teachers' judgements of student speech (Haig & Oliver 2003). Articles focusing on testing include anxiety and oral performance in a foreign language test situation (Machida 2001), and parameters of speaking for writing tests (Franken 2001). Additionally, a focus on teaching culture (Dobson 2001), the interaction of discipline and culture in academic writing (Golebiowski & Liddicoat 2002), creating cultural spaces in the Australian university setting (Eisenchlas & Trevaskes 2003) focus on various aspects of cultures. A focus issue on the contexts of tertiary literacies was the theme of the first volume in 2003 (Absalom & Golebiowski 2002; Baldauf & Golebiowski 2002; Bock & Gough 2002; Borland & Pearce 2002; Kaldor & Rochecouste 2002; Kirkpatrick & Mulligan 2002; Reid & Parker 2002).

Linguistics and applied linguistics issues are also topics of articles including those on grammars and corpora (Collins 2001), analysis of the discourse marker "so" in monologic talk (Rendle-Short 2003), an annotated bibliography on structure and variation within a genre (Starks & Lewis 2003), and a sociocultural perspective on societal support for L2 learning and L1 maintenance (Sakamoto 2001). Sociolinguistics and sociocultural issues are discussed in Ardington (2003), O'Neill & Hatoss (2003), and Winter & Pauwels (2003). Additionally, articles concerning historical perspectives on applied linguistics in North America (Angelis 2001) and Australia (McNamara 2001) are available.

Political and social issues including a focus on the discourse of hatred and the linguist's responsibility (Clyne 2003) and the children overboard affair (Macken-Horarik 2003) are topical within the current Australian context. AIDS awareness and discourse interpretation are international concerns (Paltridge & O'Louglin 2001). Two series published by the Applied Linguistics Association of Australia more recently include a focus on Asian languages and computers (Hoven & Son 2003) and using and learning Italian in Australia (Rubino 2004).

New Zealand

Topics published more recently in the *New Zealand Studies in Applied Linguistics* include studies considering Maori such as lexical expansion (Keegan 2000), Maori language revitalisation and maintenance (Christensen 2001), and its proficiency, use, and transmission (Christensen 2003). Applied linguistics issues are discussed variously in the acquisition of the subjunctive in Spanish as a second language (Torresano 2001), applied linguistics (subject to discipline) (Davies 2003), applying linguistics by developing cognitive skills through multimedia (Gough & Bock 2003), and the use of NESB immigrant resources and service provision in New Zealand's public sector organisations (Watts & Trlin 2000).

Classroom issues are discussed concerning methodology in a study of classroom multilingualism (Shameem 2000), if advanced learners benefit from the negotiation of meaning (Bitchener 2000), genre and the language learning program (Paltridge 2001), learners' perceptions of classroom reading activities (Barkhuizen 2001), direct intervention in language learning (Ellis 2002), ecology, contingency, and talk in the postmethod classroom (van Lier 2002), learning to write with a little help from friends (Turner 2002), and mother-tongue medium as foreign language object (Kim & Elder 2002).

Additional areas

Additionally, there is robust research in second language acquisition and teaching at the University of Auckland with Ellis and his colleagues (e.g., Ellis 2004a; Ellis 2004b; Ellis & Barkhuizen, forthcoming; Ellis, Basturkmen, & Loewen 2002), research in language testing at the University of Melbourne with McNamara and his colleagues (e.g., McNamara 1996; 2004; Hill & McNamara 2003) and at Victoria University of Wellington with Read (co-editor of *Language Testing*) (e.g., Read 2000; 2002; Read & Chapelle 2001), and research in various areas including critical applied linguistics (e.g., Luke 1997; 2003a; 2004; Pennycook 1999a, 1999b, 2001, 2004), language policy and planning (e.g., Baldauf 2002; Baldauf & Ingram 2003; Baldauf & Kaplan 2003; Kaplan & Baldauf 1997), and literacy (e.g., Carrington & Luke 2003; Luke 2003b; Luke & Kale 1997; Luke & van Kraayenoord 1998), among others. These are but a few more of the areas being investigated, researched, and published. Such a cursory review offers another glimpse into the continuing burgeoning applied linguistics field in both Australia and New Zealand.

Summary

The turn to the twenty-first century saw an increasing literature in applied linguistics with handbooks (e.g., Davies & Elder 2004; Kaplan 2002), introductory and monograph texts (e.g., Cook 2003; Davies 1999; McCarthy 2001; McDonough 2002; Schmitt 2002), and an edited volume that considered components of a second language education curriculum focusing on applied linguistics issues (e.g., Bardovi-Harlig & Hartford 1997). The diversity and inclusiveness of various topics make applied linguistics as a discipline, field, or area of study contestable, to say the least. Yet, in no less a manner, the programs reviewed here and research perused in this paper also offer both diversity and inclusiveness that help prepare, develop, and guide potential applied linguistics professionals. These are characteristics of a vital and growing discipline that remains quite youthful in its zest to influence, challenge, and matter to persons interested in applied linguistics in Australia, New Zealand, and the surrounding regions.

Notes

1. Thanks to Mei Hui Liu and Siti Zulaiha for their excellent assistance in helping to locate web pages, find information about programs in various places, and downloading such salient information. I also thank them for helping me scrutinise the data presented in this paper and making sure it represented the information found on the web pages. I further thank Richard Baldauf for his insights.

2. The task here is to review the compulsory and elective classes within the programs, not to compare and contrast Australian university programs with New Zealand university programs.

3. Every effort was made to photocopy each of the website pages. Furthermore, every effort was made to represent each program as depicted on the website as carefully as possible. Nonetheless, apologies for any possible misrepresentations or errors. Readers are encouraged to visit the web pages themselves; however, it should be remembered that web pages can change quickly and without notice.

4. Additional Language Learning and Additional Language Teaching offer "a contemporary up-to-date introduction to the fields of TESOL (Teaching English to Speakers of Other Languages), SLT (Second Language

Teaching), ESL (English as a Second Language), the learning and teaching of LOTE (Languages other than English) and Modern Languages generally" (see University of Sydney web page).

5. I thank Richard Baldauf for bringing this perspective to my attention.

References

Absalom, D. and Z. Golebiowski (2002). Tertiary literacy on the cusp. *Australian Review of Applied Linguistics* 25(2): 5–18.

Angelis, P. (2001). The roots of applied linguistics in North America. *Australian Review of Applied Linguistics* 24(1): 1–12.

Applied Linguistics Association of Australia. (2004). Available on the WWW: http://www.arts.usyd.edu.au/departs/langcent/alaa, accessed June 16, 2004.

Applied Linguistics Association of New Zealand, Inc. (2004). Available on the WWW: http://www.vuw.ac.nz.lals.about.alanz.alanz.html, accessed March 3, 2004 and June 16, 2004.

Ardington, A.M. (2003). Alliance building in girls' talk: A conversational accomplishment of playful negotiation. *Australian Review of Applied Linguistics* 26(1): 38–54.

Atkinson, P. and A. Coffey (1997). Analysing documentary realities. In D. Silverman (ed.), *Qualitative Research: Theory, method and practice*, pp. 45–62. Thousand Oaks, CA: Sage Publications.

Auckland University of Technology. (2004). Master of Arts in Applied Language Studies. Available on the WWW: http://www.aut.ac.nz/faculties/arts/languages/post_graduates/ma_langstudies.shtml, accessed May 2, 2004.

The Australian National University. (2004). Linguistics and Applied Linguistics Program. Available on the WWW: http://www.arts.anu.edu.au/languages/linguistics.htm, accessed April 30, 2004.

Baldauf, R.B. (2002). Methodologies for policy and planning. In R.B. Kaplan (ed.), *Handbook of Applied Linguistics*, pp. 391–403. Oxford: Oxford University Press.

Baldauf, R.B. and Z. Golebiowski (2002). Introduction: The contexts of tertiary literacies. *Australian Review of Applied Linguistics* 25(2): 1–4.

Baldauf, R.B. and D. Ingram (2003). Language-in-education planning. In *International Encyclopedia of Linguistics*, Vol. 2 (2nd ed), pp. 412–416. Cambridge: Cambridge University Press.

Baldauf, R.B. and R. Kaplan (2003). Who are the actors? The role of (applied) linguists in language policy. In P. Ryan and R. Terbor (eds.), *Language: Issues of inequality*, pp. 19–49. Mexico City: CELE/Autonomous National University of Mexico.

Bardovi-Harlig, K. and B. Hartford (eds.) (1997). *Beyond Methods: Components of second language teacher education*. Sydney: McGraw Hill.

Barkhuizen, G.P. (1998a). Discovering learners' perceptions of ESL classroom teaching/learning activities in a South African context. *TESOL Quarterly* 32(1): 85–108.

Barkhuizen, G.P. (1998b). English learners' perceptions of classroom oral activities. *Journal for Language Teaching* 32(4): 249–255.

Barkhuizen, G.P. (2001). "That's what I think": Learners' perceptions of classroom reading activities. *New Zealand Studies in Applied Linguistics* 7: 41–58.

Barkhuizen, G.P. (2002). Language-in-education policy: Students' perceptions of the status and role of Xhos and English. *System* 30(4): 499–515.

Basturkmen, H., S. Loewen and R. Ellis (2004). Teachers' stated beliefs about incidental focus on form and their classroom practices. *Applied Linguistics* 25(2): 243–272.

Bitchener, J. (2000). Do advanced L2 learners benefit from the negotiation of meaning? *New Zealand Studies in Applied Linguistics* 6: 23–52.

Bitchener, J. (2003). The effects of individual learner factors and task type on negotiation: A study of advanced Japanese and Korean ESL learners. *Australian Review of Applied Linguistics* 26(2): 63–83.

Bock, Z. and D. Gough (2002). Social literacies and students in tertiary settings: Lessons from South Africa. *Australian Review of Applied Linguistics* 25(2): 49–58.

Borland, H. and A. Pearce (2002). Identifying key dimensions of language and cultural disadvantage at university. *Australian Review of Applied Linguistics* 25(2): 101–128.

Boss, B. (2003). Swiss themes in three "pluricentric" German language textbooks. *Australian Review of Applied Linguistics* 26(1): 6–18.

Breen, M.P., B. Hird, M. Milton, R. Oliver and A. Thwaite (2001). Making sense of language teaching: Teachers' principles and classroom practices. *Applied Linguistics* 22(4): 470–501.

Burns, A. (1999). *Collaborative Action Research for English Language Teachers.* Cambridge: Cambridge University Press.

Carrington, V. and A. Luke (2003). Reading, homes and families: From postmodern to modern? In A. van Kleeck, S.A. Stahl, and E.B. Bauer (eds.), *On Reading to Children: Parent and teachers.* Mahwah, NJ: Erlbaum.

Christensen, I. (2001). Maori language revitalisation and maintenance: Issues and insights. *New Zealand Studies in Applied Linguistics* 7: 15–40.

Christensen, I. (2003). Proficiency, use and transmission: Maori language revitalisation. *New Zealand Studies in Applied Linguistics* 9(1): not available.

Clyne, M. (2003). When the discourse of hatred becomes respectable — Does the linguist have a responsibility? *Australian Review of Applied Linguistics* 26(1): 1–5.

Collins, P. (2001). Grammars and corpora. *Australian Review of Applied Linguistics* 24(2): 35–42.

Conlon, F. (2003). Searching for the semantic boundaries of the Japanese colour term 'AO.' *Australian Review of Applied Linguistics* 26(1): 71–86.

Cook, G. (2003). *Applied Linguistics.* Oxford: Oxford University Press.

Crabbe, D. (2003). The quality of language learning opportunities. *TESOL Quarterly* 37(1): 9–34.

Davies, A. (1999). *An Introduction to Applied Linguistics: From practice to theory.* Edinburgh: Edinburgh University Press.

Davies, A. (2003). Applied linguistics: Subject to discipline. *New Zealand Studies in Applied Linguistics* 9(1): not available.

Davies, A. and C. Elder (eds.) (2004). *The Handbook of Applied Linguistics.* Carlton, VIC: Blackwell Publishing.

Dobson, A. (2001). Teaching of culture within foreign language teaching and its relationship to nationalism. *Australian Review of Applied Linguistics* 24(1): 61–74.

Eisenchlas, S. and S. Trevaskes (2003). Creating cultural spaces in the Australian university setting: A pilot study of structured cultural exchanges. *Australian Review of Applied Linguistics* 26(2): 84–100.

Eisner, E. (1991). *The Enlightened Eye: Qualitative inquiry and the enhancement of educational practice.* New York: Macmillan.

Ellis, R. (2002). Direct intervention in language learning. *New Zealand Studies in Applied Linguistics* 8: not available.

Ellis, R. (2004a). Individual differences in second language learning. In A. Davies and C. Elder (eds.), *The Handbook of Applied Linguistics*, pp. 525–551. Oxford: Blackwell.

Ellis, R. (2004b). Definition and measurement of L2 explicit knowledge. *Language Learning* 54: 227–275.

Ellis, R. and G. Barkhuizen (forthcoming). *Analyzing Learner Language.* Oxford: Oxford University Press.

Ellis, R., H. Basturkmen and S. Loewen (2002). Doing focus-on-form. *System* 30(4): 419–432.

Franken, M. (2001). The parameters of speaking for writing tests. *Australian Review of Applied Linguistics* 24(1): 51–60.

Gamage, G.H. (2003). Perceptions of kanji learning strategies: Do they differ among Chinese character and alphabetic background learners? *Australian Review of Applied Linguistics* 26(2): 17–30.

Golebiowski, Z. and A. Liddicoat (2002). The interaction of discipline and culture in academic writing. *Australian Review of Applied Linguistics* 25(2): 59–72.

Gough, D. and Z. Bock (2003). Applying linguistics: Developing cognitive skills through multimedia. *New Zealand Studies in Applied Linguistics* 9(1): not available.

Grabe, W. (2002). Applied linguistics: An emerging discipline for the 21st century. In R.B. Kaplan (ed.), *The Oxford Handbook of Applied Linguistics*, pp. 3–12. Oxford: Oxford University Press.

Group of Eight. (2004). Australia's leading universities. Available on the WWW: http://www.go8.edu.au/about/facts/htm, accessed May 11, 2004.

Haig, Y. and R. Oliver (2003). Is it a case of mind over matter? Influences on teachers' judgements of student speech. *Australian Review of Applied Linguistics* 26(1): 55–70.

Hassall, T. (2001). Do learners thank too much in Indonesian? *Australian Review of Applied Linguistics* 24(2): 97–112.

Hill, K. and T. McNamara (2003). Assessment research in second language curriculum initiatives. In J.P. Keeves and R. Watanabe (eds.), *International Handbook of Education Research in the Asia-Pacific Region*, pp. 629–640. Dordrecht: Kluwer Academic Publishers.

Ho, J. (2001). The cultural significance of coda in Chinese narratives. *Australian Review of Applied Linguistics* 24(2): 61–80.

Hodder, I. (2000). The interpretation of documents and material culture. In N.K. Denzin and Y.S. Lincoln (eds.), *Handbook of Qualitative Research* (2nd ed), pp. 703–716. Thousand Oaks, CA: Sage Publications.

Hongboontri, C. (2003). *EFL University Teachers in Thailand: Reviewing their perceptions and environment.* Unpublished Ph.D. thesis, University of Queensland, Brisbane, QLD, Australia.

Hoven, D. and J-B. Son (eds.) (2003). *Asian Languages and Computers: The Australian Review of Applied Linguistics.* Series S, Number 17. Melbourne: Applied Linguistics Association of Australia.

Kaldor, S. and J. Rochecouste (2002). General academic writing and discipline specific writing. *Australian Review of Applied Linguistics* 25(2): 29–48.

Kaplan, R.B. (ed.) (2002). *The Oxford Handbook of Applied Linguistics.* Oxford: Oxford University Press.

Kaplan, R.B., and R.B. Baldauf (1997). *Language Planning from Practice to Theory.* Clevedon: Multilingual Matters.

Keegan, P.J. (2000). Recent lexical expansion in Maori: Some implications for Maori-medium classrooms. *New Zealand Studies in Applied Linguistics* 6: 53–66.

Kim, S.H. and C. Elder (2002). When mother-tongue medium becomes foreign language object: The case of native-speaker teachers in New Zealand. *New Zealand Studies in Applied Linguistics* 8: not available.

Kirkpatrick, A. and D. Mulligan (2002). Cultures of learning: Critical reading in the social and applied sciences. *Australian Review of Applied Linguistics* 25(2): 73–100.

Kleinsasser, R.C. (1993). A tale of two technical cultures: Foreign language teaching. *Teaching and Teacher Education* 9(4): 373–383.

Kleinsasser, R.C. and R.W.H. Crouch (2000). A primary LOTE program evaluation: Perspectives, insights, and challenges. *Journal of the Australian College of Education (Unicorn)* On-line refereed article. Available on the WWW: http://www.austcolled.com.au/-pubadmin/page17.html, accessed August 18, 2000.

Kubota, M. and E. Toyoda (2001). Learning strategies employed for learning words written in kanji versus kana. *Australian Review of Applied Linguistics* 24(2): 1–16.

Liu, M.H. (forthcoming). *Student EFL Teachers in Taiwanese School Contexts: Socialisation, beliefs, and practices.* Unpublished Ph.D. thesis, University of Queensland, Brisbane, QLD, Australia.

Lortie, D.C. (1975). *Schoolteacher.* Chicago: University of Chicago Press.

Luke, A. (1997). Theory and practice in critical discourse analysis. In L. Saha (ed.), *International Encyclopedia of the Sociology of Education.* London: Pergamon.

Luke, A. (2003a). After the marketplace: Evidence, social science and educational research. *Australian Educational Researcher* 30(2): 87–107.

Luke, A. (2003b). Literacy and the other: A sociological approach to literacy research and policy in multilingual societies. *Reading Research Quarterly* 38(1):132–141.

Luke, A. (2004). Two takes on the critical. In B. Norton and K. Toohey (eds.), *Critical Pedagogy and Language Learning.* Cambridge: Cambridge University Press.

Luke, A. and J. Kale (1997). Learning through difference: Cultural practices in early language socialization. In E. Gregory (ed.), *One Child, Many Worlds: Early learning in multicultural communities*, pp. 11–29. New York: Teachers College Press.

Luke, A. and C.E. van Kraayenoord (1998). Babies, bathwaters and benchmarks: Literacy assessment and curriculum reform. Available on the WWW: http://www.schools.ash.org.au/litweb/page400.html, accessed May 4, 2004.

Machida, S. (2001). The parameters of speaking for writing tests. *Australian Review of Applied Linguistics* 24(1): 31–50.

Macken-Horarik, M. (2003). The children overboard affair. *Australian Review of Applied Linguistics* 26(2): 1–16.

Macquarie University. (2004). Programs in applied linguistics. Available on the WWW: http://www.ling.mq.edu.au/programs/appling/Overview.htm, accessed June 8, 2004.

Macquarie University. (2004). Master of applied linguistics. Available on the WWW: http://www.ling.mq.edu.au/programs/appling/MasterAppLing.htm, accessed June 8, 2004.

Macquarie University. (2004). Master of applied linguistics (TESOL). Available on the WWW: http://www.ling.mq.edu.au/programs/appling/MasterAppLingTESOL.htm, accessed June 8, 2004.

Macquarie University. (2004). Master of applied linguistics (Literacy). Available on the WWW: http://www.ling.mq.edu.au/programs/appling/MasterAppLingLiteracy.htm, accessed June 8, 2004.

Macquarie University. (2004). Master of applied linguistics(Language Program Management). Available on the WWW: http://www.ling.mq.edu.au/programs/appling/MasterAppLangProgManagement.htm, accessed June 8, 2004.

Macquarie University. (2004). Doctor of applied linguistics. Available on the WWW: http://www.ling.mq.edu.au/programs/appling/DoctorAppLing.htm, accessed June 8, 2004.

Macquarie University Linguistics. (2004). About us. Available on the WWW: http://www.ling.mq.edu.au/about.html, accessed June 16, 2004.

Mangubhai, F., P. Marland, A. Dashwood, and J-B. Son (2004). Teaching a foreign language: One teacher's practical theory. *Teaching and Teacher Education* 20: 291–311.

Massey University. (2004). Languages education including TESOL. Available on the WWW: http://education.massey.ac.nz/ALE/TESOL.htm, accessed April 30, 2004.

McCarthy, M. (2001). *Issues in Applied Linguistics.* Cambridge: Cambridge University Press.

McDonough, S. (2002). *Applied Linguistics in Language Education.* London: Arnold.

McKay, S. L. (2002). *Teaching English as an International Language.* Oxford: Oxford University Press.

McNamara, T. (1996). *Measuring Second Language Performance.* New York: Longman.

McNamara, T. (2001). The roots of applied linguistics in Australia. *Australian Review of Applied Linguistics* 24(1): 13–29.

McNamara, T. (2004). Language testing. In A. Davies and C. Elder (eds.), *The Handbook of Applied Linguistics,* pp. 763–783. Carlton, VIC: Blackwell Publishing.

Monash University. (2004). Master of Applied Linguistics. Available on the WWW: http://www.arts.monash.edu.au/lcl/postgraduate_coursework/masters-appling.html, accessed April 4, 2004.

Monash University. (2004). Master of Applied Linguistics for Language Teachers. Available on the WWW: http://www.arts.monash.edu.au/lcl/postgraduate_coursework/masters-applingteach.html, accessed April 4, 2004.

Monash University. (2004). Master of Education (LOTE). Available on the WWW: http://www.monash.edu/pubs/handbooks/postgrad/pg0459.htm, accessed May 31, 2004.

Monash University. (2004). Master of Education (TESOL). Available on the WWW: http://www.monash.edu/pubs/handbooks/postgrad/pg0460.htm, accessed May 31, 2004.

Monash University. (2004). Master of Education (TESOL — International). Available on the WWW: http://www.monash.edu/pubs/handbooks/postgrad/pg0461.htm, accessed May 31, 2004.

Odgers, R. (2004, June 12). Overseas students swell coffers of seven universities. *The Courier-Mail:* 4.

O'Neill, S. and A. Hatoss (2003). Harnessing a nation's linguistic competence: Identifying and addressing needs for LOTE in the tourism and hospitality industry. *Australian Review of Applied Linguistics* 26(2): 31–45.

Paltridge, B. (2001). Genre and the language learning program. *New Zealand Studies in Applied Linguistics* 7: 1–14.

Paltridge, B. and K. O'Loughlin (2001). AIDS awareness and discourse interpretation: The travel safe campaign. *Australian Review of Applied Linguistics* 24(1): 75–92.

Pennycook, A. (ed.) (1999a). Critical approaches to TESOL. *TESOL Quarterly* 33(3): 329–348.

Pennycook, A. (1999b). Introduction: Critical approaches to TESOL. *TESOL Quarterly* 33(3): 329–348.

Pennycook, A. (2001). *Critical Applied Linguistics: A critical introduction.* Mahwah, NJ: Lawrence Erlbaum Associates, Publishers.

Pennycook, A. (2004). Critical applied linguistics. In A. Davies and C. Elder (eds.), *The Handbook of Applied Linguistics,* pp. 784–807. Carlton, VIC: Blackwell Publishing.

Ramsay, G. (2001). What are they getting at? Placement of important ideas in lengthy Chinese newstext: A contrastive analysis with Australian newstext. *Australian Review of Applied Linguistics* 24(2): 17–34.

Read, J. (2000). *Assessing Vocabulary.* Cambridge: Cambridge University Press.

Read, J. (2002). The use of interactive input in EAP listening assessment. *Journal of English for Academic Purposes* 1: 105–119.

Read, J. and C. A. Chapelle (2001). A framework for second language vocabulary assessment. *Language Testing* 18(1): 1–32.

Reid, I. and L. Parker (2002). Framing institutional policies on literacies. *Australian Review of Applied Linguistics* 25(2): 19–28.

Rendle-Short, J. (2003). So what does this show us? Analysis of the discourse marker "so" in monologic talk. *Australian Review of Applied Linguistics* 26(2): 46–62.

Rubino, A. (ed.) (2004). *Using and Learning Italian in Australia: The Australian Review of Applied Linguistics.* Series S, Number 18. Melbourne: Applied Linguistics Association of Australia.

Sakamoto, M. (2001). Exploring societal support for L2 learning and L1 maintenance: A socio-cultural perspective. *Australian Review of Applied Linguistics* 24(2): 43–60.

Sato, K. (2002). Practical understandings of communicative language teaching and teacher development. In S. Savignon (ed.), *Interpreting Communicative Language Teaching: Contexts and concerns in teacher education,* pp. 41–81. New Haven, CT: Yale University Press.

Sato, K. and R. C. Kleinsasser (1999a). Communicative language teaching (CLT): Practical understandings. *Modern Language Journal* 83(4): 494–517.

Sato, K. and R. C. Kleinsasser (1999b). Multiple data sources: Converging and diverging conceptualizations of LOTE teaching. *Australian Journal of Teacher Education* 24(1): 17–33.

Sato, K. and R. C. Kleinsasser (forthcoming). Beliefs, practices, and interactions of teachers in a Japanese high school English department. *Teaching and Teacher Education.*

Savignon, S. J. (1991). Communicative language teaching: State of the art. *TESOL Quarterly* 25(2): 261–277.

Savignon, S. J. (2003). Teaching English as communication: A global perspective. *World Englishes* 22(1): 55–66.

Schmitt, N. (ed.) (2002). *An Introduction to Applied Linguistics.* London: Arnold.

Shameem, N. (2000). Methodology in a study of classroom multilingualism: A study of primary school Indo-Fijians in Fiji. *New Zealand Studies in Applied Linguistics* 6: 67–88.

Sneddon, J. N. (2001). Teaching informal Indonesian: Some factors for consideration. *Australian Review of Applied Linguistics* 24(2): 81–96.

Starks, D. and M. Lewis (2003). The annotated bibliography: Structure and variation within a genre. *Australian Review of Applied Linguistics* 26(2): 101–117.

TESOL. (2003). *TESOL board details position on teacher quality.* News release. Alexandria, VA: TESOL, Inc.

Thompson, J. D. (1967). *Organizations In Action.* St. Louis: McGraw-Hill Book Company.

Torresano, F. d. l. C. (2001). The acquisition of the subjunctive in Spanish as a second language. *New Zealand Studies in Applied Linguistics* 7: not available.

Turner, L. (2002). Learning to write with a little help from my friends: The social construction of self and mind. *New Zealand Studies in Applied Linguistics* 8: not available.

University of Adelaide. (2004). Postgraduate programs in general linguistics. Available on the WWW: http://www.adelaide.edu.au/cesgl/general/postgraduate.html, accessed May 22, 2004.

University of Auckland. (2004). Master of Arts Language Teaching. Available on the WWW: http://www.arts.auckland.ac.nz/subjects/index.cfm?P=1215, accessed May 22, 2004.

University of Auckland. (2004). Master of Teaching English to Speakers of Other Languages. Available on the WWW: http://www.arts.auckland.ac.nz.students/index.cfm?p=210, accessed May 22, 2004.

University of Auckland. (2004). Master of Professional Studies. Available on the WWW: www.arts.auckland.ac.na/subjects/index.cfm?P=1825, accessed May 22, 2004.

University of Melbourne. (2004). Master of Applied Linguistics (Computer-Assisted Language Learning). Available on the WWW: http://psc.unimelb.edu.au/course/html/coursestreams/44-CA.shtml, accessed May 22, 2004.

University of Melbourne. (2004). Master of Applied Linguistics (English Language). Available on the WWW: http://psc.unimel.edu.au/course/html/coursestreams/44-EL.shtml, accessed May 22, 2004.

University of Melbourne. (2004). Master of Applied Linguistics (LangTest and LangProgEval). Available on the WWW: http://psc.unimelb.edu.au/course/html.coursestreams/44-LT.shtml, accessed May 22, 2004.

University of Melbourne. (2004). Master of Applied Linguistics (Teaching Engl to Speakers of Other Lang.). Available on the WWW: http://psc.unimelb.edu.au/course/html/coursestreams/44-AE.shtml, accessed May 22, 2004.

University of Melbourne. (2004). Master of TESOL. Available on the WWW: http://www.edfac.unimel.edu.au/courses/postgraduate/Courses/metesol.shtml, accessed May 11, 2004.

University of New South Wales. (2004). Master of Arts in Applied Linguistics, Master of Arts in TESOL, Master of Education (Applied Linguistics), Master of Arts in Korean Applied Linguistics, Master of Arts in Japanese Applied Linguistics. Available on the WWW: http://languages.arts.unsw.edu.au/linguistics/LING.PG.HB.2004.pdf, accessed May 3, 2004.

University of Otago. (2004). School of Language Literature, and Performing Arts. Available on the WWW: http://www.otago.az.nz/departments/humanities/h_d_lang_perform_arts.html, accessed April 30, 2004.

University of Queensland. (2004). Master of Arts in Applied Linguistics, Master of Arts in TESOL Studies. Available on the WWW: http://www.uq.edu.au/study/course_list_display.html?course_list_file_name= http://www.uq.edu.au/student/courses2004/2004MA.htm, accessed May 11, 2004.

University of Sydney. (2004). MA in Applied Linguistics. Available on the WWW: http://www.arts.usyd.edu.au/departs/linguistics/ling/study/ma_app_ling.htm, accessed May 2, 2004.

University of Sydney. (2003). Master of Education: TESOL/Languages. Available on the WWW: http://www.edsw.usyd.edu.au/future_students/postgraduate/ed_cw_med_tesollang.shtml, accessed May 11, 2004.

University of Waikato. (2004). Applied Linguistics Papers. Available on the WWW: http://www.waikato.ac.nz/wfass/subjects/linguistics/appling, accessed on May 3, 2004.

University of Western Australia. (2004). Master of Education in Applied Linguistics (Coursework). Available on the WWW: http://handbooks.uwa.edu.au/courses/c3/3055, accessed May 2, 2004.

van Lier, L. (2002). Ecology, contingency and talk in the postmethod classroom. *New Zealand Studies in Applied Linguistics* 8: not available.

Victoria University of Wellington. (2004). Master of Arts Applied Linguistics. Available on the WWW: http://www.vuw.ac.nz/lals/degrees/ma=applied.aspx, accessed May 3, 2004.

Victoria University of Wellington. (2004). Master of Arts — TESOL. Available on the WWW: http://www.vuw.ac.nz/lals/degrees/ma-tesol.aspx, accessed May 3, 2004.

Watts, N. and A. Trlin (2000). The use of NESB immigrant resources and service provision in New Zealand's public sector organisations. *New Zealand Studies in Applied Linguistics* 6: 1–22.

Winter, J. and A. Pauwels (2003). Mapping trajectories of change — women's and men's practices and experience of feminist linguistic reform in Australia. *Australian Review of Applied Linguistics* 26(1): 19–37.

Wolcott, H. F. (1990). *Writing Up Qualitative Research*. Newbury Park, CA: Sage Publications.

Zulaiha, S. (forthcoming). *Primary School Foreign Language Teaching, Learning, and Assessment: Perceptions and challenges*. Unpublished Ph.D. thesis, University of Queensland, Brisbane, QLD, Australia.

Résumé

Ce devoir passe en revue les tendances naissantes, en linguistique appliquée, à la fois en Australie et en Nouvelle Zélande. Il donne un aperçu de la situation actuelle des programmes (sélectionnés) de linguistique appliquée de troisième cycle au niveau universitaire. Il montre aussi la manière dont divers programmes universitaires définissent la linguistique appliquée grâce aux classes (titres) que les étudiants doivent valider pour obtenir leur diplôme. Une preuve des sujets ainsi que des cours obligatoires dans le programme révèlent non seulement ce que la linguistique appliquée implique en général mais donne aussi un aperçu de la manière dont la linguistique appliquée est définie et pratiquée. De plus, certains des sujets pertinents de recherche (titres) qui sont publiés dans les revues des associations de linguistique appliquée des deux pays sont examinés.

Applied linguistics in Europe[*]

Kees de Bot
University of Groningen

In this contribution developments in Applied Linguistics in Europe are linked to major social changes that have taken place over the last decades. These include: The decline of the USSR and the end of the cold war; The development of the EEC and the EU and fading of borders; The economic growth of Western Europe; Labor migration from the south to the north of Europe; The emergence of regionalism. All of these developments have shaped the role of languages in society and they have sparked research on linguistic aspects related to the languages in contact due to these developments.

Keywords: Applied linguistics in Europe, social change

Introduction

The title of this contribution is misleading. No one is able to cover the whole range of applied linguistic activities in all the countries of Europe. There is no database in which such information can be found, nor will any search machine bring all relevant information, even if we had a universally accepted definition of what constitutes applied linguistics. The definition of applied linguistics ranges from SLA to language planning, from language ecology to disorders and from mother tongue education to forensic linguistics as the list of AILA scientific commissions witnesses. Therefore some selection of applied linguistic activity had to be made. Grabe (2002: 10) defines applied linguistics (AL) as '… A practice-driven discipline that addresses language based problems in real-world contexts.' In this contribution 'language based problems in real-world contexts' will be taken as the dominant perspective. The focus will be on the roles and functions of languages in society. What is presented is for the most part typical European, which is not to say that the themes and paradigm are not of interest and studied in other parts of the world. Because of the specific focus this is not a who-is-who in European Applied Linguistics, and there will no doubt be many names that would be mentioned in the ideal complete contribution on AL in Europe. I apologize for the gaps in my knowledge and the particular bias of my position in time and space that will inevitably show. No intention is meant to exclude individuals or groups.

Defining Europe

If defining applied linguistics is a problem, defining Europe is basically impossible when we go beyond geographical definitions. Europe is clearly not a uniform community interested in the same issues. Differences in history and culture and therefore language have led to widely differing developments in different countries. The AILA list of affiliates shows in what country there is at least an association that is active enough to qualify for AILA membership, but that does not reflect what is going on: in some countries a small group of very active applied linguists are visible and make up the core of the association, but there are likely to be many more applied linguists that are less visible for various reasons. In other countries there is a larger community organized in the association and the associations' activities at least reflect some of the work going on. Then there are countries in which we know there is a lot of AL activity, but for some reason there is not an association represent-ing this. Getting information on AL activity in all those countries is difficult if not impossible. Language is likely to be one of the major obstacles for a smooth flow of information. Many associations publish on their work in the national language only, and only a part of that work is

ISSN 1461–0213 / E-ISSN 1570–5595 © John Benjamins Publishing Company

published later on in a language of wider communication. Research in some European countries is more visible because it is very much oriented towards what is going on in the Anglo-Saxon world and part of the research is published in English and accordingly available to the outside world. AILA's long standing policy of keeping French as one of the working languages has not led to a steady flow of information between the French-speaking and English-speaking communities, and is in a sense an anachronism in a world in which the role of French as an international language and a language of academia is clearly declining. Given the position of Spanish in South-America, a more privileged position for Spanish could be argued for. For some time a similar argument could be made for German which traditionally had a strong position of some of the eastern European countries, but now its position seems to be eroded very dramatically by the enormous growth of English in these countries. We will come back to this later on. Even more dramatic is the position of Russian in many countries. While it was an obligatory subject in education in former Warsaw-Pact countries, it has now been wiped out by English or by local languages.

The real world of Europe: Social changes in the last 40 years

Over the last 40 years, a number of political developments have had a tremendous impact on the role and place of languages in Europe. In the article I aim at linking those developments with developments in AL, in particular the emergence of specific research interests.

The most influential socio-political changes we have witnessed are listed more or less historically here:

- – The decline of the USSR and the end of the cold war
- – The development of the EEC and the EU and fading of borders
- – The economic growth of Western Europe
- – Labor migration from the south to the north of Europe
- – The emergence of regionalism

All of those developments are connected and apart from the ending of WWII there are no single developments that have caused all the others mentioned. This is not the place to go into deep political analyses of Europe in the last 40 years. There are excellent publications on this, such as Hobsbawm (1995) and Schöpflin (2000).

The decline of the USSR and the end of the cold war

The end of WWII also meant the beginning of the cold war and the division of Europe into two zones of influence: the western part that organized itself strategically in NATO and the eastern part that became dominated by the USSR and Warsaw Pact. Linguistically this meant that these two zones came under different influences: while in the western part English and to a lesser extent French dominated the scene, in the eastern part Russian became the language of wider communication and the language taught widely in education. German continued to play an important role in eastern Europe, in particular in academia, while its role was very limited role in western Europe. Rannut & Rannut (1995) discuss the specific problems of setting up a language policy in Estonia after the Soviet era. Estonia is faced with the difficult task of strengthening the position of the Estonian language, while at the same time taking into account the needs of the monolingual Russian speakers in Estonia. As Leontiev (1995) mentions, similar problems occur in the autonomous republics of the former USSR where large numbers of Russians migrated to, often driven by force. They now face problems in the republics they have been living in for a long time. Because of their monolingualism, they are excluded from the cultural life of the state. They cannot understand the media or official documents, unless Russian is the second official language of the new state. Many of them do not want to learn a 'new' language: they have no real experience of being bilingual or multilingual, as for instance citizens of Switzerland have.' (Leontiev 1995: 199–200)

It is obvious that in the next decade the status of many of the languages in the countries and republics of the former USSR will undergo dramatic changes (Maurais 1992), and as Takala & Sajavaara (2000) argue for the Baltic states, language policies need to be developed to ensure a stable political situation.

The development of the EEC and the EU and fading of borders
The French politician Jean Monnet became the main actor in the development of several associations between western European countries that led to the emergence of the European Economic Community and later the European Union (EU) which has now 25 members. The impact of the development of the EU on almost all aspects of language and language policy can hardly be overestimated. Here we will focus on a number of developments that are directly or indirectly related to the emergence of the EU and discuss some of the research that has been done in relation to this.

A number of issues have to be discussed here:
– Language policies in the EU
    – An early start for foreign languages
    – The development of the European common Framework of Reference
    – Content and language integrated learning
– The choice of languages in the EU
– The role of English and other languages as languages of wider communication in the EU
– The status of minority languages in the EU.

The main aim of the EU is the formation of a united Europe with open borders and active communication between residents. For this various policy measures have been taken, in particular with respect to learning foreign languages. In a meeting of the ministers of education of the EU held in 1998, a long list of intentions was presented that aimed at the development of multilingualism in the EU with the aim to 'enable all Europeans to communicate with speakers of other mother tongues, thereby developing open-mindedness, facilitating free movement of people and exchange of information and improving international cooperation' (Recommendation R (98) 6 of the European Council). Among the recommendations listed are the learning of more than one foreign language by all citizens, the use of foreign languages in the teaching of non-linguistic subjects (for example history or mathematics), an early start for the teaching of foreign languages, the promotion of life-long learning of foreign languages and a focus on learner autonomy. While the last point has not attracted much attention in the European research community, there is quite some research on various forms of content-based instruction, or what in the European context has become known as CLIL: Content and Language Integrated Learning (Maljers, Marsland & Marsh 1998). This form of language teaching is seen as much more effective than normal classrooms: 'Dieser authentischer Gebrauch der Fremdsprache fördert den Lernprozess in höherem Masse als im herkömmlichen Klassenzimmer, wo vorwiegend über pseudoreale oder fictive Inhalte kommuniziert wird' (Wolff 2002:45). In many European countries this form of language teaching has become popular, though it should also be mentioned that in the vast majorities of schools the foreign language taught is English and only few schools offer CLIL with any of the other EU languages.

Early bilingualism: Simultaneous and consecutive
In the literature on early bilingualism there are numerous studies on children who have been brought up in two languages. There is a long European tradition which goes back to the seminal work of Ronjat (1913) on his son Louis who was brought up in French and German, and Leopold (1970) who made careful analyses of the daughter Hildegardt's development in German and English. More recent work on simultaneous bilingualism includes work by Arnberg (1987), De Houwer (1990) and Lanza (1997). One of the main research questions is when and to what extent young children develop separate systems for their different languages and to what extent the well-known principle of one

parent-one language is really necessary for full bilingual development.

There is much less research on early consecutive bilingualism (Kielhöfer & Jonekeit 1983), but there is a growing interest in the development of bilingualism through early bilingual schooling that is becoming more popular due to the EU's policy to promote an early start for foreign language learning (Leman 1991; Housen & Baetens Beardsmore 1993; Baetens Beardsmore 2003). This research is a continuation of an earlier line of research in foreign languages in primary and pre-school education. Blondin et al. (1998) present and overview of findings on such education in various countries in Europe.

The choice of languages in the EU

An inevitable consequence of the establishment of the EEC and the EU was the emergence of language as a political issue in various respects: what should be the language or languages of the EU, how many languages should inhabitants of member states be able to speak, how can we test language proficiency over countries through a unified system.

In the EU in its present form there are 13 official national languages, ranging from German with 63 million speakers to Letzebuergesh with 0.4 million speakers. In addition to that there are several so-called autochthonous languages, ranging from Catalan with 10 million speakers to Gaelic with 0.1 million speakers (Ammon 1991). Of the national languages, 11 languages are official and working languages for the EU. For the running of the EU as an organization, this large number of working languages has become a heavy financial burden, because all documents have to be made available in all working languages, and in all meetings all languages can be used and so there have to be simultaneous interpreting for all possible language combinations. With the enlargement of the EU this problem becomes even more pressing, not only because the number of languages and according-ly the number of possible combinations grows dramatically, but also because it will be very difficult to find sufficient numbers of translators and interpreters for all language combinations. Van Els (2001) in his analysis of the use of languages in the EU and its institutions considers various models to simplify the language regime in the EU. The language issue is a very sensitive one, because giving up a language as one of the official languages is seen as a serious devaluation of and threat to the position of a language nationally and internationally. Defendants of national languages urge their representatives in all committees and working groups to insist on the presence of interpreters, while in the daily running of the EU at the lower levels the general practice already is that only English and French are used. Van Els discusses various options, which broadly fall into two groups: restrictive (not all languages as working languages) and non-restrictive (all languages allowed). He rejects the financial argument related to the costs of translation and interpreting with the observation that the costs of the falling apart of the EU on the language issue would be far more costly. For the restrictive options he mentions various choices, such as a smaller number of languages (German, French, English), the use of an international language (Esperanto) and English only. Most analysts (de Swaan 1999; Mamadouh 1999; Wright 2000) agree that there should be a restriction on the number of languages but they hesitate to draw firm conclusions. Van Els concludes that in the end the last choice, only English, is the only feasible one, if not because it causes less damage than any of the other options, than because no politician will be brave enough to really try to solve the issue, and doing nothing means that in practice English becomes the working language in most meetings. The use of the other languages will become more or less symbolic. At the same time English as a language will change in status because the increasing number of non-natives will use it, and in doing so change it to such an extent that it is no longer clear who 'owns English' to use Widdowson's (1994) terms.

The Common European Framework of Reference (CEFR)

One of the problems in defining a language policy with respect to the teaching and learning of languages in the EU was how to define levels of proficiency in a foreign language. The need for a common framework of reference became one of the spearheads of language policy in Europe. North & Schneider (1998) report on a large project set up to compare systems of reference for various national and commercial language tests and examinations and present a system that is primarily based on self-evaluation through the use of so-called Can-do-statements ('I am able to understand a conversation between native speakers when they speak at a normal speed about non-specialist topics' 1 = not at all … 5 = without problems). The resulting Common European Framework of Reference (CEFR, Council of Europe 1996) has become the standard for both national examinations and commercial placement tests, such as the Cambridge Exams for English. Although the use of the can-do scales is not without problems, they have now become the standard in research that aims at comparing foreign language proficiency between countries (see for instance the evaluation of English proficiency at the end of compulsory education in different countries reported on by Bonnet 2004).

The position of English and other languages in Europe
It is one of those curious developments in European history that English has become the dominant language in Europe while its country of origin has played a marginal political role on the European scene. For quite some time, Great Britain was not accepted as a member of the EU. At first the French president Charles the Gaulle opposed the entry of Great Britain, fearing it would weaken the German-French axis, later because it did not meet the economic criteria for new members. As a consequence, the English language was never actively promoted by the British, or at any rate not nearly as much as French was defended by the French government who wanted to maintain French as the language of diplomacy (Willingham-McLain 1997).

With the extension of the EU with 13 new member states the linguistic scene is changing dramatically. Holdworth (2003) mentions statistics on foreign languages skills that show that the majority of the people in the new member states are bilingual or multilingual and that in those countries Russian is the most widely spoken foreign language, followed by German. If we look at language skills in the enlarged EU as compared to the present situation an interesting picture emerges. Table 1 contains the percentages of people that claim that they can hold a conversation in that foreign language.

These figures show that the position of English and German, and in particular French is weakened. Russian still holds a strong position, but it is not clear whether that will last, since the call for English in the new states on all levels of society will inevitably go at the expense of Russian. Graddol (2004) presents data on proficiency in English in the present EU. These figures show that the knowledge of English may not be as wide spread as is sometimes assumed that its dominant position might not be as overwhelming as previously thought. As Graddol puts it:

> 'Any look into the future must entertain the idea that soon the entire world will speak English. Many believe English will become the world language to the exclusion of all others. But this idea, which first took root in the 19th century, is past its sell-by date. English will indeed play a crucial role in shaping the new world linguistic order, but its major impact will be in creating new generations of bilingual and multilingual speakers across the world.' (2004, 1330)

Table 1. Percentage of people claiming to be able to hold conversation

	EU of 15 states	EU of 28 states
English	40%	35%
German	18%	16%
Russian	>1%	11%
French	16%	10%

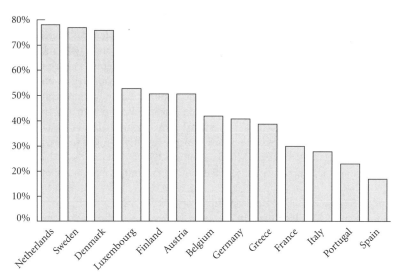

Figure 1. Percentage of European Union populations claiming that they speak English (Graddol 2004).

English now plays an important role in the live of young Europeans in many countries, in particular due to its use in the media (Berns 1995, Deneire & Goethals 1997)

From bilingualism to multilingualism

A typically European issue is the growing interest in trilingualism and multilingualism. In particular in German-speaking countries the interest in what is basically 'English plus x' has led to a range of projects on trilingualism from both a theoretical (Jessner 2000; Herdina & Jessner 2002; Dewaele 1998) and a language teaching perspective (Kjär 1997; Lindemann 1997; Dentler 2000; Hufeisen 2000). One of the most important outcomes of this research is that in multilingualism, all languages systems interact: The mother tongue can affect, but also be affected by the second or third language. In some bilingual regions in Europe, like the Basque country and the Province of Friesland in the Netherlands, English is taught as a third language.

Interestingly, most of the research on this topic has been done in Europe while most of the SLA research with a bilingual focus and a focus on the role of the mother tongue has been done in North America and Britain (see Keckes & Papp 2000). This may be the result of the more widespread multilingualism in Europe and an often personal experience of having to deal with more than two languages in the researchers themselves.

Though not a part of the EU, the small country of Switzerland serves as a model for a workable solution for the linguistic problems of Europe. With its four official languages and the problems the interaction between the linguistic communities in the country pose, Switzerland has generally managed to steer clear from the linguistic battles that have almost split up countries like Belgium and Spain. In his analysis of the Swiss situation, Berthele (2000) concludes '... dass man aufgrund der Schweizer Erfahrungen sicher sein kann, dass Investitionen in Mehrsprachigkeit grundsätzlich lohnenswert sind, und dass eine Fremdsprache nicht zwangsläufig als eigenes Schulfach unterrichtet werden muss, sondern mit anderen Fächern kombiniert vermittelt werden kann.' (127). Clearly both investment in multilingualism in the M+2 formula (Mother tongue plus two other languages of the EU) and some form of Content-Based Language Instruction or CLIL are among the main building blocks of a European language policy.

Labour migration in Western Europe

The booming of the economy in Western Europe which first came about as a result of American support for the rebuilding of Europe ('Marshall Plan') and later on the development of trade and agriculture led to the rapid growth of labour migration from countries in southern Europe, North Africa and Turkey to Germany, France, the Low Countries and the Nordic Countries. This migration quickly turned from temporary stay into permanent residence and family formation in the immigrant countries. This lead to a number of language related problems: Due to low proficiency in the language of the immigrant country, many migrant workers never integrated and in particular their children suffered from low educational achievements and accordingly higher risks of unemployment and drop-out. In many countries initiatives were taken to improve language skills of the migrants and their children and a number of large-scale projects were set up to study the language development of those groups. Probably the best-known example is the ESF project 'Second language acquisition by adult immigrants' coordinated by Wolfgang Klein and Clive Perdue. In the project the acquisition of different languages by speakers with different L1s was studied in a then well-known 'saw-tooth' pattern:

English	German	Dutch	French	Swedish
Punjabi	Italian	Turkish	Arabic	Spanish	Finnish

So, to take an example: the acquisition of German by Italian and Turkish learners was compared to the learning of English by Italian learners and Dutch by Turkish learners so enabling a cross-linguistic comparison between both source and target language. This project has led to a large number of very influential publications on SLA (Klein & Perdue 1992; Dietrich, Klein & Noyau 1995; Becker & Carroll 1997). One of the outcomes of this research was the development of what became known as 'the basic variety':

> 'One of our findings is that all our learners, irrespective of the source and target language, develop a particular way of structuring their utterances which seems to present a natural equilibrium between the various phrasal, semantic and pragmatic constraints.' (Klein & Perdue 1992: 311)

Languages in contact

There are many national languages, minority languages, regiolects and dialects in Europe and therefore language contact is a common phenomenon. There is also a long-standing interest in this. Weinreich's well known *Languages in contact* from 1953 is an early example of research that takes into account linguistic, sociolinguistic and to a certain extent even psycholinguistic aspects of language contact. There are few examples of language contact situations in which the two languages live in peace alongside each other. In most cases there is a difference in status and this implies that the weaker language is in danger to being overtaken by the stronger one. Nelde (1987) has formulated this aptly: Language contact is language conflict. As we will see later on in the discussion on maintenance and loss of minority languages, this is the reality for many languages, and, as some argue, even all languages except English.

At the same time we see the development of new varieties resulting from language contact, much along the lines proposed by Graddoll (2004). In particular in Germany, there is a growing group of researchers who are interested in the contact languages that develop in multi-ethnic cities. For some, those new varieties pose serious threats for young people with a migrant background, because the kind of input in the language they need for their education and their position on the job market is limited when they only speak these youth varieties. Schlobinski et al. (1993:9) cites several very negative comments on such youth language, including one by Lamprecht (1965): 'Die Witzigkeit des Jargons ist nur äusserlich, in Wahrheir spiegelt er sprachliche Verwilderung und emotionale Verrohung wider'. Not all comments have this sombre tone. For many linguists the development of such 'wild' varieties is a sign of the ability of languages to renew themselves and to adapt to new situations. Youth language often has a sort of 'secret language' function aimed at the exclusion of outsiders in the communication and it clearly reflects the interests of the age group of 12–18 year olds. Varieties are typically unstable, and being able to joggle with the language and be creative with new words gives prestige. The language also serves as a homogenizing force among young people with different ethnic backgrounds (Wachau 1989; Appel 1999).

Maintenance and loss of minority languages

Due to the changes taking place in Europe, two trends in language contact have emerged: on the one hand the migration to Western Europe by various groups from Southern Europe, North Africa and Turkey, and the growing impact of national languages on non-migrant minorities. Both trends have been investigated in terms of in the maintenance and loss of minority languages in various parts of Europe. Well-known examples are the work of Dorian (1989) on Scottish Gaelic, Gal's (1979) research on dialect loss in Austria and Rindler Schjerve's (1981) research on Sardinian. The loss of language skills in migrant languages has been studied in many European countries. Fase, Jaspaert & Kroon (1991, 1995) and Ammerlaan et al. (2001) present many examples of this line of research. Also from a sociolinguistic perspective there is interest in linguistic and educational characteristics of migrant groups in different countries like Sweden (Boyd 2001), Germany (Gogolin & Reich 2001), Spain (López García & Mijares Molina 2001) and France (Caubet 2001).

Regionalization

The tendency of larger and more powerful languages to dominate the smaller ones has led to a strong reaction in various countries to support and strengthen the position of smaller languages. Within the EU several resolutions have been adopted aiming at protecting regional minority languages. These actions have lead to the foundation of the *European Bureau for lesser used languages* and a very active MERCATOR network in which representatives from most regional minority languages cooperate. The *European Charter for Regional or Minority Languages* in 1992 has been a milestone in this respect, because all member states had to take positive action to protect and support their regional minority languages. This has clearly strengthened the position of those languages though there are important differences between the various regions in this respect.

The almost comfortable position of regional languages in Europe stands in sharp contrast with the weak position of migrant languages in those countries. In that sense there is an uneasy relation between proponents of migrant languages and other minority languages in Europe. Extra (1989) points to the fact that the arrangements for local or regional minority languages (like Frisian and Basque) are generally much more supportive for language maintenance than the arrangements for migrant languages. In more recent publications the defenders of the rights of the two minority communities, regional and migrant, seem to have found a common interest in campaigning for the rights of minority languages more generally. In an edited volume with the apt title 'The other languages of Europe', Extra & Gorter (2001) argue for the provision of teaching for both migrant and minority languages.

Language in Academia

Language choice in Academia is often considered an important indicator of the status of a language. If that is true, then most European languages are in a bad state. English has become the language of science, also in Europe where French and in particular German had a very strong tradition. In the Netherlands this has now reached the point that publications in national languages and even in other national languages than English are not taken into consideration by panels reviewing scientific institutions (De Wolff 1994).

A final point has to do with historical allegiances: There is a divide between the North/Western part of Europe and Southern Europe, with the German-speaking countries in between with respect to the orientation towards the English-speaking countries and accordingly research communities: while countries like Sweden and The Netherlands are almost completely focused on developments in the UK and the USA/Canada, and also contribute to the debates by publishing in English in international journals and books, the worlds of AL in France and Italy, but partly also Germany have been more inward looking, publishing in the national language and then complaining that they are never cited. Of course the number of (first/second/third language) speakers of these languages are smaller than those of English, but that is not the main explanation for the divide.

The emergence of 'econolinguistics'

As part of the discussion on the multilingualism in Europe a fairly new subfield has emerged that is concerned with economic aspects of language and language policy (Grin 1996). As Lüdi (2001) has indicated this is not just the kind of 'Alle Menschen werden Brüder' — sweet talk that can be found in many policy documents at the European level: 'Sprachlernen muss als eigentliche Investition in menschliche Ressourcen betrachtet werden, die durchaus nicht nur auf symbolisch-politischer, sondern auch auf ökonomischer Ebene früchte tragen. (61). 'Econolinguistics' has been defined by Grin (2001) as follows:

> 'L'économie de la langue s'inscrit dans le paradigme de la théorie économique et se sert des concepts et outils de celle-ci dans l'étude de relations où interviennert des variables linguistiques: Elle porte l'attention principalement, mais pas exclusivement, sur les relations dans lesquelles des variables économiques interviennent.' (43)

One of Grin's main findings at the European level of this approach is that the economic value of English as an additional language is declining because knowledge of English is so widespread that its market value has decreased, while the value of knowing other languages in various European languages is on the increase.

Final remarks

In this contribution an attempt has been made to provide a sketch of what goes on in AL in Europe at the moment. The focus was on the relationship between language in use and the complex sociolinguistic situation in Europe rather than the specific contributions to AL made by European researchers. Many if not most aspects of what is being done have not been discussed, and there are many gaps. A major gap is the virtual absence of work in and on the Romance and Slavic languages. This reflects the divide referred to earlier. Other gaps are the vibrant work on bilingual processing on which many European researchers have been working recently, text- and discourse-analysis, translation studies, linguistic aspects of SLA, language pathology and mother tongue education. They were not excluded because the research would not be worth mentioning, but because they did not fit in the structure adopted. Many researchers will be disappointed that they are not mentioned here. As I said before, this is very regrettable, but also unavoidable for an overview of such a large community of researchers. AL in Europe could easily fill a complete issue of the AILA review and even a full book. But that was not the aim of this issue. What I hope I have been able to convey, is that European Applied Linguists are very active both with respect to general theoretical issues and with issues that are specific for the European context. Some of these issues have their basis in the social and political changes that have taken place in Europe in the last 40 years, and these are the issues that have been highlighted here.

What are future developments for applied linguistics in Europe from the perspective taken here? A number of issues are likely to gain further prominence in the near future. These include:

– Further expansion of EU: what other languages, how many, what are the costs?
– Growth of English at the expense of other languages in all walks the of life and the detrimental

effect this will have on the learning of other foreign languages.

- Language and aging in migrants: The first wave of migrants in now reaching old age, and with that come problems related to physical and cognitive decline. Few countries are ready to take appropriate measures to deal with this problem at the moment.
- The Role of national language/local language/English: one scenario is that English will become the language of wider communication for all Europeans, but that they will stick to their local language as the language of comfort and solidarity. This may mean that the role of national languages is undermined since they have no role to play anymore.
- The Future of foreign language teaching: will there still be foreign language learning and teaching other than English?

Note

* The author is indebted to Jasone Cenoz, Jean-Marc DeWaele, Susan Gass and Sinfree Makoni for their comments on an earlier version of this contribution.

References

Ammerlaan, T. H. M., H. Strating, and K. Yagmur. (2001). *Sociolinguistic and psycholinguistic perspectives on maintenance and loss of minority languages.* Münster/New York: Waxmann.

Ammon, U. (1991). The status of German and other languages in the European community. In F. Coulmas (ed.), *A language policy for the European community: prospects and quandaries,* pp. 241–254. Berlin/New York: Mouton de Gruyter.

Appel, R. (1999). Straattaal. De mengtaal van jongeren in Amsterdam. *Toegpaste Taalwetenschap in Artikelen* 62(2): 38–55.

Arnberg, L. (1987). *Raising children bilingually: The pre-school years.* Clevedon: Multilingual Matters.

Baetens Beardsmore, H. (2003). Who is afraid of bilingualism? In J.-M. Dewaele, A. Housen, and Li Wei (eds), *Bilingualism: Beyond basic principles,* pp. 10–27. Clevedon: Multilingual Matters.

Becker, A. and M. Carroll. (1997). *The acquisition of spatial relations in a second language.* Amsterdam/Philadelphia: John Benjamins.

Berns, M. (1995). English in the European Union. *English Today* 11: 3–13.

Berthele, R. (2000). Die viersprachige Schweiz — Vorbild oder schlechtes Beispiel. In K.de Bot, S. Kroon, P. Nelde, and H. Van de Velde (eds), *Institutional status and used of national languages in Europe,* pp. 109–130. St. Augustin: Asgard Verlag.

Blondin, C., M. Candelier, P. Edelenbos, R. Johnstone, A. Kubanek-German, and T. Taeschner. (1998). *Foreign languages in primary and pre-school education. A review of recent research within the European Union.* London: CILT.

Bonnet, G. (2004). *The assessment of pupils' skills in English in eight European countries.* Paris: Ministry of Education.

Boyd, S. (2001). Immigrant languages in Sweden. In G. Extra and D. Gorter (eds), *The other languages of Europe,* pp. 177–192. Clevedon: Multilingual Matters.

Caubet, D. (2001). Maghrebine Arabic in France. In G. Extra and D. Gorter (eds), *The other languages of Europe,* pp. 261–278. Clevedon: Multilingual Matters.

Council of Europe (1996). *Common European Framework of reference for language learning and teaching: Draft 1 of a framework proposal.* Strasbourg: Council of Europe.

De Houwer A. (1990). *The acquisition of two languages from birth: a case study.* Cambridge: Cambridge University Press.

de Swaan, A. (1999). The European language constellation. In N. Bos (ed.), *Which languages for Europe?,* pp. 13–23. Amsterdam: European Cultural foundation.

Dewaele, J.-M. (1998). Lexical inventions: French interlanguage as L2 versus L3. *Applied Linguistics* 19: 471–490.

Deneire, M. and M. Goethals. (1997). Introduction: world Englishs in Europe. *World Englishes* 16: 1–2.

Dentler, S. (2000). Deutsch und Englisch — das gibt immer Krieg. In S. Dentler, B. Hufeisen, and B. Lindemann (eds), *Tertiär- und Drittsprachen. Projekte und empirische Untersuchungen*, pp. 77–97. Tübbingen: Stauffenberg verlag.

Dietrich, R., W. Klein, and C. Noyau. (1995). *The acquisition of temporality in a second language*. Amsterdam/ Philadelphia: John Benjamins.

Dorian, N. (ed.) (1989). *Investigating obsolescence. Studies in language contraction and death*. Cambridge: Cambridge University Press.

Extra, G. and D. Gorter. (2001). *The other languages of Europe*. Clevedon: Multilingual Matters.

Extra, G. (1989). Ethnic minority languages versus Frisian in Dutch primary schools: a comparative perspective. *Journal of Multilingual and Multicultural Development* 10: 59–72.

Fase, W., K. Jaspaert, and S. Kroon. (1991). *Maintenance and loss of ethnic minority languages*. Amsterdam: John Benjamins Publishers.

Fase, W., K. Jaspaert, and S. Kroon. (1995). *The state of minority languages*. Lisse: Swets and Zeitlinger.

Gal, S. (1979). *Language shift. Social determinants of linguistic change in bilingual Austria*. New York: Academis Press.

Gogolin, I. and H. Reich. (2001). Immigrant langauges in federal Germany. In G. Extra and D. Gorter (eds), *The other languages of Europe*, pp. 193–214. Clevedon: Multilingual Matters.

Grabe, W. (2002). Applied Linguistics: An emerging discipline for the twenty-first century. In R. Kaplan (ed.), *The Oxford handbook of applied linguistics*, pp. 3–12. Oxford: Oxford University Press.

Graddol, D. (2004). The future of language. *Science Magazine* 303: 1329–1331.

Grin, F. (1996). Economic approaches to language and language planning: an Introduction. *International Journal of the Sociology of Language* 121: 1–16.

Grin, F. (2001). L' économie des politiques linguistiques: vers un bilan critique. In K. de Bot, S. Kroon, P. Nelde, and H. Van de Velde (eds), *Institutional status and use of national languages in Europe*, pp. 41–59. St.Augustin: Asgard Verlag.

Herdina, P. and U. Jessner. (2002). *A dynamic model of multilingualism. Perspective of change in psycholinguistics*. Clevedon: Multilingual Matters.

Hobsbawm, E. (1995). *Age of extremes. The short twentieth century 1914–1991*. London: Peter Smith.

Holdsworth, P. (2003). Foreign language skills in the candidate countries. *Le Magazine. Education and Culture in Europe* 19:22.

Housen, A. and H. Baetens Beardsmore. (1993). Curricular and extra-curricular factors in multilingual education. *Studies in Second Language Acquisition* 15: 83–102.

Hufeisen, B. (2000). A European perspective: tertiary languages with a focus on German as L3. In J. Rosenthal (ed.), *Handbook of undergraduate second language education*. pp. 209–229, Mahwah. New Jersey: Lawrence Erlbaum.

Jeßner, U. (2000). Metalinguistisches Denken beim Drittsprachgebrauch — Bilingualismus ist kein zweifacher Monolingualismus. In A. James (ed.), *Aktuelle Themen in Zweitspracherwerb: Oesterreichische Beiträge*, pp. 77–88. Wien: Praesens.

Kecskes, I. and T. Papp. (2000). *Foreign language and mother tongue*. Mahwah: Lawrence Erlbaum.

Kielhöfer, B. and S. Jonekeit. (1983). *Zweisprachige Kindererziehung*. Tübingen: Stauffenberg.

Kjär, U. (1997). Deutsch as L3. Zur Interimsprache schwedischer Deutschlerner (unter berücksichtigung des Einflusses des Englischen als L2). In S. Dentler, B. Hufeisen, and B. Lindemann (eds), *Tertiär- und Drittsprachen. Projekte und empirische Untersuchungen*, pp. 41–55. Tübingen: Staufenbergverlag.

Klein, W. and C. Perdue. (1992). *Utterance structure. Developing grammars again*. Amsterdam/Philadelphia: John Benjamins Publishers.

Lanza, E. (1997). *Language mixing in infant bilingualism*. Oxford: Oxford University Press.

Leman, J. (1991). Between Bi- and intercultural education: projects in Dutch-language kindergartens and primary schools in Brussels. In K. Jaspaert and S. Kroon (eds), *Ethnic minority languages and education*, pp. 123–134. Amsterdam/Lisse: Swets and Zeitlinger.

Leontiev, A. (1995). Multilingualism for all — Russians? In T. Skutnabb-Kangas (ed.), *Multilingualism for all*, pp. 199–214. Lisse: Swets and Zeitlinger.

Leopold, W. (1970). Speech development of a bilingual child. Vols. 1–4. Evanston: University of Illinois Press.

Lindemann, B. (1997). "Da fälllt mir immer zoerst ein englisches Wort ein." Zum Einfluß der ersten Fremdsprache beim Uebersetzen ins Deutsche. In S. Dentler, B. Hufeisen, and B. Lindemann (eds), *Tertiär- und Drittsprachen. Projekte und empirische Untersuchungen*, pp. 57–66. Tübingen: Staufenberg Verlag.

López García, B. and L. Mijares Molina. (2001). Moroccan children and Arabic in Spanish schools. In G. Extra and D. Gorter (eds), *The other languages of Europe*, pp. 279–292. Clevedon: Multilingual Matters.

Lüdi, G. (2001). Vielfältige mehrsprachige Repertoires für alle Bürger Europas. Leitgedanken für ein europäisches "Gesamtsprachenkonzept". In K. de Bot, S. Kroon, P. Nelde, and H. Van de Velde (eds), *Institutional status and use of national languages in Europe*, pp. 59–76. St Augustin: Asgard Verlag.

Mamadouh, V. (1999). Institutional multilingualism: an exploration of possible reforms. In N. Bos (ed.), *Which languages for Europe?*, pp. 119–125. Amsterdam: European Cultural Foundation.

Marsh, D., B. Marsland, and A. Maljers. (1998). *Future Scenarios in Content and Language Integrated Learning.* Jyväskylä: University of Jyväskylä.

Maurais, J. (1992). Redéfinition du statut des languages en Union Soviétique. *Language Problems and Language Planning* 16(1): 1–20.

Nelde, P. (1987). Language contact means language conflict. *Journal of Multilingual and Multicultural Development* 8: 33–42.

North, B. and G. Schneider. (1998). Scaling descriptors for language proficiency scales. *Language Testing* 15: 217–262.

Rannut, M. and U. Rannut. (1995). Bilingualism — a step towards monolingualism or multilingualism? In T. Skutnabb-Kangas (ed.), *Multilingualism for all*, pp. 183–198. Lisse: Swets and Zeitlinger.

Rindler Schjerve, R. (1981). Bilingualism and language shift in Sardinia. In E. Haugen (ed.), *Minority languages today*, pp. 208–217. Edinburgh: Edinburgh University Press.

Ronjat, J. (1913). *Le development du langage observé chez un enfant bilingue.* Paris: Champion.

Schlobinski, P., G. Kohl, and I. Ludewigt. (1993). *Jugensprache: Fiktion und Wirklichkeit.* Opladen: Westdeutscher Verlag.

Schöpflin, G. (2000). *Nations, identity, Power. The new politics of Europe.* London: C. Hurst & Co.

Takala, S. and K. Sajavaara. (2000). Language policy and planning. *Annual Review of Applied Linguistics* 20: 129–146.

van Els, T. (2001). The European Union, its institutions and its languages. Some language political observations. *Current Issues in Language Planning* 2: 311–360.

Wachau, S. (1989). 'Nicht so verschlüsselt und verschleimt'. Ueber Einstellungen gegenüber Jugendsprache. *Osnabrücker Beiträge zur Sprachtheorie* 41: 69–96.

Weinreich, U. (1953). *Languages in contact.* New York: Linguistic Circle of New York Publications.

Widdowson, H. (1994). The ownership of English. *TESOL Quarterly* 28: 377–388.

Willingham-McLain, L. (1997). Arrosoir, oui, Manhattan, non: naming and the law in France. *Names* 45: 185–202.

Wolff, D. (2002). Zur bedeutung des bilingualen Sachfachunterrichts in Kontext des Mehrsprachigkeitskonzeptes der Europäischen Union. In D. Marsh (ed.), *CLIL/EMILE. The European Dimension. Actions, trends and foresight potential*, pp. 44–47. Jyväskylä: Continuing Education Centre.

Wright, S. (2000). *Community and communication. The role of language in nation state building and European integration.* Clevedon: Multilingual Matters.

Résumé

Dans cette contribution nous relions les développements en linguistique appliquée en Europe aux grands changements sociaux des dernières décennies.

Il y a ainsi la chute de l'URSS et la fin de la guerre froide; le développement de la CEE et de l'UE et la disparition des frontières internes; la croissance économique de l'Europe occidentale; la migration économique du sud vers le nord de l'Europe; et l'émergence du régionalisme.

Tous ces développements ont affecté le rôle des langues dans la société et ils ont contribué à l'éclosion de la recherche linguistique sur les langues en situation de contact.

Applied Linguistics in Asia

Pathways, Patterns and Predictions[*]

Anne Pakir
National University of Singapore

This paper examines language trends in 21st century Asia and reports on the development of Applied Linguistics (AL) in the region. It has a dual focus: the first analyses the unique preoccupations of Asian and Asia-based applied linguists that have given rise to present research directions and preferences. These, however, seem to be not much recognized in the currently BANA dominated field. A second focal point considers the larger concerns and issues that might lead to future and different directions in AL scholarship once 'proper applied linguistics' — currently originating in the West and dominating research directions — reorients and realigns itself to include these Asian research and findings. It can be predicted that with this realignment, AL will grow as a field of inquiry in leaps and bounds along with the imminent rise of Asia by the middle of the twenty first century.

Keywords: Applied linguistics, Asia

Introduction

As a discipline, Applied Linguistics (AL) originated in the west and has been dominated by western scholarship for much of the 20th century. Thus, the focus on AL in Asia brings an orientation that may prove useful as well as necessary in the 21st century, particularly in the context of a rapidly growing Asia. This paper will focus on pathways, patterns and predictions in Applied Linguistics (AL) within the Asian region in terms of both the discipline of AL, as well as how it will affect the world view of Applied Linguistics (AL). It is predicted that as a field of inquiry, AL will grow in leaps and bounds with the predicted rise of Asia by the middle of the current century. Therefore, by mid-21st century, the thrust and pace of potential AL studies worldwide might be guided and determined outside of the Western world of scholarship.

This paper addresses two concerns: Firstly, what are the unique preoccupations of Asian and Asia-based applied linguists that have given rise to present research directions and preferences? Secondly, how will these concerns and issues lead to future and different directions in AL scholarship worldwide?

Asia is a broadly defined geographical entity. It is a vast and complex continent stretching from the Middle East to the Middle Kingdom and even to Australia, if we were to include Australasia in the definition of 'Asia'. Being the continent with the largest number of people, the greatest number of living languages and the most diverse range of writing systems, Asia can be likened to a vast laboratory in which studies of who says what to whom in what languages, why, when and how can be fruitfully engaged. It is also a huge platform for understanding how languages are learnt, taught and used in communication. Following Kachru's (1984, 1985) model of the three distinctive existences of English as a global language, Asia is represented in all three circles of English users. In the inner circle we count Australia and New Zealand, countries commonly referred together as Australasia; in the outer circle are countries such as India, Malaysia, Singapore, the Philippines, and Brunei, all former colonies of Inner Circle countries (i.e., Britain and the United States). In the expanding circle are countries like China, Japan, Korea, Laos, Cambodia, Myanmar and Vietnam.

This paper will report on developments in the Kachruvian based outer and expanding circles from various sources, and will also draw upon the reflections of individual scholars from eight

AILA Review 17 (2004), 69–76.
ISSN 1461–0213 / E-ISSN 1570–5595 © John Benjamins Publishing Company

countries who responded to a questionnaire. A salient feature of all the data is that scholars in the region are studying and analysing language issues and language education without recognition from the AL scholarship in the British and North American (BANA) sphere: in fact, Asian AL research and findings are almost absent or invisible on the western front. The implication is that although much is understood about language and the discipline of language within Asia, it is not recognized sufficiently in Anglo-centric countries.

The pathways of applied linguistics in Asia

Applied linguistics traditionally focuses on language matters that apply to everyone, in both private and professional contexts. In our private lives, language is the most important means of human contact, communication and knowledge representation. In our professional lives, we communicate mainly with language to create, impart and apply knowledge.

As a discipline, AL has developed rapidly and changed significantly after nearly six decades since its recognition in the 1940s, as "'an academic arm' of English language teaching". Today, AL is seen as a fragmented field and surrounded by controversy (Seidlhofer 2003). The nature of AL is that it is not strongly definable, and like its sister discipline, sociolinguistics, it is often seen to be vainly in search of a theory or an argument. Its identity is also porous and confused: sometimes AL is assumed when SLA is mentioned, and vice-versa (Kramsch 2000). In a curious manner and in a return to its roots, AL has become identified with SLA, particularly with the rise of English as a global language. Today, much of BANA SLA pursuit is focused on the learning and acquisition of English as a second language. For example, 'Language for Specific Purposes' is centered on English for Specific Purposes and a great deal of 'Communication in the Professions' dwells on English in the Workplace. Inevitably, several orientations and take-offs in Asia are thus patterned similarly, established along the lines laid down by the notion of 'proper' Applied Linguistics, however this concept has been defined over time.

AL traditionally focuses on child language learning, adolescent language learning, adult language learning or language education in general. There are also the current and popular topics of communication in the workplace, discourse analysis and educational technology. Language learning, foreign or second language learning, interpretation and translation, language and ecology, language planning, lexicology and lexicography, literacy, mother tongue education, psycholinguistics, rhetoric and stylistics, and societal multilingualism have all also come under the ambit of what is considered AL (see, for example, the listing of the 25 scientific commissions of the International Association of Applied Linguistics (AILA)). The list whilst not exhaustive permits us to see how broadly the field of applied linguistics takes into consideration several aspects of language, culture and society, and tries to give insights into the processes related to learning language within these contexts. The current major concerns in these endeavors though, are hugely anchored in the topic of English: its learning, acquisition, assessment, translation, interpretation, and discourses. Related subject matter such as educational technology, language and the media, lexicography and lexicology are also heavily English-oriented. Intercultural communication in English with speakers from vastly different cultures and backgrounds (for example Kubota 2001) is another recurrent theme.

Given the myriad of directions in AL pursuits, it is surprising that much of the Asian scholarship in AL has had an absent history and invisible presence even as the same issues and concerns are discussed and published in Chinese, Japanese, Korean, Hindi, Thai, Tamil, Malay and other major Asian languages. These were and still are seldom seen, read and commented upon by an English-knowing, English-reading research and publishing world. For example, Tsuda's (1994) work on the diffusion of English and its negative impact on culture and communication is a fine analysis of the implications of the worldwide spread of English as a global language. Because it was published in Japanese, Tsuda's two paradigms — the diffusion of English and the ecology of languages — had to wait until Phillipson and Skutnabb-Kangas (1997) gave the English scholarship world notice of it in an issue of *World Englishes*. These are examples of pioneering, laudable attempts to make such scholarship known to an English reading audience. However, it is still noticeable that scholars who write in their own language are being read and are successful only when an English language audience is targeted, or has its attention brought to them.

In a recent review of a Chinese publication *Shijie yingyu gailun* (*Introduction to World Englishes*) (Yan 2002), Zhang (2003) stated that "this book …serves well as a reference to the Chinese research community on English-related issues". As a country in the Expanding Circle, China has many issues with language teaching, much of which concerns Chinese ELT (Yan 2002). Another reviewer (Hino 2003) recently called attention to a Japanese publication, *Ajia no Saishin-eigo-jijo: The Encyclopedia of the English Language Situation in Asia* (Honna 2002). Comprising 21 chapters, the encyclopedia is written by 15 Japanese experts on Asian Englishes in 21 countries. Six aspects of each country or region are included: historical, geographical, ethnic, and social background; language policies; social use of English; English language teaching; features of local varieties of English, and prospects for the future use of English (Hino 2003). In addition, a handsomely produced encyclopedia of applied linguistics was published in Japan in 2003 and it is now the definitive Japanese reader in AL in the country. This volume remains unknown to AL scholars from the western world because it has yet to be made visible by being reviewed in an English or U.S. based journal. These examples of Asian AL publications written in the native languages are typical of the scant attention paid to non-English research, and they are also an indication of the fine standards of research to come.

The patterns of applied linguistics in Asia

Much of the AL work in Asia is linked to the English-knowing bilingualism that is prevalent in the world today because of the spread and diffusion of English as a world language. This paper, another Anglo-centric report, does pay attention to established scholarship in the field of BANA-directed AL, with its heavy emphasis on English language learning and teaching concerns. However, beneath the surface of AL English-based rhetoric, it will also attempt to uncover the common patterns in the field usually classified under the umbrella term of 'Applied Linguistics'.

Two sources were used to uncover the patterns and trends in Asia: the Directory of English Language Scholars and Researchers in the SEAMEO countries (for Southeast Asian AL scholarship) and the responses from authoritative voices in Southeast, South and East Asia. They represent views from both the Outer and Expanding circle countries that use English.

The Directory of English Language Scholars and Researchers in SEAMEO Countries is a readily accessible online resource identifying and listing — on a self-selecting basis — "the innumerable individuals who have been involved in teaching English at national and institutional levels… and thus those who are able to make significant contributions to the improvement of English language teaching and research". Table 1 indicates all 10 of the ASEAN countries, (previously often referred to as Southeast Asian countries) and the number of English language teachers and scholars from each country who registered themselves in the directory.

Each of the online self-registering teachers/scholars had to list their three main areas and rank them hierarchically using the numbers 1, 2, and 3 with 1 being the most important. Not every individual reported on these main areas or ranked them, but of those who did the pattern in Table 2 emerged.

The primary concerns of the 337 "English language scholars and researchers in SEAMEO countries" were: English for Specific Purposes (138), Methodology (128), and Instructional Materials Development (122). These concerns are heavily pedagogical in nature, focusing on efficiency in English language teaching and learning, with the implication that the inspiration and model for these main areas would come from the Inner Circle countries or 'western' traditions.

The second set of data was of greater interest. Between January to June 2004, I conducted an informal survey among Asian 'young and old voices' in AL from the following countries: Peoples' Republic of China, Japan, Korea, Malaysia, the Philippines, Singapore and Sri Lanka, the first three

Table 1. Countries and the number of registrants in the directory

Country	Number of Registrants (TESOL/TESL/TEFL teachers and scholars)
Brunei	7
Cambodia	3
Indonesia	94
Lao PDR	12
Malaysia	57
Myanmar	28
Philippines	46
Singapore	56
Thailand	21
Vietnam	13
TOTAL	337

Table 2. Main areas of teaching/scholarship and their rankings

MAIN AREA	RESPONSES (3)	Overall Ranking
Curriculum Design	85	
Discourse Analysis	102	
English for Special Purposes	138	1
Grammar	78	
Instructional Materials Development	122	3
Language Policies	39	
Methodology	128	2
Psycholinguistics	44	
Sociolinguistics	105	
Testing and Evaluation	68	
Others (please specify)	7 (no specifications)	

being countries in the Expanding Circle and the last four in the Outer Circle of English users. They were invited to answer a questionnaire made up of eight open-ended questions regarding: (1) their country's prime language issues, (2) how these issues could contribute to a global view of AL, (3) the development of AL in their country, (4) the current issues being dealt within AL in their country, (5) the unique features of AL research in their country, (6) who their leading researchers were, (7) whether these were contributing to a global view of applied linguistics and (8) their opinion on what research in AL in their country could contribute to a global view of AL.

Below is a summary of the key features and common concerns, along with the two different views taken by the Outer Circle countries (Malaysia, the Philippines, Singapore and Sri Lanka) and the Expanding Circle countries (China, Japan and Korea).

Applied linguistics in Outer Circle countries

The common feature regarding language issues in the former colonies of the British Empire is that of the complexities inherent in the teaching of any language, not just English. The societies within the outer circle countries of Malaysia, the Philippines, Singapore and Sri Lanka have lived, comfortably or uncomfortably, with many linguistic and ethnic traditions, and have always been made acutely aware of the cultural politics of language. Having the status of former colonies, they grapple in their own ways with the legacy (to some) and the curse'(to others) of the English language left behind by colonialists. Complicating their emerging nationhoods and need for policies (including language) in determining their individual destinies has been the inadvertent rush by these countries into a 'modern' existence and a bowing to the pressures of globalization and its tandem language, English.

One major language concern is the Medium of Instruction (MOI) policy, in terms of its centrality in achieving specific agenda and its implications. For example, in Malaysia, this concern has precipitated the move to reintroduce English as a medium of instruction after three decades of Bahasa Malaysia MOI. Malaysia's scrutiny of their own nationalistic language policy has led successfully to the recent decision to have English as the MOI for science and mathematics. In the Philippines, the debate is often whether English, Filipino or a vernacular among its more than 300 major languages should be the MOI especially at elementary school level. The MOI issue in the Philippines is inextricably tied to the larger, politically volatile issue of what the national language is (now established as Filipino, although not readily accepted everywhere and by every citizen of the country). In Singapore, English was chosen as the working language and this MOI is taught together with the three other official languages, Malay, Mandarin and Tamil. However, the main concern in the small city-state Republic is not so much the MOI but rather the standards expected and achieved in it. In Sri Lanka, the MOI issue hovers around the choice of English, Tamil and Sinhala, each having its own socio-cultural-political dimensions and implications.

AL is regarded as a vastly complex discipline in these countries and emerges from a base of problematic language issues firmly rooted in historical, traditional, ethnographic, socio-cultural, political, as well as ideological realities.

Having such grounded language scenarios, these countries could contribute to an innovative and strategic direction for AL: for example, by pointing out first that AL must not be taken as a neutral discipline; it is not shielded from the bare bone facts of human existence, and it allows multilateral perspectives (Tupas personal communication.). In addition, the language issues in these Outer Circle countries could contribute to redefinitions of bilingualism, bilingual education and the links between language and identity. These issues should, in particular, be able to contribute to a better understanding of what is meant by the term, "English as a world lingua franca" (Ho personal communication.). As someone working in the field of AL, I have described in my research the phenomenon of 'ascendant English-knowing bilingual communities' in Outer Circle countries and suggested that discourses on English as a 'Glocal Language' (Pakir 2003) could be an apt response in order to counterbalance the discourses on English as a Global Language.

Applied linguistics in Expanding Circle countries

The Expanding Circle countries of China, Japan and Korea have also had to grapple with the issue of English in a globalizing world where the flows of peoples, goods and cultures are aided by English, the language of greatest currency in the world at the start of the 21st century. Thus, the teaching of English as an international, national or foreign language and its impact on local identities, communities, and culture is a prime concern.

However, the paths taken so far by these countries also include a constant and undivided attention to their own language that is tied to a strongly identifiable monocultural-cum-monolingual existence (Chinese, Japanese, Korean). The study of the clearly defined national languages in these countries (the Han language in China, the Nihon-go in Japan, and the Hanggul in Korea) is paramount and strongly focused on, albeit complemented by the study of ethnic languages and the study of foreign languages.

Data responses from active scholars publishing in the field of AL point to the fact that the work being done in historiography of Chinese, Japanese and Korean languages, and in the areas of orthography, dialectology, literacy, terminology, language planning, and language in information processing is of an advanced level. These studies in turn, will make the process of transition and exchanging templates or frameworks specifying the introduction of English as a necessary foreign language in the respective countries, easier. Dictionary compiling has become innovative with the introduction of bilingual dictionaries and 'tri-bi' dictionaries in which three languages and two scripts are used — an example being the alphabetic script for English and the logographic script for Mandarin and Cantonese. Translation studies, cross-cultural studies, and contrastive studies using English and Chinese/Japanese/Korean are all making remarkable progress. For instance, how the Chinese learn English can be compared and contrasted with how the Japanese or the Korean learn English. Without doubt these can all contribute significantly to the AL community.

Unfortunately, as with the trend in AL thus far, exciting as these studies may be, they are mostly inaccessible or invisible to the BANA world unless and until translations into English or reviews written in English make their worth more widely acknowledged. However, the attempt to surface AL issues in the outer and expanding circle countries has been made. We must note the significance of the two most recent AILA Congresses held at the turn of the century and the millennium. The 13th World Congress of Applied Linguistics (AILA 1999, Tokyo) and the 14th World Congress of Applied Linguistics (AILA 2002, Singapore) were held in Asia. With these Asian venues, there has been an intense increase in AL activities, interests, and publications not only in English but in several other important languages.

Patterns in AL research as described above bear testimony to the fact that valid and valuable scholarship is emanating slowly from Asia to the rest of the world.

Consider another set of data: the rise in numbers of professional associations in Asia linked with AL and/or English. TEFLIN (Teaching of English as a Foreign Language in Indonesia) was established in Yogjakarta in 1970 and is the leading Indonesian association of teachers of English as a foreign language having held 51 international and local conferences. ASIALEX, the Association for Asian Lexicography is now into its 7th year of existence, having had Asian board members, and presidents serving two-year terms from China, Korea, Japan and now Singapore. Working with JACET (the Japan Association of College English Teachers) and other organizations such as ELTAS (the English Language Teachers' Association of Singapore) in order to centralize these related organizations under one umbrella association, AsiaTEFL was established in March 2003. It is a vast pan-Asian organization based in Korea with 134 founding committee members from 16 Asian regions, and was set up "to promote scholarship, disseminate information, and facilitate cross-cultural understanding among persons concerned with the teaching and learning of English in Asia".

These new rallying centers for research and exchange in matters concerning teaching and learning languages with a special focus on the English language will benefit and flourish from the synergy of several linguistic and applied linguistic traditions from Asia. As a result, AL development in these regions in turn can only benefit from further research, combined understanding and mutual support.

Predications for applied linguistics in Asia

Although the current description paints a picture of the increasing use of English as a lingua franca, and the corresponding predicted rise of ascendant English knowing bilingual communities in the world, especially in the metropolitan centers, it is possible to envision another future.

It has been predicted that by 2050, the world could be a radically different one. China and India, each with a population far exceeding 1 billion, and the United States with its predicted population of 450 million would be the three largest economies in the world (Wilson and Puroshothaman 2003). In another forecast of 2050 by British applied linguist Graddol (2004), the English language would probably drop in prominence ranking after Chinese and become comparable to Hindi, Arabic and Urdu.

Given the rise of China and India as two of the world's largest economies, the world's focal points could shift toward Asia. A key question is: will English remain the language universally sought after? A relevant subsequent question is: will AL with much of its current focus on the teaching of English as a first, second, or foreign language have to change its orientations, directions, and make new alignments in its mission of solving language issues?

Should "proper" applied linguistics — originating in the West and currently dominating research directions — reorient and realign itself to the emerging realities of a possible future world, AL could rise to greater heights. There would then be a fuller understanding of the complexity of trying to be a problem-oriented and problem-solving discipline.

By the end of this century, the ground may have shifted. TOMIL and TOHIL could become major enterprises, rather than the current TOEFL or TESOL: The rise of Teaching of Mandarin as an International Language (TOMIL), and the Teaching of Hindi as an International Language (TOHIL) may not be all that surprising in a world where these would be the languages of the numerically superior or the most powerful economies. The English language may not always be the forbearer for patterns and trends in AL research.

Conclusion

AL is fundamental to reflecting and explaining not only how we deal with the problems of language but also how we see the world, how we encounter and encourage difference, and how we apply principles of equity and justice. In particular, AL as a discipline that is currently grounded in western practices, should allow for more inclusive practice, seeking out researchers who are on the fringe of the present discourses.

This paper has hinted at the necessity of identity politics for AL and its future. To become a more 'Inclusive Applied Linguistics', AL as a discipline, a field, a practice, needs to be available by all, to all, and for all. AILA has to identify the barriers to access and the barriers to participation. Many of these barriers have to do with different kinds of ignorance that exist about AL research in Asia. For example, because research in languages other than English is invisible and absent, it has followed that research in languages other than English is not considered important. AL in its current practice articulates privileged relationships and privileged positions and it may even be expanded and improved upon by contributions from those writing from the less privileged positions.

AL orientations have to be re-visioned, re-worked, and must acquire flexibility in order to grow as well as accommodate Asian-based AL and potential shifts in dominant languages of the world. The growth of Asia, with the high level of research available there, makes this all the more imperative. With new contexts emerging, AL can then as a discipline develop and be known, both within Asia and without.

Note

* The author wishes to acknowledge the Asian Association for Lexicography (ASIALEX); the Association for the Teaching of English as a Foreign Language in Indonesia (TEFLIN); and the Asia Research Institute (ARI, National University of Singapore) for the support at their various conferences. The ASIALEX 2003–3rd Biennial Conference, Tokyo, Japan; the TEFLIN 2003–51st annual conference, Bandung, Indonesia; and the Language Trends in Asia 2003 conference organized by ARI allowed me to present my initial ideas and obtain feedback on this topic of AL and English language education. Thanks are also due to the SEAMEO RELC which provided the online database and to ASIATEFL, a new organization for English education in Asia. Last but not the least acknowledged are the following individuals who responded to my questionnaire on applied linguistics in Asia between January to June 2004: Ho Wah Kam (Singapore), Hu Wen Zhong (People's Republic of China), Joo-Kyung Park (Korea), Saran Kaur Gill (Malaysia), T. Ruanni Tupas and Beatriz P. Lorente (the Philippines), Thiru Kandiah (Sri Lanka) and Yasukata Yano (Japan). While all help is acknowledged all mistakes are mine only.

References

Directory of English Language Scholars and Researchers in the SEAMEO Countries. Singapore: SEAMEO Regional Language Centre. Available on the WWW: http://www.relc.org.sg/directory/, accessed July 2004.
Graddol, D. (2004). The Future of Language. *Science* 303(5662):1329–1331.

Hino, N. (2003). Review of *Ajia no Saishin-eigo-jijo:* The Encyclopedia of the English Language Situation in Asia. *World Englishes* 22(3): 336–338.

Honna, N. (ed.) (2002). *Ajia no Saishin-eigo-jijo:* The Encyclopedia of the English Language Situation in Asia. Tokyo: Taishukan.

Kachru, B. (1984). World Englishes and the teaching of English to non-native speakers, contexts, attitudes, and concerns. *TESOL Newsletter* 18: 25–26.

Kachru, B. (1985). Standards, codification, and sociolinguistic realm: the English language in the outer circle. In R. Quirk and H. Widdowson, *English in the World*, pp. 11–30. Cambridge & New York: Cambridge University Press.

Kramsch, C. (2000). Second language acquisition, applied linguistics and the teaching of foreign languages. *The Modern Language Journal* 84(3): 311–326.

Kubota, R. (2001). Teaching world Englishes to native speakers of English in the USA. *World Englishes* 20(1): 47–64.

Pakir, A. (2003). Which English? The Nativization of English and the Negotiations of Language Choice in Southeast Asia. In R. Ahrens, D. Parker, K. Stierstorfer and K. Tam (eds), *Anglophone Cultures in Southeast Asia: Appropriations, Continuities, Contexts*, pp. 73–84. Heidelberg: Universitätsverslag.

Phillipson, R. and T. Skutnabb-Kangas. (1997). Linguistic Human Rights and English in Europe. *World Englishes* 16(1): 27–43.

Seidhlhofer, B. (2003). *Controversies in Applied Linguistics.* Oxford: Oxford University Press.

Tsuda, Y. (1994). The diffusion of English: its impact on culture and communication. *Keio Communication Review* 16: 49–61.

Wilson, D. and R. Purushothaman. (2003). Dreaming with BRICS: the Path to 2050. Global Economics Paper 99. New York: Goldman Sachs. Available on the WWW: ⟨http://www.gs.com/insight/research/reports/99.pdf⟩, accessed, July 2004.

Yan, Z. (2002). *Shijie yingyu gailun [Introduction to World Englishes].* Beijing, China: Foreign Language Teaching and Research Press.

Zhang, H. (2003). Review of *Shijie yingyu gailun* [Introduction to World Englishes]. *World Englishes* 22(3): 334–336.

Résumé

Cet article examine les tendances du langage dans l'Asie du 21e siècle et étudie le développement de la Linguistique Appliquée dans cette région. Cette étude a deux centres d'intérêt: tout d'abord, elle analyse les préoccupations particulières des linguistes appliqués asiatiques mais aussi des linguistes appliqués basés en Asie qui ont influencé les préférences ainsi que les directions des recherches actuelles. Cependant, celles-ci ne semblent pas être beaucoup reconnues dans le champ dominé à l'heure actuelle par les Anglais et les Américains. En deuxième lieu, cet article examine les inquiétudes et les problèmes plus importants qui pourraient conduire à des directions différentes dans le domaine de la Linguistique Appliquée une fois que 'la Linguistique Appliquée adéquate' — qui a sa source en Occident et qui domine les directions de recherche — se réoriente et se réaligne pour inclure les recherches et découvertes asiatiques. On peut prédire qu'avec ce réalignement, la Linguistique Appliquée deviendra un champ de recherches aux limites inimaginables et fera un bond extraordinaire avec la montée imminente de l'Asie vers le milieu du 21e siècle.

Western perspectives in applied linguistics in Africa

Sinfree Makoni and Ulrike Meinhof
Pennsylvania State University / University of Southampton

The aim of this article is to analyze the nature of the historical and contemporary social contexts within which applied linguistics in Africa emerged, and is currently practiced. The article examines the challenges 'local' applied Linguistics in Africa is confronted with as it tries to amplify applied linguistic programs emanating from Europe and North America. The article argues that seemingly progressive applied linguistic projects interconnect in consolidating a western view of Africa in postcolonial Africa. In this way these projects end up mirroring the very theories which they seek to challenge.

Keywords: Western and local perspectives, applied linguistics in Africa

Introduction

This article like many others since the 1970's (see Towa 1979; Hountodji 1977, 1994; Mudimbe 1988; Masolo 1994) is a critique of western theories of African realities. Unlike earlier critiques which were mainly of religion, history and philosophy, this article addresses the field of applied linguistics. It critiques not only western theories but also emerging Africanist responses to the alleged eurocentricism of some linguistic scholarship on Africa. (Mazrui and Mazrui 1998). The objective of the analysis is to create conditions which facilitate more independent production of knowledge about Africa in applied linguistics (Bates, Mudimbe and O'Barr 1993), and avoid the pitfalls of critiques of western theories from Africa which inadvertently have ended up mirroring the very theories which they are challenging.

The idea of focusing an article specifically on western perspectives on Africa raises a number of issues which demand immediate clarification: (i) the label 'western' in our title (ii) the apparent contradiction of viewing applied linguistics through western lenses while writing an article on Africa.

Said, in his book *Orientalism,* comments on the conceptualization of 'western' which is relevant to our overall argument when he writes:

> Labels purporting to name very large and complex realities are notoriously vague and at the same time unavoidable. If it is true that 'Islam' is an imprecise and ideologically loaded label, it is also true that the west and Christianity are just as problematic. Yet there is no easy way of avoiding these labels, since Muslims speak of Islam, Christians of Christianity, westerners of the west, Jews of Judaism, and all of them about all the others in ways that seem to be both convincing and exact. Instead of trying to propose ways of going round the labels, I think it is more immediately useful to admit at the outset that they exist and have long been in use as an integral part of cultural history rather than as objective classifications. (Said 1978: 86)

The second issue we want to address at the outset is a focus on western sources while addressing issues about applied linguistics in Africa. In a recent study Prah points to the dominance of western scholarship in African studies, however misconstrued, a situation which is markedly different from that in China, where sovereignty of Chinese scholarship on China is widely accepted (Prah 1998: 25). In contemporary scholarship, the same holds true for the Japanese, for India and the Arab world who have created their own epistemologies for studying their own cultures and societies. Yet much of our systematic knowledge of African societies is derived from and continues to be produced by western sources.

AILA Review 17 (2004), 77–104.
ISSN 1461–0213 / E-ISSN 1570–5595 © John Benjamins Publishing Company

The real power of the west is not located in its economic muscle and technological might. Rather, it resides in its power to define. The west defines what is, for example, freedom, progress and civil behavior; law tradition and community; reason, mathematics and science; what is real and what it means to be human (what is applied linguistics and what is not — our addition) The non-western civilizations have simply to accept these definitions or to be defined out of existence. (Sardar 1999:44)

The historical and continuing 'hold' of western knowledge over Africa does not devalue the importance of clearly articulated arguments aimed at developing African perspectives on applied linguistics which have emerged over the years (see for example, Mazrui and Mazrui 1998; Robinson 1996; Webb and Kembo-Sure 1999). In as much as we are critical of western perspectives on applied linguistics in Africa we are also at the same time skeptical of the validity of ethnicising epistemologies in applied linguistics in Africa as an intellectually viable way of reacting to the 'dominance' of such western perspectives. The ethnicisation of epistemologies is typically expressed in the form of *African Voices, African Perspectives*, and we feel it forecloses rather than provides opportunities for continued debate. We therefore argue that some criteria for establishing 'local or regionally shared knowledge practices' are necessary (Crossman 2003; Canagarajah 2002).

In the article we explore ways in which diverse areas such as 'indigenous languages', the policies of the Summer Institute of Linguistics International (SILI) lexicography, orthography, New Englishes (NE), interconnect in consolidating a western view on Africa in the postcolonial period in spite of the seemingly progressive and egalitarian developments encaptured in them.

Historical contexts in which applied linguistics in Africa emerged

Because 'language' has always been a companion of imperialism and 'Empire' (Hardt and Negri 2000) it can be argued that there has always been one version or other of applied linguistics in Africa's colonial and neocolonial encounters with the west. Deliberately misreading Kaplan's (1980) argument that there is no site in which applied linguistics cannot play a role, we suggest, that there is no historical period of African colonial and postcolonial encounters with the west and where ethnic groups have been in contact within a polity, which did not include some version of applied linguistics. To understand the nature of these we propose a distinction between applied linguistics as a formal discipline and applied linguistic 'activities' (Makoni and Meinhof 2003:4).

We construe applied linguistic activities to refer to applied linguistic projects such as lexicography or the development of language teaching materials to facilitate the acquisition of African languages. These were carried out in the late 19th and early 20th centuries in Africa either as part of mission linguistics, or as part of a concerted colonial policy of control and containment (Cohn 1996). These applied linguistic activities predated the emergence of applied linguistics as a formal discipline, which did not take place until the late 1950's and early 1960's. Historically, this much later 'inauguration' of applied linguistics 'proper' coincided with Africa's decolonization. The emergence of applied linguistics as an academic discipline in Africa was, in part, driven by the British concern about the 'quality' of English language teaching after the end of British colonial rule-as if the impending loss of explicit and formal British colonial control compelled the British to 'rediscover' the importance of English in postcolonial Africa. 'The British Empire was giving way to the empire of English' (Phillipson 1992:1). The concern about the 'quality' of English language teaching after Africa's 'flag' independence is revealing because during the colonial period the British were less preoccupied with the teaching and learning of English particularly at primary school levels, but rather with the 'development' of what in our view is incorrectly described and conceptualized as a series of 'indigenous' languages. We shall return below to the implications this has for the prolific field of language planning in Africa.

The 'decolonization' of Africa and the Cold War period also resulted in a greater US involvement in Africa. Academically this contributed towards the establishment and 'flowering of what became known as African Studies in the US. African Studies is a western project, a way of explaining the other in the western mind' (Prah 1998: 31). Particularly in the USA a strand of African applied linguistics was subsequently subsumed within African Studies. However, the objective of this strand of applied linguistics in African Studies was not to create applied linguistic alternatives, but alternatives to applied linguistics.

If applied linguistic 'activities' were shaped by and contributed to shaping colonialism, applied linguistics as a discipline in Africa is still struggling to confront the 'hold' of what Hardt and Negri (2000) aptly refer to as 'Empire' because with political independence in Africa has come no freedom from the imperial grip (and local African dictatorship we hasten to add), but mediated command. The example par excellence is French West Africa which by way of a sophisticated and somewhat Machiavellan French strategy was divided into a dozen potentially functional, but in reality dysfunctional newly independent states. Nominally independent, these countries were dysfunctional from their inception because of their small populations and tiny national economies coupled with a convertible currency. These factors made these states 'poor countries with a currency of rich people' Charles De Gaulle quoted in Breton (2003: 207). With political systems which had no robust institutional past nor political structure (Breton 2003: 206), the newly independent African countries, particularly former French countries became more rather than less dependent on France after they had attained independence. This created ideal conditions for Africa's neo-dependence or 'extra-version' (Crossman 2004: 40) as Africanists prefer to call it in economic terms as well as in the academic sector, especially as regards our own discipline. Applied linguistics in particular has not yet systematically confronted its own colonial legacy as other disciplines in Africa such as anthropology (Prah 1994: 95), which has shown considerable reflexivity under the pervasive influence of colonial and postcolonial theories. We therefore conclude our essay with some recommendations on how applied linguistics particularly in higher education might be 'developed' as a strategy to construct and initiate new and alternative futures in our discipline.

The inauguration of applied linguistics as an academic discipline was important because it occurred at an important historical juncture in Africa's decolonization process ushering in a new epistemological trend in language studies in Africa. While the main focus of applied linguistic activities in the colonial period had been the construction and 'development' of African languages for Europeans, applied linguistics as a discipline concentrated on the teaching and learning of European languages by Africans. This led in some parts of Africa, particularly South Africa, to a conceptualization of applied linguistics as synonymous with English language teaching (Young 2001). The trend of using indigenous languages as key sites of applied linguistics was to be continued by the Summer Institute of Linguistics International (SILI) and its domestic arm the Wycliffe International (WI) previously known as the Wycliffe Bible Translators. WI is generally responsible for the domestic 'fund' raising of the SILI in the US. According to its own stated mission, the goal of the SILI is to bring the 'word to Bible-less tribes' (Laitin 1992: 98). SILI was to be one of the key 'International Organizations' which was to subsequently shape and influence the direction of applied linguistics in Africa. Besides the SILI, there are other organizations which have contributed to the development of applied linguistics in Africa such as the Ford Foundation, the French sponsored Comité Linguistique Africaine Africain à Dakar (CLAD), and the British Council (Laitin 1992: 98). Until recently AILA was not one of the major forces in the development of applied linguistics in Africa. There is only one AILA affiliated association in Africa, the Southern African Association of Applied Linguistics (SAALA) which in spite of the 'Southern African' nomenclature concentrates largely on applied linguistics in South Africa. SAALA was formed in 1980, during the period of academic boycott of South Africa when it was not strategic to use South Africa in the title of the association. There are, however, some other associations such as the Linguistic Society of Southern African Universities, the Linguistic Society of Nigeria and the English Studies of Nigeria which amongst other areas also engage in some applied linguistic research, but the influence of these associations pales in comparison to the historical and on-going impact of SILI.

It is not our objective to provide a comprehensive summary of all applied linguistic activities in Africa. Given the diversity and range this would be an impossible undertaking. Our objectives are much more modest than that. We have three main aims: First to examine how western perspectives are embedded in seemingly progressive areas of applied linguistics in Africa. Secondly, to analyze the contradictions which emerge in African attempts at amplifying such projects. Thirdly, to discuss ethnicising epistemologies in Africa as a reaction to the dominance of the west in applied linguistics in Africa, and thus show their problematic nature.

Lexicography in applied linguistics in Africa

Christianity, lexicography, anthropology and more recently 'descriptive' linguistics particularly corpus linguistics, have been the key driving forces behind the development of Africa's modern day lexicography (Prinsloo and de Schruyver 2001, 2002).

Lexicography in Africa has its origins in word lists, 'Vocabulary-collecting was something visitors to the continent did' (Irvine 2001:79) The earliest word lists were produced between 1643 and 1660 by Jesuit and Capuchian priests. Most of these early 'dictionaries' were bilingual and were produced for European language learners of African languages. For example, a quadrilingual dictionary of Italian, Latin, Spanish and kiKongo was published in 1650, predating by about a century the famous monolingual English dictionary by Samuel Johnson which was published in 1755 (Benson 2001). The dictionaries together with the language primers produced during the colonial period were targeted at Europeans. As other language teaching materials used to teach African languages, they are extremely revealing about the nature of European perspectives on Africans and their languages, and if seen from a contemporary African stand point are amenable to charges of eurocentrism. However, eurocentrism in this case should not be defined negatively, since such a critique suggests denigrating lexicographers for succeeding in their objectives. Not all 19th century lexicographers were Europeans, one notable exception was the Nigerian Samuel Ajayi Crowther who wrote a dictionary on his first language, Yoruba. He also worked on a range of other West African languages, notably Temne, Igbo, Nupe and Hausa (Irvine 2001:77).

It is also important to stress that in the 19th century there was a much closer relationship between literary studies and the study of African languages in two key respects, in terms of the 'source material' which was used, and in what applied linguistics today might call the genre used in the 'linguistic' studies of African languages. The source material included proverbs which were seen as an important component of lexicography. Currently studies in proverbs are seen more as a key component of oral African literature than of applied linguistics in Africa. The dictionaries were also not only written for their linguistic sophistication but for their literary merits as well (Irvine 2001:64).

The applied linguistic question worth posing is thus not so much whether the dictionaries and primers were Eurocentric as such, but rather focus on the effects of the eurocentrism when the dictionaries and primers were subsequently used in the provision of literacy in African education. Rather than targeting children's own cultural life dictionaries and language teaching materials were resources for the learning of African languages by Europeans as part of a strategy of containment. Underlying the policy of containment was the belief that one way to control people is to create European versions of African languages, and subsequently superimpose them when used as medium of instruction.

There have been extensive and on-going discussions on linguistic imperialism and the suppression of vernaculars (cf. Phillipson 1992; Davies 1996; Joseph 2004). Our perspective on this important topic is slightly different. Historical evidence shows that in African contexts, and particularly in British colonies, it was the victorious who were keen to learn the languages of the defeated rather than the other way round. Hence in such contexts linguistic imperialism is not to be seen as the imposition of a colonial language on the colonized but entails the imposition of a colonial version of an indigenous language on Africans. For example, in the Republic of the Congo, the colonial 'indigenous' variety associated with the state was referred to as the *kikongo ya leta* (The kikongo of the rock) and *kikongo ya matari* (The kikongo of the stone breaker) (Mufwene 2001:176). The chiShona associated with the state and missionaries in Zimbabwe was called *chibaba* the language of the missionaries (Chimhundu 1992). It is these versions which became the local vernaculars used as medium of instruction.

Our perspective of linguistic imperialism also entails a redefinition of expertise in African languages: in this case a shift from oral performance to textual analysis. As a rule, most of the analysts adept at textual analysis were either European professional linguists who typically had learnt African languages as second languages or they were western educated Africans. Thus the native speaker was displaced as a legitimate expert in his/her own language.

Currently, there is considerable interest and excitement in a more innovative production of African language dictionaries based on electronic corpora (Prinsloo and de Schryver 2001, 2002). The relative ease with which African corpora can now be established has led to a proliferation of corpus-based dictionaries often covering closely related languages/language varieties as is illustrated in the following lexical items:

Table 1. A comparative analysis of the Bemba/Lamba & Kaonde lexicon

English	Bemba	Lamba	Kaonde
All	Onse	Onsi	Onse
Animal	Nama	Nyama	Nyama
Ashes	To	Toi	To
Belly	Fumo	Kati	Vumo
Big	Kulu	Kulu	Katampe
Bone	Fupa	Fupa	Kupa

(Kashoki and Mann 1978:82–93).

It is questionable whether it is justifiable to compile separate dictionaries for Bemba, Lamba, and kaonde because of the considerable similarity in spite of the different labels. The converse does apply, that in some cases considerable diversity is masked by using a single language label. For example, there is both lexical and grammatical variability within Swahili. As illustrated in the following:

Table 2. A Comparative analysis of Ugandan kiSwahili and Tanzanian KiSwahili

KiSwahili (Uganda)	Swahili (Tanzania)	English
Bado	Mapema	Soon
Nguo za serikali	Sare	Uniform
Maktab	Ofisi	Office
Ndito	misicha…	Girl
Muro	chakula…	Food

(Mukama 2002:67).

The differences also apply at a grammatical level. For example, Swahili in Uganda operates with 9–10 noun classes, while Swahili in Tanzania like any other Bantu languages has over 20 noun classes. Noun classes are the central organizing principle for the organization of Bantu languages. The presence of diversity within the same label does not preclude the possibility of compiling a single dictionary which accommodates that diversity. Research and dictionaries on African especially South

African sign language (Penn and Reagan 1991, 1995, 2001; Reagan 1996) provide examples of how this can be achieved. In enumerating different types such as American sign language, British sign language, pidginized sign languages, they reflect the great diversity within sign languages. Penn and Reagan (1995) report that 98% of the words they compiled were represented by more than one sign. But the dictionary was compiled in such a way as to accommodate that range of diversity.

Rather than seeking to compile a dictionary for each variety which, as the above examples illustrate, might entail producing dictionaries which greatly overlap with one another, it should be feasible to compile a common dictionary, especially in situations of limited financial resources. To us the model to follow is not the development of one dictionary for each variety but a pluralistic one: the 'one dictionary = many varieties' model reflected in African sign language research and indeed in the dictionary of South African English which incorporates the different 'varieties' of South African English in its tradition. The South African lexicographical tradition started in 1913 under the auspices of Pettman (1913) cited in Bolton (2004), and continued to the present day with Branford (1987), and Silva's (1998) monumental dictionary of South *African English on Historical Principles* (Bolton 2004: 381).

Sociolinguistics of urban vernaculars

In the sociolinguistic and psycholinguistic literature it is treated as established fact that in Africa code-switching and mixing are extremely widespread (McCormick 1995; Myers-Scotton 1993; Kamwangamalu 1998; Slabbert and Finlayson 2002). There are three discernible orientations towards code-switching and mixing research: psycholinguistic, sociolinguistic and linguistic. The objective of this section is not to review the voluminous literature on code-switching and mixing, but to examine the assumptions which form the basis of this literature, to investigate what it might tell us about the researcher's perceptions about Africa. From the perspective of an educated speaker it is plausible to assume that code-switching and mixing is the result of the speaker/author's choice of linguistic material from different languages. This assumption is particularly valid for educated speakers who have been exposed to 'school language versions', since as a rule 'School language' is unmixed. However, whilst this may hold for educated speakers, it may not necessarily be true of non-educated speakers. For such speakers, unmixed forms are an exception, whereas the norm is a linguistic amalgam based on material from diverse languages as illustrated in the two extracts below.

The mixing may occur so frequently and so pervasively that it constitutes the norm for those speakers. The following two extracts illustrate the extent to which the mixing may be so intricately intertwined that it might be more plausible to describe it as a single code rather than a product of two or more separate codes. Thus what may be perceived analytically as bilingualism and a hybrid language from an analyst's perspective may indeed be a form of monolingualism from a non-educated language user's perspective. It is important to stress that when we call a language a hybrid we are making statements about its history, that it, is derived from many sources, but as we all know people do not necessarily inherit the history of their language when they are learning it!

> Extract 1
> Mi igioinki ki ndozala
> '(I'm on my way to the market') contains words from different languages: mi (I < Swahili mimi), gouink (go < English going), ki (LOC.,) French qui and ndozala (market < Lingala zando) (Goyavertz 1996: 125)

These mixed forms are not restricted to spoken medium only, but are apparent even in written discourse, and at times include different writing conventions as illustrated in the following extract from an electronic communication:

English in normal font, chiShona in italics, informal discourse in bold

Extract 2

Hi sekuru (uncle) compliments of the new year, I hope *makapinda mairi mushe mushe*. (you had a pleasant new year) Do you know how long the PR (permit res) is **gonna** take?

The short extract above seems to be an amalgam of different languages, and different styles and writing conventions. From the perspective of an educated analyst, it may be assumed that the author is astutely combining different styles and languages. But from the perspective of the language user, what a western educated linguist may construe as a mixture might simply be a single code albeit variable in the way in which it brings together 'elements' from different languages. To describe the codes as chiShona and English may be introducing distinctions which although available in the analysts mind are absent from the speaker's perspective. Most of the speakers and writers of the linguistic amalgams do not necessarily have separate competence in the 'named' languages. But when they do not know the languages in the unmixed forms, is is not plausible to argue that they are combining material from different languages. The truth may be that for many African speakers whether in speech or writing it may now be impossible to separate African languages from different varieties of English. We may be witnessing a formation of a linguistic amalgam which is so complete that even for some educated speakers it may be difficult to identify the different 'varieties'. Nor are they strictly speaking 'street languages' restricted to urban areas since such mixes are even recorded in rural areas. It is the urban vernaculars which now constitute a threat to 'indigenous' African languages and not English. We refer to the linguistic amalgams as urban even though they are spoken in rural communities as well because they transcend physical location and stand in sharp contrast with indigenous (standardized) African languages deemed to be rural (Cook 2002:108; Finlayson, Calteaux and Myers-Scotton 1998). Thus Urban and rural are not understood not as purely geographical locations only but as key aspects of an individual's identity, articulated in part through language. It is an open question whether it is appropriate to define the urban vernaculars as 'languages'. One possible way of defining them would be to regard them simply as 'expressive inventories, that not only enable people to communicate with each other, but also allow people to communicate something about themselves' (Cook: 2002:111). These 'expressive inventories' pose a serious conceptual challenge to the neocolonial constructions of African languages which underpin most of the notions about language in language planning in Africa.

From a western perspective, the spread of the urban vernaculars such as Town Bemba in Zambia, Iscimatho in South Africa, Wolof in the Gambia and Senegal is of interest because although language loss is rare in Africa, its the urban vernaculars and not ex-European languages such as French or English which constitute a threat to 'indigenous' African languages. In situations of economic collapse, 'petty' trading is one of the key professions, and it requires the command of urban vernaculars more so than either French or English, or 'indigenous' African languages. More importantly, English is closely tied to western models of modernization, Christian conversion and modernist social and capitalist development which since the late 1980s has come to represent a 'dead-end for most suburban dwellers' (Devisch 1995, 1999).

While the endangerment of 'indigenous' languages may be read as potentially catastrophic by some linguists, from an Africanist perspective, the spread of the urban vernaculars reflects the extent to which African speakers are creatively adapting to new urban contexts. This underscores the importance of sociolinguistic frameworks which would be able to capture the nuances of the local contexts An attrition framework may not be relevant (Mufwene 2001, 2002, 2004). The issue of language endangerment raises fundamental problems about the underlying notions of language, and the relative importance being attached to speakers as opposed to the languages themselves. We would like to argue that the endangerment of language does not necessarily mean the endangerment of the speakers of those languages. Indeed the creative adaptation by urban African speakers may enhance rather than reduce their chances of survival (Mufwene 2004).

In Africa according to Brenzinger (1998) 54 African languages are already extinct, and another 116 are at various stages of extinction. The statistics of the numbers of endangered languages raises issues which are extremely important in applied linguistics in Africa. It touches directly on the issue of enumerability/countability of languages in Africa. We are not questioning either the statistics of the number of existing African languages nor the ones regarded as threatened or indeed the numbers of those regarded as likely to be extinct. What we seek to draw attention to is a much more fundamental problem. We are seeking to challenge the nature of the linguistic thinking, which makes it possible to think in terms of the enumerability of those languages in the first instance, and to foreground the role of enumerability as one of the modalities of governance. 'To census is an important gesture of power' (Hill 2002: 127).

Analytically, urban African vernaculars are comparable though not equivalent to creoles in so far as they arise in 'contexts of extreme domination (slavery, apartheid) and where one more or less dominant group presides over several subordinate groups. The new social contexts created by the political/economic formation, (e.g., urban centers and shantytowns rather than plantation) create new identities and ethnicities. Depending on the specific historical and social setting, urban vernaculars arise to express and complement these new identities, drawing from the linguistic landscape in different ways and gender-specific ways (Spears personal communication). For example, male urban vernaculars in South Africa draw more upon Afrikaans, than English, while the converse is true for young Black female South Africans (Cook 2002) analysis of 'street Se Tswana' in South Africa.

An analysis of language mixing in urban vernaculars provides an invaluable opportunity for understanding the nature of language contact in real time. Although we are not claiming that urban African vernaculars are creoles or pidgins as such, an analysis of the urban vernaculars sheds light on the processes which pidgins and creoles underwent because of the similarity in the basic processes of variation and simplification.

That urban vernaculars are being acquired as first and second languages pose important sociolinguistic questions with crucial educational implications. Is it always necessary to standardize languages if they are to be used and taught educationally? Without a standard variety what type of language teaching materials would be useful? We suggest that in that case such materials should reflect the heteroglossic (Bakhtin 1981) nature of African sociolinguistics; the materials should therefore be made up of diverse authentic texts. Although standardization might be useful in some contexts, it is possible that the absence of a single standard relieves users of urban African vernaculars of the intense pressures of a monolithic standard. If the urban vernaculars are subsequently standardized, one challenge is how to produce an orthography which allows variation within it. Issues about orthography have been at the core of a great deal of research into African languages, because of the inconsistencies within the orthography. At times the 'same' language may also have more than one orthography (Yanga 1980, 1998; Nyombe 1977). A solution might be to have a general agreement about the phonetic values of the letters, but no standard spelling for individual words. English followed a similar pattern for centuries one could encounter the same word on the same page, spelt differently.

African varieties of English-initiating an African response to new Englishes

The New Englishes (NE) paradigm has been extensively used by some of Africa's most prolific and talented applied linguists (Owusu-Ansah 1991; Kamwangamalu and Chisanga 1997; Arua Arua 2001; Dako 2001; Gough 1996; Wolf and Igboanuasi 2003; Letsholo 2000; Moyo and Kamwangamalu in press) to analyse the ways in which phonologically, lexically, semantically, and pragmatically English has been adapted to Local African contexts in Nigeria, Cameroon, Ghana, Swaziland, South Africa, Zimbabwe, Botswana and more recently the Sudan. NE research has thus served as a counter to 'centrist' arguments about English. However, the main focus of our analysis is different. We explore the ideological implications of using NE within African contexts from the perspective of a majority of Africans with restricted, if any proficiency in English as a way of shedding light onto the status of English in Africa. A comparable ideological analysis of NE within non-western contexts has been carried out in Asia (Canagarajah 1999; Dasgupta 1993; Krishnasway and Burde 1998; Kandiah 1998). In New Englishes the sociolinguistics of landscape of Africa seems to be viewed through the prism of a national identity, and a national culture ('Leitkultur' (Nigerian English, South African English, Zambian English etc). Because the main prism is that of a nation state, the research overlooks the inescapable historical, economic and cultural inter-dependencies of contemporary Africa and the modern world. Such interconnections might shape the use of language particularly of English in Africa much more strongly than the nation state. It might therefore be useful for those working in the New Englishes paradigm in Africa to seriously consider developing paradigms where language in use is situated in transitional and transnational social networks. Such models have already begun to be developed in migration research in which the 'state' is conceptualized as an 'imagined community' (Anderson 1983), or through the 'narration of the nation' (Hall 1995). Unless such a conceptual shift is made away from a nation state towards more transitional networks, research in Englishes will find it difficult to account for the effects of Africa's voluntary and involuntary massive migration on language use. Because of the massive migration both within and across borders, speakers of Nigerian, Zambian, South African English rarely live in isolation from other nationalities.

There are three main types of English users in Africa:

i.   monolingual English speakers, a majority of whom are white and 'settled' in South Africa.
ii. English/African language bilinguals with English as a second language (ESL).
iii. Trilingual speakers fluent in English/French or English/Portuguese and an African language. For these trilingual speakers, English is a foreign language. The trilingual speakers are largely but not exclusively in 'Lusophone' and 'Francophone' Africa.

Lanham and Macdonald (1979) distinguishes between three types of varieties of White South African English, also called General South African English: *conservative, respectable*, and *extreme*. Conservative is based on what White South Africans perceive to be Received Pronunciation *respectable* is a locally cultivated South African variety, associated with middle class South Africans. *Extreme* SAE is associated with lowly educated and low social class White South Africans (Gough 1996xii).

If the other types of English users in Africa, apart from the White South Africans are framed in terms of Kachru's (1986) and Graddol's (1996) concentric circles model of *inner,* and *outer* then the bilingual ESL group can be categorized as belonging to the *outer circle*. Such outer circle speakers are said to be *norm-dependent*. Trilingual speakers can be situated within the *expanding circle* (Kachru 1992:2).

But how applicable is this model to Africa? If most speakers do not have access to native speakers of English in everyday encounters is it really feasible to claim that they are *norm-dependent*. Instead of using the construct of *norm-dependence* it may be more appropriate to refer to the use of English in such contexts as examples of what Pennycook describes as 'crucial acts of semiotic reconstruction' (Pennycook 2003). *Norm-dependency* also undermines what NE framework seeks to celebrate, namely the creativity of non-native speakers of English.

The NE framework purports to move 'from linguistic authoritarianism of the native speaker variety to a speech fellowship-specific realism' (Kachru 1995:25), and thus ostensibly displaces the construct of the native speaker as central organizing principle. Yet norm-dependency reintroduces it by the backdoor. The Kachru framework in such a context appears to apply double standards. This ambivalence towards the epistemological role of English arises because English is defined through 'cross-referential or anaphoric meaning, which depends on the meaning of English in its native habitat'. (Dasgupta 1993:48), rather than being seen potentially independent, locally and contextually determined reference system 'the dictionary draws the reader's attention to semantic links between

South African English with those found, for example, in the English of Britain, the United States, Jamaica, or Nigeria' (Silva: 1998:xv). There are also further problems with the applicability of the NE in Africa. There are no principled reasons why some linguistic forms are selected as typical of NE and other hybrid forms excluded. For example, it is not clear why Owusu-Ansah identifies some features as typical of Ghanaian English and excludes others. Similarly, there are no principled reasons why Gough (1996) selects the following features as typical instantiations of General South African English, African English, Colored English, South African Indian English:

> **General South African English**
> a. 'Busy' as a marker of the progressive: I'm busy cooking'
> b. Reduplication of adverb 'now' as 'now-now', which denotes either 'immediately' or 'soon'.
>
> **African English**
> a. Use of indefinite article before certain 'non-count' nouns: 'He was carrying a luggage'.
> b. Use of 'do' or 'did' in unemphasized statements and questions: 'I did tell him to come': Who did throw that? (Mesthrie 1993:31)
>
> **'Coloured' English**
> a. Use of the dative of advantage": I'm gonna buy me a new car'
> b. Retention of ordinary question order in indirect questions with the verb 'be': I don't know what's that' (Mesthrie 1989:6).

Each of the above varieties is best construed as part of a continuum.

It is indeed possible that the above features represent the English used by different ethnic and racial groups in South Africa. It is, however, not clear what criteria were used to determine which linguistic features fall under each ethnic/racial category. Consequently, methodologically, NE reads like an elitist standardization of periphery Englishes relying on the 'prescriptive and elitist tendencies of center linguistics' which the framework wants to distance itself from (Canagarajah 1999:180) another telling example of intellectual double standards! If the descriptions of the ethnic/racial Englishes cited above are largely linguistic, an alternative approach which is largely political emerged in what was referred to as 'People's English'. This perspective emphasizes the role which English played in shaping the identities of African users of English in South Africa during the apartheid 'People's English' is political because it represents a challenge to the current status of English in South Africa in which control of the language, access to the language, and the teaching of the language are entrenched within apartheid structures' (Norton Peirce1995:108; see also Norton Peirce 1989). The objective of 'People's English was to wrestle the control of English from white South African native speakers. With the strategic advantage of hindsight a decade after the end of apartheid we can safely say 'People's English' failed to meet its political objectives, because English in South Africa is now firmly within the hands of white South African native speakers perhaps even more so than it was during the apartheid era.

Since the NE are describing the English used by formally educated Africans, some insights into African responses to notions about NE would be revealing. Educated African users of English find the categories' Nigerian' or 'Ghanaian English' sociolinguistically offensive as Kofi Sey, the founding father of Ghanain English Linguistics wrote, thus anticipating the discussion of NE in Africa:

> … Nothing disgusts an educated Ghanaian more than being told that the English he uses is anything but standard. The linguist may be able to isolate features of Ghanaian English and describe them. But once these are made known to him, the educated Ghanaian would strive to avoid them altogether. The surest way to kill Ghanaian English, if it really exists, is to discover it and make it known to him. (Sey 1973:10)

One of the most powerful arguments advanced in support of the NE framework is its supposed inclusivity, underwritten by a heterogeneous philosophy and not the homogeneity typical of discourses of monolithic English emerging from Anglo-American centers. But from whose perspective is English heterogeneous or inclusive?

In comparison with or as a challenge to the monolithic and 'centrist' views of English in Anglo-American centers, the NE framework is clearly inclusive. But in the context of the language spoken and understood by the majority of Africans, it is clearly not inclusive at all. Even when the localized varieties of English are taken into account they clearly exclude a large majority of Africans who use pidgins and creoles (Mufwene 1998). Speakers who do not use English, that is the majority of Africans do not perceive any linguistic distinctions between British Standard English and Africanized adaptations of English. It is not possible to distinguish between types of what you do not know. In other words, for non-English users distinctions between British English and Africanized Englishes are rightly construed as part of the language games of professional elites.

English whether adapted or not remains an elitist code. Therefore, from the perspective of non-English speakers the homogeneity/heterogeneity distinction is not relevant. That NE, in contrast to popular French-should be so class marked is highly significant, and part of an important sociolinguistic process-particularly in South Africa as a caste-like social stratification is gradually replaced by social class. Paulston (personal communication 2004) points to a 'growing middle class of people of color and concurrently the growing number of private schools' where English is one of the, if not the primary, means of instruction. Belief in the neutrality of English will foreclose discussion in an important area of research at exactly the time when we need to focus on the complex interaction between social class and language. Pennycook (2003) takes this further in forging a connection between the apparent tolerance of different variations of NE with an already achieved world-wide dominance.

Applied linguistic concerns: The role of the non-native teacher

Given the amount of research which has been carried out on NE, and the contributions of non-native English teachers in Africa, it is odd that there is very limited research which has focused on the role of the non-native teacher of English in the teaching and learning of English in Africa; yet the non-native teacher is increasingly becoming a focus of educational research in North American and European research (Kramsch 1993, 2002, 2004). Research into English in Africa also needs to examine much more systematically the nature of the relationship between the teaching of English and the use of English particularly in the workplace. Insights from such research will not only be useful linguistically, but might have an impact in terms of African governance as well. Some scholars (King 1986) attribute the slow functioning of African bureaucracy to the hesitation to commit ideas to paper in English!

Constructing indigeneity

Language planning in Africa is a rapidly expanding and contentious area. (Ridge 2001; Roy-Campbell 2003, 2002; Kamwangamalu 1998; Moyo 2003; Omoniyi 2003). One of the central concepts underlying language planning is the notion of 'indigenous languages'. The objective of this section is to examine how indigeneity is constructed. Our goal is not to provide an overview of language planning in Africa, especially since a number of excellent overviews already exists (cf. Fafunwa et al.1989; Bambgose 1976, 1991; Mazrui 2000). These texts should be read in conjunction with Robert Kaplan and Richard Baldauf's edited monographs on *Current Issues in language planning* which focus on individual African countries. To date monographs have been written on Botswana, South Africa (Nkonko Kamwangamalu), Tunisia, Ivory Coast (Paulin Djite), Malawi (Edrinnie Kayambazinthu), Nigeria. Monographs on other African countries are also being prepared.

The construct of *indigenous languages* is significant for two reasons. At a very general level, it involves 'local knowledge' (Geertz 1983), a vital ingredient in the growth of applied linguistics in Africa. At a more specific level, since one of the purported objectives of language planning is to ensure the survival of indigenous languages against the encroachment of dominant languages, the discussion is relevant to language planning. Our main objectives here are neither to suggest that applied linguistics in Africa should dispense with 'western' modern sciences, nor simply oppose local knowledge with western knowledge, but to initiate a discussion which would lead towards a construction of a more legitimate framework for understanding site specific applied linguistics and western applied linguistics. Seen from a different perspective, Western applied linguistics is in itself local from a different perspective.

The concept of indigenous languages been used extensively in academic discussions of language planning in Africa, usually with a focus on the technical, pedagogic, and economic contexts rather than on the conceptualization of the construct of indigenous languages itself (cf. Stroud 2002).

Although, the concept of indigenous has not been analyzed critically, it has even acquired a quasi-legal status in the Organization of African Unity (Organisation De l'Unité Africaine) Language Plan of Action and the 1996 Constitution of the Republic of South Africa.

In the Founding Provisions of the 1996 South African Constitution all the indigenous languages are official languages, but not all official languages are necessarily indigenous languages.

In spite of quasi-legal status of indigenous languages in these significant documents there are four questions which we seek to raise:

1. How valid is the binary distinction between *indigenous languages* and ex-*colonial languages*?
2. To what extent is the notion of the indigenous a postcolonial reaction to the legacy of colonialism, rather than a description of a pre-colonial state of affairs?
3. In what ways is the construct of the indigenous itself part of western nomenclature?
4. If you racialise and ethnicise epistemology through the use of constructs such as the indigenous are we not reinforcing colonial thinking?

The term *indigenous languages* is used uncritically in applied linguistics, even though the term *indigenous* is regarded as problematic in anthropology and political science. The term was used interchangeably with the so-called 'customary law', and 'traditional medicine'. The term gained wide currency after it was used extensively by Warren et al. in 'developmentalist' discourses. Mamdani demonstrates the problematic nature of the construct, when he writes:

> ... The anthropologist considered the illiterate native a more reliable authority on customary law than the literate native, the authority was construed in terms of a primary source, to be sifted through, analyzed, its central contradictions smoothed over, its gaps and lapses filled in, all to arrive at a coherent, consistent, and comprehensive secondary formulation. (Mamdani 1996: 113)

Mamdani's analysis shows that indigenous knowledge systems (IKS) were seen by the colonialists not as true representatives of a pre-colonial past, but as products of their intervention. Hence, those accounts, whereby indigenous systems-including languages-become representative of a pre-colonial era, reflect a postcolonial orientation to colonialism rather than an accurate analysis of a pre-colonial social and historical state. Indigenous languages were created through a process of mediation which is irreversible. Breckenbridge and van de Veer's account of India resonates here very well with the African experience.

> The very languages that are called 'native' are products of an intricate dialectic between colonial projects of knowledge and the formation of group identities' (Breckenbridge and van de Veer 1993). Notions about customary law, traditional medicine, ethnocosmology undermine the holism of indigenous knowledge. (Semali and Kinchele 1999: 21)

Fortune who played a key role in descriptions of Bantu languages takes the argument further still when he observes that the separation of language from cultural practices as implied in structuralist descriptions of African languages is inconsistent with an African world view (Fortune 1977). Reformulating Fortune's argument we can say that the idea of African grammars having an ontological existence outside discourse and cultural practices is part of a tradition of African linguistic scholarship which in its preoccupation with grammar and linguistic structure 'often metaphorized as bringing grammar and structure to the languages' (Blommaert 1999:178).

The 'complex dialectic' which Breckenbridge and van der Veer has in mind is analogous to Mamdani's 'secondary formulation'. Both 'complex dialectic' and 'secondary formulation' highlight the fact that the institutions may not be as 'natural/indigenous' to Africa as we may be inclined to believe. That the secondary formulation and by implication 'unnaturalness' was not restricted to customary law, and traditional medicine but extended to the so-called 'indigenous' languages as well can be illustrated by analyzing how European oriented meanings emerged in African vernaculars. A close analysis of 'indigenous' language raises issues about what is natural and what is not in 'indigenous languages'. What is 'authentically' African in indigenous languages are the linguistic forms, the meanings of the words arose as a result of active social intervention. On the basis of linguistic evidence drawn from chiShona, a language used in Zimbabwe, and phonetic examples from Luwo, Lugbara and Ateso/Akarimojong spoken largely in Uganda.

In order to demonstrate how some of the European meanings of African words were created, distributed, circulated and legitimated-drawing on some of the work by Jeater & Hove (in press) we focus on an analysis of the *Mashonaland Quarterly* (MQ). The MQ was launched in 1925 at Morgenster Mission. The mission station was run and administered by the Dutch Reformed Church. Geographically Morgenster is situated in south-central parts of Zimbabwe. The MQ is an ideal text to analyze because it was the first publication to be used by Europeans in then Rhodesia (now Zimbabwe) to communicate their world views to an African audience on issues about education, religion and how to carry out small scale farming. Since it was the first such publication, an analysis of the use of some of the lexical items will give us insights into how the meanings of some words were reconfigured rendering them amenable to control.

The term '*vanhu*' in chiShona for example, meant people, a generic word category not marked for race. After European intervention the term 'Vatema' emerged within the MQ and in subsequent publications on chiShona, to refer to 'Black people'. It replaced the generic *vanhu*: a creation of meanings for Europeans. The replacement of '*vanhu*' with '*vatema*' introduced racial distinctions which were absent in *indigenous* thoughts (Jeater and Hove in press). In a different noun class the root '*tema*' is '*nhema*' which means color '*nhema*' (black cow) and '*kutaura nhema*' (lies) creating a collocation linking in the MQ and subsequent standard chiShona publications, which links racial categorization with lies.

Although Africans were racially categorized, the Europeans did not use such categories to refer to themselves in African vernaculars. They simply referred to themselves in terms of their social status as 'bosses' or 'masters' using the word '*murungu*'. The term reflected social status and not racial categorization. Africans referred to Europeans as '*vasinamabvi*' — those without knees — meaning a people who couldn't bend to work on their knees, grinding, and digging, or as *mabvakure*. By sharp contrast to the racial categories about Africans central for the Europeans, there was no racial marking in African descriptions of either Europeans, nor in reference to themselves. (Jeater 2002; Jeater and Hove in press). Furthermore, Europeans frequently described Africans in the possessive: *wanhu wedu watema wari mu Afrika (our people who are in Africa)*(Jeater and Hove in press) Since European world views were embedded in the constructed vernaculars, the development of literacy in indigenous languages involved a shift away from an indigenous world perspective towards a European based one.

The introduction of European perspectives on African linguistic forms was not restricted to the lexicon only, it is also evident phonetically, for example in the superimposition of five vowels on Eastern Nilotic languages, and the absence of a standard orthography for Lwo, Lugbara and Ateso/Akarimojong (Walusimbi 2002:15).

African scholars have argued quite forcefully for the use of '*indigenous*' languages as medium of instruction highlighting the problematic nature of using so-called excolonial languages (Bamgbose

1976; Rubagumya 1998; Fafunwa et al. 1989). What has been absent from the debate is an analysis of the assumptions about language, and education which form the basis of the construct of 'medium' in 'medium of instruction'. The notion of 'medium' seems to be based on a Lockean idea of communication and instruction through language as 'telementation' the transference of messages from one mind to another (Cameron 1990: 55; Makoni and Pennycook in press). This is only possible if one accepts the idea of African languages as fixed codes. The construct of 'medium' of instruction also seems to reinforce the notion of instruction as consisting of a transference of information from the teacher to the student. The idea of medium of instruction thus reinforces a hierarchical relationship between teachers and students, and validates a one way flow of information. That the learning through and the teaching of English creates problems for learning in Africa is a well known fact. A logical but inaccurate inference to draw from such studies is, however, that the use of 'indigenous' languages as 'medium' of instruction of instruction will be a panacea to Africa's educational problems.

The lesson we can draw from the above analysis of *indigenous* languages is that there is a danger of falling prey falling prey to reductionist western binarism between excolonial and indigenous *languages* and thus to overlook the imprint of colonialism/European perspectives on indigenous languages. The use of the term indigenous may be politically correct, but it is a romantic, idealistic and ahistorical notion, subverting the efforts to address contemporary African language problems. Its use also highlights the dangers of an ethnicising and racializing epistemology which reinforces the very categories which the analyst is tying to escape from.

The notion of indigenous languages is founded on a conception of language as made up of discrete units, which Grace (forthcoming) refers to as 'Autonomous Text Languages' (AT), whose primary function is to serve as 'codes for expository prose' for communicating factual information by encoding and decoding propositions (Grace forthcoming). Such a conceptualization is problematic. The idea of indigenous languages as AT languages is a continuation of a long prescriptive tradition in western epistemology and cultural history. In other words, the notion of indigenous languages is an heir to western cultural history. It is a product of anthropological discourse about the 'other', which has analytically tried to supercede the discourses of racial and biological inferiority as a way of framing and conceptualizing differences. Clearly, indigeneity is a much more welcome concept for explaining difference than that of racial and biological inferiority. However, the discourses of indigeneity remain western constructs which do not successfully capture how indigenous people experience themselves. More importantly the discourses of indigeneity emerge from a series of unsuccessful 'development' discourses, and thus offer only an apparent escape from the evolutionary and scientist paradigms of applied linguistics. Epistemologically, Mufwene (2002: 393) reviewing Nettle and Romaine demonstrates that the use of indigenous is exemplified in sentences such as 'the greatest biolinguistic diversity is found in areas inhabited by indigenous peoples' (Nettle and Romaine 2000: ix, see also page, 13, 21, and 22 for what Mufwene calls 'semantic oddities' in the use of indigenous). Although the usage is odd, it is politically revealing because it 'erases' from view indigenous populations in Western Europe, creating the impression that Western Europe is one of those places without indigenous populations! (Mufwene 2002: 393).

From indigenous to endogenous

Although the significations of the concept of endogenisation have been explored (Devisch 1999; Crossman 2002; Crossman and Devisch 2002), the concept itself was coined by French-speaking West African scholars (Ki-Zerbo 1990; Hountodji 1977, 1995; Ela 1994, 1995, 1998) in an effort to avoid some of the historical 'baggage' and misunderstandings that have accrued to the term 'indigenous' and its derivatives in both French and English. In French the term has acquired bad connotations because of the wide spread use of the homonym 'indigent'. With the exception of econometrics, the term endogenous has not been used in the social sciences. It has however been used to good effect in botany revealing the key differences between the two terms i.e. indigenous and endogenous. Here 'indigenous' primarily refers to a species that is native to a particular topography while 'endogenous' denotes a plant's capacity to *develop on the basis of its own resources,* or 'growing or originating from within *Concise Oxford Dictionary 9th Ed.)* The major difference here is that topographical definition tends to portray the subject as static, its only descriptor being a quasi-permanent link to a geographic locality or area, whereas the second allows for a more organic and dynamic understanding in that it evokes autonomously oriented growth' (Crossman 2004: 24).

Reflecting on endogeneity

The construct of endogeneity clearly has the advantage that it enables us to capture, *hybridity, difference and mobility* more effectively than indigeneity. In a sub-discipline of applied linguistics such as language planning in which scholarship and political activism merge it is important to be aware that hybridity, difference and mobility are not necessarily always liberating. For example, for refugees in Africa—(and Africa currently has the largest number of refugees in the world) a 'certain immobility, a fixed place to call home is an urgent need. 'In contexts of state terror and mystification, clinging to the primacy of the concept of truth can be a powerful and necessary form of resistance. The master narratives of the Enlightenment do not seem particularly repressive here, and the concept of truth is not fluid or unstable on the contrary' (Hardt and Negri 2000: 155). Hybridity is another postmodern construct which has come under criticism in applied linguistics for not being grounded in material reality. This is frustrating because at a historical juncture when Third World scholars are celebrating their identities they quickly realize that Postmodern discourses deny them of their particularity (Canagarajah personal communication). It is crucial to extend Canagarajah's argument by stressing that as a notion hybridity is a metaphor originating from 'taxonomic biology'. It is founded on the presupposition that the offspring-the hybrid is a heterogeneous mixture of relevant constituent parts. On the one hand, it is founded on the assumptions of purity/essentialism, on the other, purity itself is an epistemological construction because every pure form is a hybrid by one criteria or other (Bauman and Briggs 2003: 5).

Hybridity is the result of the appropriation which takes place in all contexts of cultural encounters. However, even though hybridity takes place in moments of cultural encounters, its usage is unfortunately restricted to describe the cultural appropriation by colonized subjects leading Lynn Mario de Souza to make the pertinent observation: 'So when a former colonized appropriates he is called a hybrid as if the former colonizing cultures and persons are above hybridity (Lynn Mario de Souza personal communication). 'We therefore conclude that hybridity, like indigeniety are two of the terms used in applied linguistics to consolidate the description of the 'Other'.

Educational research into the teaching of 'indigenous' languages either as L1, or L2 is still at an early stage, yet in spite of limited research two trends are emerging in Africa. First, in countries like Zimbabwe language teaching materials and syllabuses are designed for second language speakers to teach L1 speakers. In Nigeria, the opposite is the case, L2 speakers of Hausa, Igbo, and Yoruba typically use materials designed for L1 users. Perhaps the issue worth addressing here is whether within African contexts L1 and L2 distinctions are applicable or pedagogically of much relevance.

Even if such distinctions were valid, the scarcity of material resources makes the production of materials tergeted specifically at either L1 or L2 users of African languages unlikely. In such situations what is important is the training of teachers in methods of adapting their materials and 'methodologies' to suit the appropriate sociolinguistic situation.

African applied linguists are in an enviable position which enable them to create opportunities to formulate alternative ways of thinking, if they seriously take issues about African languages. Most applied linguists working in Africa have a real footing in at least two or more cultures. It is reasonable to expect from them an interest in examing the different ways in which knowledge about language is constructed in the communities they are affiliated to. It has been suggested that a large percentage of English metalanguage is constructed around the 'conduit' metaphor. If English is organized around a 'conduit' metaphor African languages are not necessarily organized around a similar metaphor. For example, most of the Hausa (spoken in west Africa) is constructed around ontological metaphors which provide ways of viewing it as events, emotions, ideas, touch, and smell.

Reflecting on research on African multlingualism at the level of the individual African sociolinguistics seems to find itself in an anomalous situation. On the one hand, it has argued quite vociferously against the continued use of so-called ex-colonial languages in education particularly English and French, because such policies marginalize African 'indigenous' languages. On the other hand, African sociolinguistic research into individual African multilingualism seems to be organized around the very same languages which are an object of sustained African critique. Although a majority of African individual multilingualism includes languages other than English and French, most of the studies nevertheless comprise either English or French and an African language. Wolff (2000) cites a sample of 20 studies which all follow this pattern. In other words, there was no study in which bilingualism consisted only of a combination of exclusively African languages, or of a bilingualism in which Africans spoke either a pidgin or a Creole and an 'indigenous' language. Yet arguably even such types of bilingualism are much more widespread than those which include an African language and either French English, or Portuguese (Lucko, Peter and Wolf 2003).

Popular and standard French in Africa

In this section we examine issues relating to French in the so-called Francophone countries. In our discussion we are excluding the literature which is gradually developing which focuses on French in former British colonies (cf. Omoniyi 2003 for his account of French in Nigeria). Following Djite (1998) we maintain a distinction between SF — also called 'French French' in local Ivorian idiom and Popular French (PF). PF is a local simplified non-elite variety of SF. For example, the variety of PF in the Ivory Coast-one of the Francophone countries is referred to as Français de Moussa. It has a simplified verb system, is characterized by a general absence of articles, and has phonetic and prosodic features strongly influenced by African languages (Djite 2000: 35).

Table 3. Some examples of Popular French

Popular French	Standard French	English
C'est verse à Abidjan	C'est chose courante à Abidjan	This is a common thing in Abidjan
Il'veunt mouiller mon pain	Il veut me créer des ennuis	He wants to get me into trouble
Tout pres n est pas loin près n'est pas loin	Maintenant	Let's do it here and now

(Djite 2000: 34).

Not only does PF adapt SF to local African contexts. It is also slowly becoming a linguistic pastiche drawing selectively from other languages in the Ivorian landscape such as English, and Dyula (the local lingua Franca) as apparent in expressions such as Boro d' enjaillment. Enjaillment is a PF adaptation of English enjoyment (Djite 2000: 35).

Typically PF is used as the language of non-elites. It is also used extensively in publications with a mass circulation such as popular drama, cartoons, and newspapers targeted at the lowly educated, even in a national daily newspaper such as *Ivoire-Dimanche*.

PF is predominantly a combination of Standard French, and local African languages, and at times it also includes elements from Standard English. PF is thus increasingly becoming a lexical pastiche and going beyond being a simple adaptation of SF only. Sociolinguistically, PF is unlike NE because the latter is an elite code for educated speakers, while PF is a 'code' widely used by lowly educated persons.

Paradoxically, the policy of legislating the use of French only as the medium of instruction from kindergarten to university has resulted in the spread of locally adapted versions of French, PF. By contrast, the British policy of introducing 'indigenous' languages and subsequently shifting to English has limited the spread of English, and restricted the use of NE to the educated class.

Wycliffe international and the summer institute of linguistics international

This section reviews some of the work carried out by the WI formerly Wycliffe Bible Translators (WBT) cum SIL. There are four main reasons for carefully reviewing the work by WI/SILI. First, the WI/SILI is one of the most expansive organizations involved in applied linguistics in Africa. Secondly, it has taken part in applied linguistics for a relatively long period of time, in some cases for over half a century. Thirdly, it has contributed directly towards shaping the nature of applied linguistics in Africa by creating administrative structures within which applied linguistics in Africa is conducted. Fourthly, although the work of the WI/SILI has been carefully reviewed in Latin America and the Pacific Region we are not aware of any such review in Africa. We therefore see this contribution as preliminary review of the work by an important player in applied linguistics in Africa.

The WI/SILI has had a dual identity since the WBT & SIL were institutionalized separately in the US in 1942. This dual identity of the WI/SILI has served the organization well. It enables WI/SILI personnel to 'play missionaries at home and linguists abroad' (Havalkof and Aaby 1981: 10). WBT/SIL was founded by Cameron Townsend. In 1934 he established camp Wycliffe in an abandoned farmhouse near Sulphur Springs Aarkansas in the United States and held the first summer course in linguistics for two students (Havalkof and Aaby 1981: 10). WBT is the domestic arm of the SILI tasked with the responsibility for raising funds within the US, while the SILI does the missionizing and applied linguistics abroad as it brings the 'Word to the Bibleless tribes' and to preserve languages.

Reviewing the impact of 'applied linguistics' of the WI/SILI is necessary because it is one of the biggest organizations working on language in Africa. In some countries it has worked on African languages for over half a century. In Cameroon it has been active since 1969, in Benin since 1981. Its activities in other parts of Africa are much more recent. For example, it initiated its activities in the Chad in 1989.

WI/SILI has worked in language development which they construe as translation, literacy, and the development of orthographies and the recording of local folklores. The range of its work is apparent when one takes a look at the bibliography of the 2002/3 SILI Africa Area report where it catalogues the list of activities which the SILI was engaged in. Below is an extract of the Africa Area Report cited below:

> **'Other literacy activities, events and milestones'**
> A primer workshop was held to train individuals and language teams to design effective basic primers for local languages. Fourteen Central Africans and one Congolese participated alongside several SILI members. Eight languages were represented. Booklets containing 10 lessons each were designed for CAR's Bogoto, Gbanu, Gbeya, Kaba, Manza, and Ngbugu languages (Area Report: 2002/3: 22)

WI/SILI established administrative centers which have played a key role in applied linguistics in Africa. For example, setting up the Ghana Institute of Languages in 1962, and in 1974 a Translation Center in Abidjan (the Ivory Coast). In the Central African Republic it has worked in close cooperation with the *Institut de Linguistique Appliquée* (ILA). In Mali it works closely with the *Institut des Langues Abdoulaye* (ILAB), and in Chad with the Linguistics department at the University of N'Djamena.

A review of the WI/SILI raises important issues which are not unique to Africa but which do seem to acquire special poignancy in Africa. Since a majority of American applied linguists working through the SILI are missionaries. This raises issues about the nature of the relationship between applied linguistics and religion particularly that of Christianity. To what extent do SILI or the local Africans perceive applied linguistics as a secular exercise? (Snow 2001). The relationship between applied linguistics and religion has not been systematically examined in Africa. Smith's writing about Peru in Latin America resonates with our African experiences: 'native peoples under the influence of the WI/SILI, have become fundamentalist Christians as they become literate. They are offered no choice'. Because of the impact of the WI/SILI, literacy and bilingualism have become intertwined with Christianity, difficult to separate from applied linguistics as a secular project. Bilingualism and literacy are therefore seen as ways of projecting Christian ways of thinking.

Another issue tied to the SILI is their impact on 'indigenous' languages particularly their objective to translate the bible into all of the world's languages. There are two key issues which the work of the WI/SILI on indigenous languages raises. Firstly, SILI members are astute and highly motivated at learning African languages. Their learning of the vernaculars has, perhaps rightly, been characterized as motivated by the desire not 'to learn the meaning of things, but to acquire the means of transmitting their own message. The learning of African languages in such contexts results in a sophisticated use of vernaculars to articulate profoundly European modes of thought. The idea of translating the bible into all of African languages however commendable it might be, is based on the assumption that there are a definite number of discrete languages in Africa-an issue which is quite controversial in African linguistics. Philosophically, the orientation towards African languages on which the translation of African languages into all of Africa's languages is based on a descriptive 'tradition which focuses on linguistic structure rather than linguistic praxis' (Blommaert 1999: 178).

Christian English teachers: The need for 'prayerful thoughts'

If the focus of the SILI was on 'indigenous languages' the main focus of the Christian English Teachers (CET) as might be expected is on English. English has been conceptualized in a number of different ways. In this section we focus on a way of conceptualizing English which does not yet have wide currency in applied linguistics, namely English as a missionary language (EML) (cf. Pennycook and Coutard-Marin 2003). It is intriguing that in spite of the magnitude of the EML project it has not been the focus of systematic study in applied linguistics — perhaps because it is a type of English which is more widely spread in non-western contexts than in Anglo-American communities. Non-western perspectives or the perspectives of the 'other' easily reveals the connection between English and religion, particularly Christianity in this case. Christian English Teachers (CETS) explicitly state that English is not only a western language but a Christian language as well.

The framing of English as a Christian language is particularly important because it brings English Language Teaching directly into potential 'conflict' with Islam. Because of the link between Christianity and English the African student who associates English with conversion to Christianity is not completely wrong, because it is indeed the type of connection which CETS and EML would like language learners/converts to make. In other words, the distinction between religious conversion and linguistic categories on which some, if not most, of western applied linguistic research is predicated may be difficult to sustain both theoretically and in practice in non-western contexts.

Concluding remarks

In the concluding section we propose some strategies which may be pursued to consolidate applied linguistics in Africa. Some of the problems confronting this project are typical of the African academy, while others may be peculiar to applied linguistics as a discipline. Hence some of the strategies we are proposing are generally applicable to the African academy, while others may be much more specifically relevant to applied linguistics only.

One of the suggestions we proposed recently to the AILA Executive to enhance the development of applied Linguistics in Africa was to encourage the formation of more national and regional associations in Africa. On the face of it such a recommendation seems reasonable because to date the Southern African Association of Applied Linguistics in Africa (SAALA) is the only AILA affiliated association in the entire African continent. However, efforts to set up 'newer' national or regional applied linguistics associations in the rest of Africa have to date not been successful, and are unfortunately unlikely to succeed in the foreseeable future. Most of African countries with the exception of Nigeria, and South Africa do not have a 'critical mass' of applied linguists to make the formation of national or regional associations of applied linguistics a viable alternative.

The formation of Applied Linguistics Associations are also likely to fail because they will be faced with an acute shortage of financial and material resources necessary for a successful administration of the Associations-a problem which would not be unique to Applied Linguistic Associations, but one which they would share with the African academy generally. For national and regional associations to function successfully they will have to depend to a large degree on the 'generosity' of the African nation/state. Unfortunately, African state authorities have not been forthcoming in their financial support of the academy 'Regarding African scholarship more as a threat than a constructive stake holder. They have thrown African scholarship to the winds. So off we go, riding into the sunset, looking for kinder masters and honorable or dishonorable patrons' (Prah 1998: 28).

A more modest but perhaps more feasible strategy standing a better chance of succeeding is the strengthening of already existing academic networks through the exchange of external examiners and shared doctoral supervision. Facilitating more intellectual exchanges between African applied linguists within Africa would enhance **South to South** cooperation which could be complemented by well structured **North** to **South** cooperation. Unfortunately, the success of North to South 'collaboration' has been varied and has been subjected to severe criticism by some Northern European scholars for enhancing rather than reducing African dependence on the North (Devisch 2004: 15; Gaillard, Krishna and Waast 1997; Yesufu 1973).

African academy generally, and applied linguistics in Africa in particular has not escaped the criticism, — perhaps rightly so-, of being psychologically and academically unduly dependent upon Northern scholarship. Mazrui and others have argued that rather than being a source of development, the African university has played a key role as an agent of neo-dependency by perpetuating academic and cultural dependency upon the North. 'African universities have been the highest transmitters of Western culture in African societies' (Mazrui 1992: 105).

The key strategy which has been proposed to overcome African academic and cultural dependency on the North is what is referred to in African studies as the effort to domesticate the modern project, what has been felicitously described by Chakrabarty an Asian scholar (1992) as 'provincialising' the west. By this we mean efforts to bridge the gap between the contexts in which some of the applied linguistic ideas are generated and the contexts in which they are subsequently applied in Africa. The mediation is a common practice in applied linguistics but it becomes even more so in Africa because the theoretical ideas which underpin our work in Africa are not typically produced with Africa in mind. This is not to say that ideas generated elsewhere are not relevant to applied linguistics in Africa but that their relevance has to be demonstrated rather than assumed. Applied linguistics in Africa has to constantly distinguish between that which is globally current and that which is locally relevant if it is to be a problem-oriented discipline. Unfortunately in some cases that which is locally relevant might be regarded as outdated in other regions in which applied linguistics is practiced. This creates pressures for applied linguists in Africa which scholars in other regions might not necessarily feel: a need to constantly refer to some work which is globally current, even if it is not immediately relevant, so as to protect the 'quality' of their work in the eyes of their 'western' colleagues. Although there is a growing interest in the development of local versions of applied Linguistics in Africa, the 'prestigious' journals in Applied Linguistics and indeed in most disciplines are published in English and 'from western locations' (Cangarajah 2002:254). In such contexts, and irrespective of subject matter and methodology, African scholars are underprivileged in relation to western colleages especially when quality of scholarship is assessed in terms of frequency of publishing in internationally refereed journals (Crossman 2004).

There are more publications in internationally refereed journals by western scholars on Africa than by African scholars themselves! The 'domestication of modernity' does not, however, exclude the use of western sources but proposes that they cannot remain the centre of gravity of knowledge of Africa. They should be complemented by (Prah 1998:27) drawing parallels between African applied linguistics and utilizing other non-western sources from other 'Third World' communities such as India, Latin America and indeed even immigrant communities in North America and Europe (Spivak 1987).

The 'domestication of modernity' also has an important methodological dimension. It requires that African applied linguistics be both 'local' and national before it can become fully international. It cannot proceed in the opposite direction i.e. from being international to the local. This should not be construed to mean that African applied linguistics should not be concerned with international readership. It simply means that applied linguistics in Africa can only arrive at internationalism through the local. If local applied linguistics has sufficient 'cognitives cold' it will soon register internationally (Prah 1998; Ki-Zerbo 1990; Ngugi wa Thiongo 1993).

Failure to achieve this has adverse effects not only on the type of African scholarship but on staff retention because African institutions ions in a single minded pursuit of excellence have trained researchers with little stamina to address issues about development which ostensibly they should be spearheading (Mamdani 1993:15).

'Domestication of modernity' unless handled circumspectly has serious pitfalls. It seems to encourage a proliferation of academic material claiming to be presenting 'African perspectives' or African Voices'. Such approaches although clearly welcome create the impression that academic authority is determined by cultural affiliation. When expertise is determined solely or largely by cultural affiliation we run the danger of losing an invaluable opportunity to develop a reflexive relationship between applied linguistics and African constituencies-something which should be a hallmark of applied linguistics in Africa.

The development of applied linguistics in Africa has also been adversely affected by the scarcity of academic materials with an African focus. Serious efforts to address this lack of resources is gradually being redressed in that there is some progress in the development of academic materials with African perspectives. For example, the following is a list of some of the notable publications seeking explicitly to develop African perspectives:

- Spencer (1971a) *Colonial Language Policies and their legacies*
- Spencer (1971b) *The English Language in West Africa*
- Mazrui (1975) *The Political Sociology of the English language: an African experience*
- Adegbija E (1994) *Language attitudes in Sub-Saharan Africa.*
- Robinson (1986) *Language use in a rural development: an African perspective.*
- Mazrui and Mazrui (1998) *The Power of Babel. Language Governance in the African experience.*
- Webb and Kembo-Sure (1999) *African voices: an introduction to the languages and linguistics of Africa.*

Some of the publications not only focus on Africa but seek to compare African experiences with the experiences of other ethnic minorities particularly in North America. A recent example, of such scholarship is Makoni, et al. (2003) *Black Linguistics, a study of the social, political and linguistic problems of languages in Africa and the Americas.*

Most of these Africa based materials have the explicit objective of developing 'African-oriented training programs' because as Webb and Kembo-Sure aptly observe:

most 'introductory textbooks in linguistics are (understandably, we suppose) shaped by North American or British/European perspectives… while students of linguistics in Africa need, in addition to the knowledge, insights, and skills, relevant to Africa'. (Webb and Kembo-Sure 1999:x)

Initiatives for the development of Africa based materials is progressing not only in Africa but outside Africa as well. For example, Kaplan and Baldauf have initiated a series of monographs as part of the journal of *Current Issues in Language Planning*. Although focusing on language planning these publications provide useful and up to date information on different aspects of the social, political, linguistic and educational aspects of African countries. Monographs on Botswana, South Africa (Kamwangamalu 2000), Malawi (Kayambazinthu 1998; Côte d'Ivoire (Djite, 2000), Tunisia have already been published and a number of monographs on other African countries may be prepared in future. These monographs update and complement earlier publications reporting on research funded by the Ford Foundation on Language in Africa in the 60s and 70s, for example, John Spencer's article 'Colonial language Policies and their legacies' in the edited collection by Thomas Sebeok: *Current Trends Linguistics*. More recently, a special issue focusing on Applied Linguistics in Africa, *AILA Review* (16) was published (Makoni and Meinhof 2003).

The production of academic materials and syllabi on African applied linguistics should be construed as part of a broader strategy of Africanization or contextualization. In this article we construe Africanization as a strategy to 'domesticate modernity'. Because Africa is socially, and politically and geographically diverse we do not anticipate Africanization to take the 'same form and expression' across Africa (Crossman 2003:23). This means that a version of applied linguistics might emerge in North Africa which would be different from that in southern Africa.

It is important to reflect on whether it is always and necessarily desirable or indeed feasible to develop African perspectives in applied linguistics and what epistemological objectives which we are seeking to achieve in doing so. Because so much of applied linguistics is based on English scholarship the relevance of assumptions about what constitutes 'language', being 'human' learning cannot be uncritically accepted. The following are some examples of English linguistic scholarship which have to be carefully scrutinized in applied linguistics in Africa:

1. the belief in distinct word classes
2. the belief in the possibility of using the same descriptive labels for all languages
3. the belief in the separability of language from so-called non-linguistic phenomena
4. the belief in the existence of separate languages.
    (Mühlhausler 1996:328)

The development of applied linguistics in Africa demands not only a critical evaluation of western versions of applied linguistics, but more importantly a careful and systematic reflexivity clearly articulated by Sole (1997:215) when he writes:

> In my opinion black 'post-colonial' intellectuals cannot accept tenure as spokespeople for their community without the constant interrogation of their own positions demanded by their own post-structuralist predilections. What is most striking about the approaches of both white and black critics of this ilk, though, is a tendency to use post-structuralists techniques when scrutinizing the 'oppressor', but to slide back into positivism and liberal humanism when faced with the products of the 'oppressed'.

Expressed differently, the development of African applied linguistics is not likely to succeed as long as 'the historical construction of what constitutes 'language' remains unquestioned' (Heryanto in press). It is also not likely that African applied linguistics will succeed unless it takes full cognizance of the implications arising from the fact that applied linguistics is a western cultural construct, which means that some of the assumptions it makes about language, 'humanity', 'learning' might need to be questioned.

'Domestication of modernity' has stronger chances of succeeding at this historical juncture because parallel reforms are taking place in Europe and America to an extent not possible until postmodernism, and the hiatus between so-called empirical and interpretive traditions in western scholarship (Wallerstein 2001) In spite of these changes, we should not underestimate the material and psychological pressures on scholars on Africa because of the sheer weight of the modernistic western paradigm.

Whatever is the ultimate outcome of efforts to develop African perspectives on applied linguistics, there is no shortage of interest in the discussion both within and outside the academy. A constituency demonstrating (surprisingly) special interest in the Africanization of the academy are radical non-formally educated African feminists. Their interests are different from those of the African intellectual. They are interested not so much in the impact of African scholarship on the west, but the impact of western scholarship on Africans. It is therefore appropriate to bring this article to a close by giving them a final say by quoting from one of their representatives, the poet Okot'pTek, and her *Songs of Lawino*,

'There is no single true son left
The entire village
Has fallen into the hands of war captives and slaves!
Perhaps one of our boys
Escaped with his life!
Perhaps he is hiding in the bush
Waiting for the sun to set
But will he come
Before the next morning?
Will he arrive in time?
Bile burns my inside!
I feel like vomiting
For all our young men
Were finished in the forest,
Their manhood was finished in the class-rooms,
Their testicles
were smashed
With large books!'

References

Adegbija, E. (1994). *Language attitudes in Sub-Saharan Africa*. Clevedon: Multilingual Matters.

Ajayi, J., L. Goma and G. Johnson. (1996). *The African experience with higher education*. London: James Currey.

Anderson, B. (1983). *Imagined Communities: reflections on the origins and spread of nationalism*. London: Verso.

Arua, Arua. (2001). Swazi English. In E. Ridge, S. Makoni and S. G. Ridge (eds), *Freedom and discipline: essays in Applied Linguistics from southern Africa*, pp. 129–138. New Delhi: Bahri.

Bakhtin, M. (1934/1981). *The dialogic imagination*. [edited by Michael Holquist].Austin, TX: University of Texas Press.

Bamgbose, A. (1976). *Mother tongue education: the West African experience*. London: Hodder and Stoughton.

Bamgbose, A. (1991). *Language and the nation: the language question in sub-Saharan Africa*. Edinburgh: University Press.

Bates, R. H., V. Y. Mudimbe and J. F. O'Barr (eds) (1993). *Africa and the Disciplines: the contributions of research on Africa to the social sciences*. Chicago: Chicago University Press.

Bauman, R. and C. Briggs. (2003). *Voices of Modernity: Language ideologies and the politics of Inequality*. Cambridge: Cambridge University Press.

Benson, P. (2001). *Ethnocentrism and the English Dictionary*. London and New York: Routledge.

Bolton, K. (2004). World Englishes. In A. Davies and C. Elder (eds), *The Handbook of Applied Linguistics*, pp 387–396. Malden: Basil Blackwell.

Blommaert, J. (1999). Reconstructing the sociolinguistic image of Africa: Grassroots writing in Shaba Congo. *Text* 19 (2): 175–200.

Branford, W. (1987). *The South African pocket Oxford dictionary.* Cape Town: Oxford University Press.

Breckenbridge, C. and P. van de Veer (eds) (1993). *Orientalism and its postcolonial predicament: perspectives from south Asia.* Philadelphia: University of Pennsylvania Press.

Brenzinger, M. (ed.) (1998). *Endangered languages in Africa.* Cologne: Rudinger Koppe Verlag.

Breton, R. (2003). Sub-Saharan Africa. *Languages in a Globalizing World.* Cambridge: Cambridge University Press.

Cameron, D. (1990). Demythologizing sociolinguistics, why language does not reflect reality. In J. E. Joseph and T. J. Taylor (ed.), *Ideologies of language,* pp. 79–93. London and New York: Routledge.

Canagarajah, A. S. (1999). On EFL teachers, awareness and agency. *ELT journal* 53(3): 207–214.

Canagarajah, A. S. (2002). Celebrating local knowledge on Language and Education. *Journal of Language, Identity, and Education* 1(4): 243–261.

Chakrabaty, D. (1992). Postcoloniality and the artifice of history. *Representations* 37:1–26.

Chimhundu, H. (1992). Early missionaries and the ethno-linguistic factor during the invention of tribalism in Zimbabwe. *Journal of African history* 33: 87–109.

Cohn, B. (1996). *Colonialism and its forms of knowledge: The British in India.* Princeton: Princeton University Press.

Cook, S. E. (2002). Urban language in a rural setting: the case of Phokeng, South Africa. In G. Gmelch and W. P. Zenner (ed.), *Urban life: readings in anthropology of the city* 4th edition, pp. 106–113. Prospect Heights: Waveland Press.

Crossman, P. (1999). *Endogenisation and African universities. Initiatives and issues in the quest for plurality in the human sciences.* Belgian Administration for development Cooperation.

Crossman, P. (2002). *Teaching Endogenous Knowledge: Issues, Approaches. Teaching Aids.* DAE, Sovenga: University of the North. Pretoria: Cindek, University of Pretoria. Leuven: ARC, Kuleuven.

Crossman, P. (2003). Endogenous knowledge: an anthropological perspective. In C. Odora-Hoppers (ed.), *Towards a philosophy of articulation: IKS and the integration of knowledge systems,* pp. 30–45. Cape Town: New Africa Education Publisher.

Crossman, P. (2004). Perceptions of Africanisation or endogenisation at African universities: issues and recommendations. In P. Zeleza and A. Olukoshi (eds), *African Universities in the twentieth-first century: knowledge and society.* Volume 11, pp. 24–42. Dakar: CODESRIA.

Crossman, P. and R. Devisch. (2002). Universiteiten in Zuid-Saharisch Afrika in de 21 seeuw. *Mededelingen der Zittingen van de Koninklije Academie voor Ovrzee Wetenschappen – Bulletin des séances de'l Academie royale des sciences d'Outre-Mer* 45: 443–463.

Dako, K. (2001). Ghanaianisms: towards a semantic and a formal classification. *English World Wide* 22(1): 23–53.

Dasgupta, P. (1993). *The otherness of English: India's Auntie Tongue Syndrome.* New Delhi: Sage Publications.

de Schruyter and D. J. Prinsloo. (2000). The compilation of electronic corpora with special reference to African languages. *Southern African linguistics and applied language Studies* 18(2): 89–100.

deKlerk, V and D. Gough. (2002). Black South African English. In Mesthrie, R. (ed.), *Language in South Africa,* pp. 356–38. Cambridge: Cambridge University Press.

Devisch, R (1995). Frenzy, violence, and ethical renewal in Kinshasa. *Public culture* 7:593–629.

Devisch, R. (1999). Universiteiten in Zuid Saharisch Afrika in de 21 ste eeuw. *Koninklijke Academie voor Overzeese Wetenschappen-Bulletin des séances de l' Académie royale des sciences d'Outre-Mer* 45:443–463.

Devisch, R. (2004) Endogenous Knowledge Practices: Cultures and Sciences: Some Anthropological Perspectives. In F. Nahavandi (ed.) Repenser le development et la cooperation internationale p 109–134. Paris, Karthala.

Devisch, R. (in press). *Endogenous Knowledge Practices, Cultures and Sciences: Some Anthropological Perspectives.*

Djite, P. (1998). Correcting Errors in Language Classification: Monolingual Nuclei and Multilingual Satellites. *Language Problems and Language Planning.* 12(1): 1–14.

Djite, P. (2000). Language Planning in Cote d'Ivoire Non scholea sed vitae discimus. We do not study for academia, but for real life. *Current Issues in Language Planning* 1(1): 13–46.

Ela, J-M. (1994). *Restituer L' histoire aux societes Africaines: prouvoir les sciences socials en Afrique Noire.* Paris: Harmattan.

Ela, J-M. (1995). Afrique L'irruption des pauvres Societe contre Ingerence, Pouvoir et Argent. L, avenir de L' Afrique: enjeux strategiques et politique. *Alternatives Sud* 4:101–112.

Ela, J-M. (1998). *Innovations sociales et renaissance de l' Afrique noire.* Paris: Harmattan.

Fafunwa, B. A., I. Macauley, J. Ii and J. A. Sokoya. (1989). *Education in the mother tongue the primary education research project (1970–1978).* Ibadan: University Press. Ltd.

Ferrant, J. and L. Alfonso. (1997). Strategic planning at African universities: how relevant are Northern models? *Higher Education policy* 10:23–30.

Finlayson, R., K. Calteaux and C. Myers-Scotton (1998). Orderly mixing and accommodation in South African code-switching. *Journal of Sociolinguistics* 2(3):395–420.

Fortune, G. (1977). *Shona grammatical constructions.* Part 11. PhD dissertation, University of Rhodesia.

Gaillard, J., V. Krishna and R. Waast (eds) (1997). *Scientific communities in the developing world.* New Delhi: Sage.

Geertz, C. (1983). *Local Knowledge: further essays in interpretive anthropology.* New York: Basic Books.

Gough, D. (1996). The English of black South Africans. In V. De Klerk (ed.), *English around the world; focus on south Africa,* pp. Amsterdam: John Benjamins.

Goyvaerts, D. L. (1996). Kibalele: form and function of a secret language in Bukavu (Zaire). *Journal of Pragmatics* 25:123–143.

Grace, G. (forthcoming). Collateral damage in Linguistics. In Makoni, S and A. Pennycook (eds), *Disinventing and Reconstituting Language.* Clevedon: Multilingual Matters.

Graddol, D. (1996). And is it English? *English-World Wide* 17:153–74.

Hall, S. and Gay, P. (1995). *Questions of Cultural Identity.* Thousand Oaks: Sage Publications.

Hardt, M. and A. Negri. (2000). *Empire.* Cambridge/Massachusetts: Harvard University Press.

Havalkof, S. and P. Aaby (eds) (1981). Is God an American? *An anthropological perspective on the missionary work of the Summer Institute of Linguistics.* London: Survival International.

Heryanto, A. (in press). Then there were languages: Bahasa Indonesia was one among many. In Makoni, S and A. Pennycook (eds), *Disinventing and Reconstituting languages.* Clevedon: Multilingual Matters.

Hill, J. (2002). "Expert Rhetorics" in advocacy for endangered languages: who Is listening, and what do they hear? *Journal of Linguistic Anthropology* 12 (2):120–133.

Hountodji P. (1977). *Sur la 'philosophie africaine': critique de'l ethnophilosphie.* Paris: Maspero.

Hountodji, P. (ed.) (1994). *Les saviors endogens: pistes pour une recherché.* Paris: Karthala.

Hountodji, P. (1995). Producing Knowledge in Africa today. *African Studies Review.* 38(3):1–10.

Hountondji, P. (1977). *Sur la 'philosophie africaine': critique de l'ethnophilosophie.* Paris: Maspero.

Hountondji, P. (1995). Producing knowledge in Africa today. *African Studies Review* 38 (3):1–10.

Irvine, J. (1995). The family Romance of colonial linguistics: gender and family in 19th century representations of African languages. *Pragmatics: Quarterly publication of the International Pragmatics Association* 5:139–153.

Irvine, J. (2001). Genres of Conquest: from literature to Science in Colonial African Linguistics. In K. Knoblauch and H. Kotthoff (eds), *Verbal Art across cultures: the aesthetics and proto-aesthetics of Communication,* pp. 63–89. Tübingen: Gunter Narr Verlag.

Jeater, D. (2002) Speaking like a native. *Journal of African History* 43: 449–468.

Jeater, D. and C. Hove (in press). And the God was made word: exploring the limitations of translation and power in the 1920's. *Southern Rhodesia Quarterly.*

Joseph, J. (2004). 'Language and Politics'. In A. Davies and C. Elder (eds), *The Handbook of Applied Linguistics,* pp. 347–367. Malden: Blackwell.

Kachru, B. B. (1986). *The alchemy of English: The spread, functions and models of non-native Englishes.* Oxford: Pergamon.

Kachru, B. B. (1992). Teaching world Englishes. In Kachru, B. B. (ed.), *The other tongue: English across cultures,* pp. 353–366. Urbana: University of Illinois Press (2nd edition).

Kachrus, B. B. (1995). English as an Asian Language. In M. L. S. Bautista (ed.), English is an Asian Language: the Philippine context., pp. 1–25. Manila: The Macquarie Library.

Kamwangamalu, N. (1998). Identities of English and codeswitching in post-apartheid South Africa. *Multilingua* 17(2/3): 277–296.

Kamwangamalu, N. (2000). The Language Planning Situation in South Africa. *Current Issues in Language Planning* 2(4): 361–445.

Kamwangamalu, N. and T. Chisanga. (1997). Owning the Other Tongue: the English language in Southern Africa. *Journal of Multilingual and Multicultural development* 18 (2): 89–99.

Kandiah, T. (1998). Epiphanies of the deathless native users' manifold avatars: A postcolonial perspective on the native-speaker. In Singh, R. (ed.), *The native speaker: Multilingual perspectives,* pp. 79–110. New Delhi: Sage Publications.

Kaplan, R. (1980). On the scope of linguistics, applied and non. In R. B. Kaplan (ed.), *On the scope of applied linguistics,* pp 76–86. Rowley, MA: Newbury House.

Kashoki, M. E. and M. Mann. (1978). A general sketch of the Bantu languages of Zambia. In S. Ohannessain and M. E. Kashoki (eds), *Languages in Zambia,* pp. 9–46. London: International Africa Institute.

Kayambazinthu, E. (1998). The language Planning Situation in Malawi. *Journal of Multilingual and Multicultural Development* 19 (5&6):369–400.

King, K. (1986). Concluding comments. In A. Davies (ed.), *Language in Education in Africa.* Centre for African Studies, University of Edinburgh.

Ki-Zerbo, J. (ed.) (1990). *Educate or perish: Africa's impasse and prospects.* Dakar: Unesco-Unicef.

Kramsch, C. (1993). *Context and culture in language teaching.* Oxford: Oxford University Press.

Kramsch, C. (ed.) (2002). *Language acquisition and language socialization: ecological perspectives.* London: Continuum.

Kramsch, C. (2004). Language, thought and culture. In Davies, A. and C. Elder (eds), *The Handbook of Applied Linguistics,* pp. 235–262. Malden: Basil Blackwell.

Krishnaswamy, N. and A. Burde. (1998). *The politics of Indians' English: Linguistic colonialism and the expanding English empire.* Delhi: Oxford University Press.

Laitin, D. (1992). *Language repertoires and state construction in Africa.* Cambridge: Cambridge University Press.

Lanham, L. W. and C. A. Macdonald. (1979). *The standard in South African English and its social history.* Heildelberg: Julius Groos.

Lanham, L. W. (1985). The perception and evaluation of varieties of South Africa English in South Africa society. In S. Greenbaum (ed.), *The English language today.* Oxford: Oxford University Press.

Letsholo, R. (2000). English in Botswana: a sociolinguistic description. In. S. Makoni and N. Kamwangamalu (eds), *Language and Institutions in Africa,* pp. 161–179. Cape Town: Centre for the Advanced Studies of African Societies.

Lucko, P., L. Peter and H-G. Wolf (eds) (2003). *Studies in African Varieties of English.* Frankfurt: Peter Lang.

Makoni, S. and U. Meinhof. (2003). Africa and Applied Linguistics. *AILA Review 16,* pp. 1–11. Amsterdam: John Benjamins.

Makoni, S. and Pennycok (eds) (in press). *Disinventing Language.* Clevedon: Multilingual Matters.

Makoni, S., G. Smitherman, A. Spears, and A. Ball (eds) (2003). *Black Linguistics: the social, linguistic and political problems of languages in Africa and the Americas.* London: Routledge.

Mamdani, M. (1993). University crisis and reform: a reflection on the African experience. *Review of the African Political Economy.* 5(8):7–19.

Mamdani, M. (1996). *Citizen and Subject: contemporary Africa and the legacy of late Colonialism.* Princeton: Princeton University Press.

Masolo, D. (1994). *African philosophy in search of identity.* Bloomington: Indiana University.

Mazrui, A (1975). *The political sociology of the English language: an African perspective.* The Hague: Mouton.

Mazrui, A. (2000). The mirror of Africanity: reflections on scholarship and identity. In T. Falola (ed.), *Tradition and change in Africa, essays of J. F. Ade Ajayi.* Trenton, NJ: African World Press.

Mazrui, A. and A. Mazrui. (1998). *The Power of Babel: Language and Governance in the African Experience.* Chicago: University of Chicago Press.

McCormick, K. (1995). Code-switching, code-mixing and convergence in Cape Town. In R. Mesthrie (ed.), *Language and Social History,* pp. 193–208. Cape Town: David Phillips.

Mesthrie, R. (1989). The origins of Fanagalo. *Journal of Pidgin and Creole Languages* 4(2):211–40.

Mesthrie, R. (1993). *Language and social history.* Cape Town: David Phillips.

Moyo, T. and N. Kamwangamalu. (in press). Some characteristic features of Englishes in Lesotho, Malawi and Swaziland, *Per Linguam.*

Moyo, T. (2003). The democratization of indigenous languages: the case of Malawi. *AILA Review* 16: 26–38.

Mudimbe, V. (1988). *The invention of Africa: gnosis, philosophy, and the order of knowledge*. Bloomington: Indiana University Press.

Mufwene, S. (1998). Jargons, pidgins, creoles and koines. What are they? In Spears and D. Winford (eds), *The structure and status of pidgins and creoles, pp.* 35–70. Amsterdam: John Benjamins.

Mufwene, S. (2001). *The ecology of language evolution*. Cambridge: Cambridge University Press.

Mufwene, S. (2002). Colonisation, Globalisation, and the Future of Languages in the Twenty-first Century. *MOST Journal of Multicultural Societies* 4(2): 165–197.

Mufwene, S. (2004). Multilingualism in linguistic History. Creolization and indigenization. In T. Bhatia and W. Ritchie (eds), *The Handbook of bilingualism* Malden: Blackwell.

Mühlhausler, P. (1996). *Linguistic Ecology: language change and linguistic Imperialism. In the Pacific region*. London: Routledge.

Mukama, R. (2002). The use of Swahili as a (male) code in the security sector. In K. Glanz and O. Benge (eds), *Exploring Multilingual Community Literacies: Workshop at the Ugandan German Cultural Society* Sonderforschungsbereich 538 Mehrsprachigkeit, *pp.* 65–72.

Myers-Scotton, C. (1993). *Social Motivations for code-switching*. Oxford: Oxford University Press.

Nettle, D and S. Romaine. (2000). *Vanishing Voices: the extinction of the world's languages*. Oxford: Oxford University Press.

Norton Peirce, B. (1989). Toward a pedagogy of possibility in the teaching of English internationally: People's English in South Africa. *TESOL Quarterly* 23:401–420.

Norton Peirce, B. (1995). Social Identity, investment, and language learning. *TESOL Quarterly* 23: 410–420.

Ngugi wa Thiong, O. (1993). *Moving the Centre: the struggle for cultural Freedom*. London: James Currey.

Nyombe, B. G. V. (1977). Survival or Extinction: the fate of the Indigenous languages of Southern Sudan. In M. H. Abdulaziz (ed.), *International Journal of the Sociology of language* 125. Berlin: Mouton de Gruyter.

Omoniyi, T. (2003). Language ideology and politics: A critical appraisal of French as second official language in Nigeria. *AILA Review 16, pp.* 13–26. Amsterdam: Benjamins.

Owusu-Ansah, L. (1991). Is it or is it not an interlanguage? A head on confrontation with non-native English. *Edinburgh Working Papers in Applied Linguistics* 2:119–116.

Penn, C. and T. Reagan. (1995). On the other hand, implications of the study of South African sign language of the deaf in South Africa. *South African Journal of Education* 15:92–96.

Penn, C. and T. Reagan. (1991). Toward a National Policy for deaf education in South Africa. *South African Journal of Communication Disorders* 38:19–24.

Penn, C. and T. Reagan. (2001). Linguistic social and cultural perspectives on Sign Language in South Africa. In E. Ridge, S. Makoni, and S. G. Ridge (eds), *Freedom and Discipline: Essays in applied linguistics from southern Africa, pp.* 49–65. New Delhi: Bahri.

Pennycook, A. (2003). Turning English inside out. *Indian Journal of Applied Linguistics* 28(2): 25–35.

Pennycook, A. and S. Coutand-Marin. (2003). Teaching English as a missionary Language. *Discourse Studies in the Cultural Politics of Education* 17(3) 337–353.

Pettman, R. C. (1913). *Africanerisms. A glossary of South African words and phrases and their names*. Green and Company. London: Longmans.

Phillipson, R. (1992). *Linguistic Imperialism*. Oxford: Oxford University Press.

Prah, K. (1994). *Beyond the color line: Pan-Africanist Disputations*. Academic Literature, Africa World Press.

Prah, K. (1998). African scholars and Africanist scholarship. *CODESRIA*. 3:425–431.

Prinsloo D. and G-M. de Schryver. (2001). Taking Dictionaries for Bantu languages in the New Millenium-with special reference to Kiswahili, Sepedfi and isi Zulu. In J. S. Mdee and H. J. M. Mwansoko (eds), Makala ya *Kongamano la kimataifa, pp.* 188–215. Dar es Salaam: TUKI Chuo Kikuru cha.

Prinsloo, D. and G-M. de Schryver. (2002). Designing a Measurement Instrument for the Relative Length of Alphabetical Stretches in Dictionaires, with Special reference to Afrikaans and English. In A. Braasch and C. Povlsen (eds), *Proceedings of the Tenth EURALEX International Congress. EURALEX 2002, Copenhagen, Denmark, August 13–17*, 4:583–494.

Reagan, T. (1995). Neither easy to understand nor pleasing to see: the development of manual sign codes as language activity. *Language problems and language planning* 19:133–150.

Reagan, T. (1996). Bilingualism and the culture of the deaf. South African medical journal. *Suid-Afrikaaanse mediese tydskrif* 86: 797–799.

Reagan, T. (2001). The promotion of linguistic diversity in multilingual settings: Policy and reality in post-apartheid South Africa. *Language Problems and language Planning* 25:51–71.

Ridge, S. (2001). Discourse constraints on language policy in South Africa. In E. Ridge, S. Makoni and S.G. Ridge (eds), *Freedom and Discipline: Essays in Applied Linguistics from Southern Africa*, pp. 15–30. New Delhi: Bahri.

Robinson, C. (1996). *Language use in rural development: an African perspective*. Berlin: Mouton de Gruyter.

Roy-Campbell, Z.M. (2003). Promoting African languages as conveyors of knowledge in educational institutions. In S. Makoni, G. Smitherman, A. Spears and A. Ball (eds), *Black Linguistics: language, Society, and Politics in Africa and the Americas*, pp. 83–103. London/New York: Routledge.

Roy-Campbell, Z.M. (2001). *Empowerment through language: the African experience, Tanzania and Beyond*. Trenton, NJ: Africa World Press.

Rubagumya, C. (eds) (1998). *Teaching and researching language in African classrooms*. Clevedon: Multilingual Matters.

Said, E. (1978). *Orientalism*. New York: Pantheon books.

Sardar Z. (1999). Development and the locations of Eurocentrcism. In R. Munck and D.O. Hearn (eds), *Critical development theory*, pp. 44–62. London. Zed.

Sardar Z. (1977). *Science, technology and development in the Muslim world*. London: Croom Helm.

Seidlhofer, B. (2003). *Controversies in Applied Linguistics*. Oxford: Oxford University Press.

Semali L. and J. Kincheloe (eds) (1999). *What is Indigenous Knowledge: Voices from the academy?* New York: Garland Press.

Sebeok, T. (1971). *Current Trends in Linguistics*. The Hague: Mouton.

Sey, K. (1973). *Ghanaian English: an exploratory survey*. London: Macmillan.

Silva, P. (1998). *A dictionary of South African English on historical principles*. Oxford: Oxford University Press.

Slabbert, S. and R. Finlayson. (2002). Code-switching in South African townships. In R. Mesthrie (ed.), *Language in South Africa*, pp. 216–235. Cambridge: Cambridge University Press.

Snow, D. (2001). *English Teaching as Christian Mission*. Scottdale, Penn: Herald Press.

Sole, K. (1997). South Africa Passes the Posts. *Alternation* 4:116–151.

Spencer, J., (1971a). Colonial language policies and their legacies. In Sebeok, T.A. (ed.), *Linguistics in Sub-Saharan Africa (Current Trends in Linguistics, 7)*, pp. 537–547. Paris-La Haye, Mouton.

Spencer, J. (1971b). *The English language in West Africa*. London: Longman.

Spivak, G. (1987). *In Other Worlds: Essays in Cultural Politics*. London: Routledge.

Stroud, C. (2002). Framing Bourdieu socioculturally: alternative forms of legitimacy in postcolonial Mozambique. *Multilingua* 21:247–273.

Summer Institute of Linguistics International Annual Reports 99–02. Dallas, TX: SIL International. Available on the WWW: ⟨www.sil.org⟩, accessed July 2004.

Towa, M. (1979). *L'idée d'une Philosophie Africaine*.Yaonde, Cle.

Wallerstein, I. (2001). *Unthinking social science: the limits of 19th century paradigms*. Philadelphia: Temple University Press.

Walusimbi, L. (2002). Multilingual Literacy in Uganda. In Glanz and Okot.P. Benge (eds), *Exploring Multilingual Community literacies*. Sonderforschungsbereich 538. Mehrsprachigkeit 8–12.

Webb, V. and Kembo-Sure (eds) (1999). *African Voices: an introduction to the languages and linguistics of Africa*. Cape Town: Oxford University Press.

Wolff, H.E. (2000). Pre-school Child Multilingualism and its educational implications in the African context. *PRAESA Occasional Papers* 4.

Wolf, H-G. (2003). The contextualization of common core terms in West Africa: evidence from computer corpora. In P. Lucko, L. Peter, and H-G. Wolf (eds), *Studies in African varieties of English*, pp 3–21. Frankfurt: Peter Lang.

Wolf, H-G. and H. Igboannusi. (2003). Semantic Dislocation in Nigerian English. In P. Lucko, L. Peter and H-G. Wolf (eds), *Studies in African varieties of English.*, pp. 69–83. Europaischer Verlag der Wissenschaften: Peter Lang.

Yanga, T. (1980). *A sociolinguistic Identification of lingala*. Ph.D.thesis, University of Texas, Austin.

Yanga, T. (1998). Harmonisation, standardization and the emergence of state Languages: a case from Zaire. In K. Prah (ed.), *Between Distinction and Extinction: the Harmonization and standardization of African languages*, pp. 173–187. Johannesburgh, South Africa: Witwatersrand University Press.

Yesufu, T. (ed.) (1973). *Creating the African University: Emerging Issues in the 1970's*. Ibadan: Oxford University Press.

Young, D. (2001). Why Applied language studies and not Applied Linguistics aspects of the evolution of Applied language studies in South Africa since the 1960's into the new millennium-a personal view? In E. Ridge, S. Makoni and S. G. Ridge (eds), *Freedom and Discipline Essays in Applied Linguistics from Southern Africa*, pp. 149–170. New Delhi: Bahri.

Résumé

Le but de cet article est d'analyser la nature des contextes sociaux historiques et contemporains dans lesquels la linguistique appliquée en Afrique est apparue, et est actuellement pratiquée. Cet article examine les défis auxquels la linguistique appliquée locale est confrontée lorsqu'elle essaie de développer des programmes de linguistique appliquée venant de l'Europe et de l'Amérique du Nord. Cet article indique que des projets apparemment progressifs de linguistique appliquée sont étroitement liés les uns aux autres en ce sens qu'ils consolident une vue occidentale de l'Afrique dans l'Afrique post-coloniale. Cet article montre que ces projets, apparemment progressifs, finissent par consolider les perspectives occidentales sur l'Afrique et créent un dilemme pour la Linguistique Appliquée en Afrique car une critique de la linguistique appliquée occidentale finit pas être le miroir des théories mêmes qu'elles cherchent à rejeter.

Perspectives in applied linguistics

A North American view[*]

William Grabe
Northern Arizona University

This overview focuses on the work of Applied Linguistics in North America with an emphasis on publications in the past 6 years. Follow a brief interpretive section on the nature and status of Applied Linguistics, the article reviews a number of major areas of research in Applied Linguistics. These areas include second language acquisition (and its various sub-domains), L2 reading and writing research, language learning and teaching, language and culture, corpus linguistics, critical perspectives, language assessment, language policy and planning, language uses in professional contexts, and technology in Applied Linguistics. The overview closes with comments on seven possible areas for growth in Applied Linguistics in addition to the mainstream fields noted above.

Keywords: Applied Linguistics, North America

Introduction

The field of Applied Linguistics has evolved over the past 10 years in ways that indicate a growing maturity. It has maintained its core purposes of resolving serious language-based problems in society, enhancing language use and language learning outcomes, and building interdisciplinary networks to support its work. At the same time, Applied Linguistics has drawn on information from related disciplines in ways that recognize the diverse needs of its own discipline. For example, many, if not most, applied linguists look at linguistic theories as a resource for their own needs and their own work, not as dominating theories that must be learned and used regardless of relevance and applicability. Similarly, language assessment practices are no longer single-minded as to the benefits of reliability above other validity criteria. Rather, reliability is now incorporated into a larger view of validity, a view that gives greater attention to the test taker, to fairness in assessment, and to the consequences of assessment. These and several other changes can be observed in the work of applied linguists across the world, and not just in North America. So what can one say of North American work in Applied Linguistics in particular?

Perhaps the clearest answer that can be given is that applied linguists in North America are active participants in many key areas that signal the evolution of Applied Linguistics. It is these contributions that can be explored in some detail, though not in isolation from work in other parts of the world. In the way that Applied Linguistics itself is interdisciplinary, applied linguists in different parts of the world work collaboratively on language-related issues. This article will attempt to capture a range of North American contributions in this collaborative enterprise.

As a way to situate these contributions, I will first briefly interpret an endorsed view of the American Association for Applied Linguistics on the purpose and goals of the discipline. Then I will note briefly the contributions of several recent volumes on Applied Linguistics, commenting on the domains covered and issues addressed. Finally, I will provide a more personal perspective on the current state of Applied Linguistics from a North American perspective and close with some modest suggestions for continuing trends.[1]

AILA Review 17 (2004), 105–132.
ISSN 1461–0213 / E-ISSN 1570–5595 © John Benjamins Publishing Company

Interpreting a AAAL perspective

In 2003, the American Association for Applied Linguistics (AAAL) endorsed a statement describing the activities of applied linguists, at least in North America.[2] The initial purpose of the document was to seek greater recognition for Applied Linguistics with federal funding agencies in the US. The document was seen by the AAAL Executive Committee as a reasonable short description of Applied Linguistics that could be used in future documentation and publicity for the field and the Association. This document defines Applied Linguistics from a North American perspective and outlines its contributions to higher education and to the wider society. The statement affirms the interdisciplinary nature of Applied Linguistics and the real-world problem-driven focus of the discipline. It also points out the growing popularity of Applied Linguistics in North America, noting that there are now 45 doctoral programs in Applied Linguistics in North America, that there are many job postings for Applied Linguistics in North American universities, and that there are many widely recognized conferences and professional journals in Applied Linguistics.

As a second disciplinary-defining activity, the planning committee for the annual AAAL conference is asked each year to create the sub-domain categories for abstract submission. These categories represent a de-facto outline of the sub-domains that delimit Applied Linguistics in North America. While most members of AAAL see the categories for its utilitarian purpose — deciding which sub-domain to submit their abstract to — the overall listing provides one frame for understanding current views on Applied Linguistics. The list below represents an amalgamation of the sub-domains used in the last three annual conferences of the Association (2001–2003).

Table 1. Sub-Domains in Applied Linguistics: AAAL 2001–2003

1. Assessment & Evaluation
2. Bilingual, Immersion, Heritage, Language Minority Learners
3. Critical Linguistics & Language Ideology
4. Discourse Analysis
5. Language Acquisition & Attrition
6. Language, Cognition & the Brain
7. Language, Culture & Socialization
8. Language Policy & Planning
9. Reading, Writing & Literacy
10. Research Methods & Applied Linguistics
11. Second & Foreign Language Pedagogy
12. Sociolinguistics
13. Technology & Language
14. Translation & Interpretation

This conference listing does not mean that Applied Linguistics cannot be represented elsewhere among academic disciplines. For example, many Speech pathologists see themselves as applied linguists even if the large majority does not. Similarly, some rhetoricians would be happy to be considered applied linguists as well as rhetoricians, although the very large majority of rhetoricians are not willing to be seen as applied linguists. Of more important annual concern is whether any persons who identify themselves as applied linguists feel shut out by the above categorization. With few exceptions, AAAL conference planners have not had major difficulties with AAAL members wishing to participate in the conference but feeling that they are not represented anywhere in the above categories. It is also worth pointing out that these categories are meant to assist conference participants and represent an inclusive set of the whole of Applied Linguistics rather than a representation of equally important sub-domains. For example, the AAAL section on Language Acquisition and Attrition represents a large number of sub-categories within it and it receives a very large number of abstract proposals for the conference. The same observation holds for Second and Foreign Language pedagogy.

One might look at the AAAL list of domains and ask where the defining core is. I do not think that such a question is either useful or appropriate. A common complaint directed at Applied Linguistics, at least in the US, is that it is becoming more fragmented with sub-disciplines splitting off by themselves. While there is a definite trend for sub-disciplines to define themselves more clearly, this is not the sign of a discipline's demise. In many more-mature disciplines, a careful examination will reveal many splits, fizzures and sub-disciplines, along with many different grand narratives, research methods, and practical applications (serious looks at psychology and biology should satisfy most readers). Applied Linguistics is alive and well, and will continue to do just fine.

Overall, the AAAL categorizations provide one starting point for establishing a North American perspective on Applied Linguistics. A second resource for establishing the domain of Applied Linguistics relevant to North America is through published volumes that have appeared recently (since 2000).

Recent volumes on applied linguistics

There have been a number of recent publications on Applied Linguistics that demonstrate the broad range of the discipline, its interdisciplinarity, and issues that are at the forefront of scholarship and debate. These volumes are not specific to North America; indeed, some are decidedly not North American in orientation. Yet they all represent ways to conceptualize Applied Linguistics (Cook 2003; McCarthy 2001; Seidlhofer 2003; Widdowson 2003). Two recent edited collections on applied linguistics have a large North American representation.

Schmitt's (2002) *Introduction to Applied Linguistics* includes 15 chapters covering key areas of Applied Linguistics, with a strong orientation to language learning. The volume provides coverage of language description and use (e.g., vocabulary, grammar, discourse analysis, pragmatics, corpus linguistics), research fields supporting language learning (SLA, psycholinguistics, sociolinguistics, motivation and learning), and language skills and assessment (e.g., speaking, writing, assessment). It is primarily oriented to teachers and the support that Applied Linguistics provides for learning and teaching. One half of the authors are not from North America so it is fair to say that this volume has an international orientation, though certainly it reflects North American views as well.

The second volume, Kaplan's (2002) *The Oxford Handbook of Applied Linguistics*, is designed to be a true reference handbook with 39 chapters, and 8 chapters on sub-areas of SLA alone (formal approaches, sociocultural approaches, identity and culture approaches, cognitive approaches, variationist approaches, social psychological approaches, interactionist approaches, and pragmatic approaches). The volume covers many topics and areas centered on language learning and teaching, but it also addresses issues involving language use, the bilingual individual, societal multilingualism, translation and interpretation, technology applications and more. Because 26 of the 39 chapters are written by North American authors, this volume is a reasonable contemporary representation of Applied Linguistics in North America.

A more personal view of applied linguistics

As past editor of the *Annual Review of Applied Linguistics* (*ARAL*), I was able to follow general trends in various sub-domains of Applied Linguistics and also observe key topics discussed by many contributors. One way to track changes in Applied Linguistics is with a simple type of content analysis — in this case examining the topics covered in the last five years of *ARAL* — and observe emerging trends.

In the years from 2000–2004, ARAL has included volumes on language and psychology, discourse analysis, language contact and change, Applied Linguistics as emerging discipline, and language teaching. In the volume on discourse analysis (2002), issues include various approaches to discourse analysis; discourse analysis applications in genre, stylistics, and pragmatics; discourse in the classroom; and discourse and language assessment. In the volume on language contact (2003), issues addressed include language maintenance and revitalization, bilingual interpretation, language rights, various sites of language contact (e.g., education, legal settings, health care, business), and specific causes of language change. In the most recent volume, on advances in language pedagogy (2004), issues include research on teaching each of the fours skills, research on current approaches to teaching, research related to issues in curriculum development, and explorations of the relation between language learning research and teaching practice.

Tucker (2000, 2003), in a set of summaries for *ARAL* volumes, highlights a number of issues that should be given careful consideration by all Applied Linguists. In Tucker (2000), he points out that all language use and language learning occurs in complex contexts. These contexts and their impact on language performance need to be considered in applied linguistic research and practice. Moreover, every individual carries multiple identities when using and learning a language, and the complex interplay of these identities will influence both language learning and use. He notes that several issues remain relatively neglected in Applied Linguistics despite multiple calls for research, including research on training non-native teachers of a language, research on sign language, and language program effectiveness in third world countries. With regard to research approaches, he argues that evidence needs to be collected and analyzed from multiple perspectives, and research involving longitudinal data, including data over several years, needs to be encouraged and supported. He also notes that future work in Applied Linguistics needs to examine the effectiveness of technology for language learning: Does technology make a significant difference in learning outcomes and who will have access to appropriate technology as a matter of equity? In concluding, he points out that the US is a recipient of over a million immigrants a year and immigrant populations are the fastest growing segment of the population. Thus, there will be a continuing need to explore applied linguistics issues for the foreseeable future as a matter of educational and national priorities.

In his more recent volume summary (Tucker 2003), Tucker notes that sites of language contact and the ways that individuals interact at these sites of contact profoundly influence issues of language rights, language maintenance, language revitalization, bilingual education, multilingual language uses in various non-educational contexts, and bilingual interpretation. Tucker points to a number of ongoing and emerging trends that have a major bearing on future applied linguistics research: 1) It is still the case that language shift is hard to reverse for many reasons. 2) Language discrimination is still and will likely continue to be a major source of discrimination against individuals, particularly those of language and ethnic minority status. 3) Some language communities will chose to shift their language resources to a second language, typically a language of wider communication. 4) Understanding complex language dynamics among multilingual speakers will require many case studies in different settings and much longitudinal research. 5) Research will be needed to understand advanced bilingualism and exceptional bilinguals; for example, what makes a person a skilled interpreter beyond knowing two languages? How do individuals become exceptional and what might this say about training programs? 6) Research will be needed to determine the ways in which other major languages, aside from English, dominate minority and lesser languages within their spheres of influence. Much is made of English as a hegemonic language, but many other large languages fit this role in international and regional settings. Further information on these six topics would be welcome by researchers, educators, and policy makers to understand the dynamics of language use, maintenance, and shift in various contexts.

These issues explored in recent ARAL volumes indicate the range of topics, issues, and problems that Applied Linguistics addresses. All of the above issues are ones that are either being explored by applied linguists in North America or that deserve greater attention. At the same time, this review has yet to identify those issues that most North American applied linguists would see as central concerns of the field. In a recent article (Grabe 2002), I sought to highlight main lines of applied linguistics research and applications that many North American applied linguists regularly engage in. The article reviews key areas that have taken on greater prominence for applied linguists in the past ten years. That discussion was organized around the following seven topics:

1. Language learning and language teaching
2. Critical Applied Linguistics
3. Language use in professional contexts
4. Descriptive linguistics for applied research
5. Multilingualism and language contact
6. Language assessment
7. Applied Linguistics as mediating discipline

Language learning and language teaching included discussion of SLA, language teaching practices and their effectiveness, and teacher training. Critical applied linguistics issues recognized the emergence of this field in the late 1980s and its growth through the 1990s, covering issues of critical pedagogy, student rights, ethics and fairness in language assessment, and uses of discourse by institutions to shape social, moral, and political views of readers and listeners. The third area involved the study of language use in professional, academic, and social services contexts. A key aspect of this area of research is how language can be used for gatekeeping purposes and how language can lead, even unintentionally, to miscommunication and loss of services or support. In academic settings, a major theme is the role of genres and registers in differing academic and professional domains, and the need to learn appropriate genre expectations to become a member of an academic community. The fourth theme involves the trend in Applied Linguistics toward descriptive linguistics as a resource for applied research, including recent work on corpus linguistics over the past decade. The fifth theme focused on multilingualism and bilingual interactions across community, school, and work contexts. The sixth theme addressed changing perspectives in language assessment. The changing views on construct validity have generated important discussion of assessment consequences for students, ethics and fairness in testing, critical assessment practices, and technology applications in testing. The seventh theme emphasized the mediating role that applied linguists must play between research in language and other disciplines (e.g., Linguistics, Education) on the one hand, and the various groups of people that are affected by language issues and language problems, and that need assistance on the other.

Current issues and themes for applied linguistics in North America
The review of current issues that follows attempts to focus primarily on work by North American researchers and, in a few cases, involves issues that are primarily North American in nature. Table 2 outlines the topics and issues that will be addressed. This overview is not intended to be comprehensive. In fact, each sub area indicated below can be the topic of several volumes. Here, I can only provide a road map of the applied linguistics territory and hope that the resources cited will be useful to readers.

Second language acquisition
Second language acquisition research is the largest research sub-field in North American Applied Linguistics. While there is much SLA research done outside of North America, it is evident from published research in books and journals that SLA is a major part of applied linguistic work in North America. There are many ways to try to organize SLA so I make no claim to authority with the sub-categories I have created to organize my discussion (see Gass 2000; Larsen-Freeman 2000; Lightbown & Spada 1999 for three different overviews). I have created two cognitive categories for SLA: one for research on the language knowledge base and its acquisition, the second for the processing operations carried out by learners and the acquisition of these processes. Two further categories can be

Table 2. Areas of Research in North American Applied Linguistics

Second language acquisition
    Cognitive SLA focusing on representational knowledge
    Cognitive SLA focusing on processing systems
    Neurolinguistic views
    Social psychological views
    Sociocultural views
    Sociolinguistic views
    Pragmatic views
L2 reading and writing research
Language learning and teaching
    Second language teaching (English for Academic Purposes)
    Foreign language teaching
    Bilingual and language minority education
    Instructional Approaches
Language and culture
Corpus Linguistics
Critical perspectives in Applied Linguistics
Language assessment
Language policy and planning
Language use in professional contexts
Technology in Applied Linguistics

associated with psychological approaches: neurolinguistic views and social psychological views. These four categories are followed by three categories that are more contextual in nature: sociocultural, sociolinguistic, and pragmatic approaches. Looking at the range of research on SLA coming out of North America, one would have to devote at least a full chapter to this work alone just to begin to do it justice. I will only note and highlight aspects of this field with selected references for interested readers.

Cognitive SLA, representational knowledge. The area of cognitive SLA that emphasizes knowledge of language forms and its acquisition can be divided into functional/descriptive approaches and formalist approaches. Two current functional approaches to acquisition involve research on Focus-on-Form (FonF) (Doughty and Williams 1998; VanPatten 2003) and interactional approaches to acquisition. FonF research seeks to demonstrate that meaningful input which presents frequent use of specific grammatical forms — a type of grammatical input flood — when combined with appropriate instruction, will lead to the acquisition of these forms faster than by specific direct instruction alone or by incidental learning of forms through processing of meaning (see Norris & Ortega 2000). Interactional approaches focus on the role of language input for the learner and the nature of interaction patterns that occur between native and non-native speakers or between two non-native speakers. A general finding of this approach is that negotiated interaction while carrying out different types of language tasks can improve language acquisition (Gass 2002; Mackey 1999). Additional key notions for interaction are the roles of negotiated feedback (recasts, questions, or direct correction), attention (noticing the input), and output (language production) as influences on acquisition. Work by Gass, Lightbown, Long, Spada, and Swain have all been influential in this approach (Gass, Mackey & Pica 1998; Lightbown 1998; Long 1996; Spada 1997; Swain 2000a).

    Formalist approaches to SLA center primarily on research that adopts a UG framework (see White 2000) and then generates data to examine how (or whether) SLA development conforms to UG theory. Work in formal aspects of SLA has become somewhat less popular recently as it is difficult to do currently relevant experimental work with a changing theory (but see Eubank & Juffs 2000; Hawkins 2001; Schwartz 1999; Schwartz & Sprouse 2000). Work by Juffs seeks to combine formal theories of language with language processing influence on SLA and represents a current effort to bridge the representational research and the processing research (see Harrington 2002; Juffs 2002, 2004). For example, in recent research, Juffs (2004) explores the relationship between working memory processes, structural complexities in sentences, and on-line parsing constraints using response time data. Formalist approaches should also include phonology acquisition research as a sub-category, and this line of SLA work is represented by Major (2001) and Flege (e.g., Flege, et al. 1995).

Cognitive SLA, processing systems. The second variety of cognitive approaches to SLA involves a cognitive processing perspective. This approach seeks to understand the influence of specific cognitive processes on SLA such as attention, memory, transfer, word recognition speed, syntactic parsing, and fluency (see Robinson 2001; Segalowitz & Lightbown 1999). It also incorporates more general issues of language transfer and the critical period hypothesis. SLA processing research has explored word recognition processes (Koda 2004), bilingual effects on word recognition (Jiang 2002; Kandil & Jiang 2003; Kroll et al. 2002), connectionist explanations for learning (Ellis & Schmidt 1997), fluency as a factor in SLA performance (Segalowitz & Hulstijn, in press), and the influence of processing factors on individual differences in SLA student performance (Robinson 2001). Transfer research could be viewed as a separate sub-field of SLA, and considerable research is done in this area (see MacWhinney 1997; Odlin 2003). A further area of research that would fit under psychological processing more generally is the ongoing research on the critical period hypothesis (see Scovel 2000; Singleton 2001). Research in the area of components of cognitive processing in SLA is still somewhat limited at this time because this work requires lab resources and a fair amount of start-up funds (as opposed to exploring acquisition in a classroom setting, for example). However, this area of SLA research will grow considerably in the future, forming a closer connection with cognitive psychology research on learning. A final related area of cognitive processing and SLA involves the study of individual differences in terms of aptitude, attitude, motivation, anxiety, and cognitive individual differences (Dörnyei & Schmidt 2001; Horwitz 2001; Larsen-Freeman 2001; Oxford 2002; Robinson 2002; Sparks & Ganschow 2001).

Neurolinguistic views. Neurolinguistic perspectives on SLA are only beginning but are generating considerable interest. Schumann (1997) explored in some detail the working of the brain for motivation and cognition as it applied to language learning (see also Schumann 2001; Schumann, et al. 2004). Segalowitz (2001) points to recent research on brain scans and neuroimaging to understand better the notions of language modules and language faculties (see also de Bot 2000; Perfetti et al. 2001). There is little direct work being done with neuroimaging in SLA research specifically, though it is only a matter of time before such approaches lead to new insights into language learning and language use.

Social psychological views. A final area that primarily involves cognition and SLA is social-psychological perspectives on learning. This field is dominated by the work of Gardner (2000, 2002; Masgoret & Gardner 2003) and focuses on the social and psychological intersection of motivation, attitudes, and expert performance. The key notion is that language learning is closely tied to attitudes and views about the target culture and the learning environment. Specific issues that apply to SLA include the relation between integrative motivation and success in learning a second language, the role of instrumental motivation as a support for academic language development, and the range of wider social and environmental factors that influence language learning.

Sociocultural views. Sociocultural perspectives in SLA have grown considerably in the past decade, and they are likely to continue to increase in influence. North American educational researchers have become increasingly interested in Vygotskean perspectives for learning, and especially for language learning (Frawley & Lantolf 1985; Moll 1990; Wells 1999). From the early 1990s on, Lantolf has argued that adapting Vygotskean orientations to learning would be both insightful and productive as a research direction for SLA (Lantolf 2002; Lantolf & Appel 1994). Other early contributions include a synthesis of SLA and Vygotskean views by Schinke-Llano (1993), a study of oral practice and its role in SLA by Hall (1993), and a study of private speech by McCafferty (1992). Since the mid-1990s, several other researchers have become strongly engaged with this orientation. Swain et al. (2002) reviews the role or peer-peer dialogues as a means of L2 learning, Hall and Walsh (2002) survey studies on teacher-student interaction and their impact on L2 learning. Hall and Verplaeste (2000) provide a collection of studies on SLA from a sociocultural perspective as does a recent volume by Lantolf (2000).

Sociolinguistic view. Sociolinguistic perspectives on SLA cover a wide territory. Key areas include language variation and variability in SLA, conversational analysis in SLA, cross-cultural communication, classroom language, language and identity, and language and culture (though this could be a separate category). Variationist perspectives on SLA, and especially interlanguage variation, are reviewed in Bayley and Preston (1996), Preston (2002), and Young (1999). A particularly important line of work, one that intersects with sociocultural work, is the impact of context on SLA. In particular, the research by Tarone on context influences on learning represents an important counterbalance to the strongly cognitive orientation of much of SLA (Tarone 2000; Tarone & Liu 1995). Work on classroom discourse not solely in a sociocultural framework is also an important site for sociolinguistic SLA research (Duff 2002; Poole 2002; Zuengler & Mori 2002). Language and identity has become more important as an area in SLA over the last 10 years (Norton 2000, 2001; Norton & Toohey 2002). Closely aligned with Vygotskean learning theory, identity studies also involve the role of institutional, authority, and power relations in learning, as well as the responses of the individual in constructing an identity that will learn effectively or not.

Pragmatic views. Pragmatic perspectives in SLA could be included in either sociolinguistic perspectives or cognitive perspectives, but they are becoming more commonly viewed as part of their own sub-field. Key issues include the role of pragmatics in language learning, particularly in communicative language teaching, the nature of cross-cultural miscommunication due to pragmatic factors, the nature of pragmatic transfer, and the learning and performance of pragmatic knowledge. Recent overviews are provided by Bardovi-Harlig (1999, 2002), Boxer (2002), and Kasper & Rose (2002). At present, a greater emphasis has been given to descriptions of pragmatic interlanguage and its uses in different contexts, while less attention has been given to the impact of pragmatics on enhancing (or impeding) SLA outcomes.

Second language reading and writing research
Research on second language reading and writing are two areas that reside on the borders of SLA, language teaching, English studies, literacy research, and educational and cognitive psychology. Both areas make important and useful connections with SLA in areas of language transfer, vocabulary learning, language input and student output, and classroom-based research. L2 reading and writing research both have the potential to contribute importantly to issues of elementary and secondary student L2 language development in schools, but little has been done to take advantage of this linkage (Harklau 2002). Relations between L2 reading and K-12 educational research are growing as educational researchers are now beginning to recognize the increasing numbers of English L2 students in school systems and their needs (Alvermann & Eakle 2003; Bernhardt 2003; G. Garcia 2003). L2 reading and cognitive psychology have also strengthened their relationships with explorations of L2 fluency, lexical access, vocabulary growth, text structure awareness, and comprehension development (Geva & Siegal 2000; Koda, 2004; Segalowitz & Hulstijn in press). L2 writing research has linkages with both educational psychology and English studies, though the recognition, by researchers in related disciplines, of the specific contexts on L2 writing has yet to be widely recognized. It is worth noting that the relations between reading and writing on one hand, and SLA,

on the other, are not always straightforward. For example, most SLA introductory texts have no discussion of either reading or writing.

Research on L2 reading is reviewed in Bernhardt, (2000), Carrell and Grabe (2002), Grabe and Stoller (2002), and Koda (2004). Bernhardt (2000) highlights the growth of L2 reading research as it begins to separate its own concerns from that of L1 reading development. She also reviews work on models of L2 reading development and makes the argument that L2 reading research liberates L1 educational research from assumptions of reading in a single linguistic system. Carrell and Grabe (2002) examine research on issues of the L2 language threshold, language transfer, reading strategies, vocabulary learning, reading rate, and text structure awareness, as well as implications for reading instruction. Specific discussions of the L2 reading needs of language minority children in schools are addressed in Bernhardt (2003), Fitzgerald (2003), Garcia (2000) and Jimenez (2003). The majority of researchers in this latter area would not consider themselves applied linguists, but rather educational researchers with interests in language minority students.

Recent reviews of research on L2 writing from a primarily North American context are presented in Belcher and Hirvela, (2001), Casanave (2004), Ferris and Hedgcock (1998), Johns (1997, 2001), Kroll (2003), and Silva and Matsuda (2001). Because North American universities place a strong emphasis on entry-level writing courses for all students, the field of second language writing is heavily influenced by the needs of L2 students who must take university writing courses and more advanced courses that require extensive writing. Most discussions of L2 writing among elementary and secondary students appear in educational and literacy journals and few applied linguists in North America write about these populations (cf. Merino & Hammond 2002).

Language learning and teaching
Second language teaching. The largest number of research and scholarly articles on L2 language teaching by applied linguists focuses on the teaching of English for Academic Purposes. A similar emphasis may be asserted as well for other parts of the world, but in North America, this emphasis is unarguable. ESL methods books in North America are heavily oriented to pre-university and university ESL students. Where books are directed primarily to elementary (and occasionally secondary) populations in public schools, they are often written by researchers in bilingual education, most of whom do not identify themselves with Applied Linguistics (or with ESL teaching). Celce-Murcia's (2001) recent methodology book represents a strong example of a North American applied linguistics orientation to ESL teaching. It makes an effort to cover K-12 issues in ESL instruction, but the majority of articles are directed more to groups of EAP students. Other standard ESL foundations books, such as Brown (2000), are similarly oriented towards EAP contexts.

Because most applied linguists are not housed in education departments, they have relatively little influence on K-12 instructional issues and relatively little access to L2 students in K-12 settings (cf. Faltis & Wolfe 1999). The most influential work by applied linguists in K-12 settings involves the various projects and outreach support provided by the Center for Applied Linguistics (CAL). In their many research activities, publications, and information clearinghouse functions, they are actively engaged in learner and teacher research studies, teacher training, curriculum development, language assessment, policy studies, and a range of other applied linguistics activities. Their extensive work is well detailed on the CAL website (www.cal.org).

Influential research on advanced EAP teachers, students, student learning needs, and classroom interactions are discussed in Bailey (1996, 2001), Johns (1997, 2001), Swales (2000), and van Lier (1996) among others. In their work with many types of university students, important issues of genre knowledge, differing disciplinary demands, student needs, learner autonomy, and classroom-based research on teaching and learning are among the many issues that comprise language teaching research in North American contexts. In a recent article, Scarcella (2002) argues forcefully that the move to emphasize oral language abilities and 'natural learning' has led to students with limited advanced L2 academic language abilities. She recommends that pre-university L2 language instruction focus more attention to form and provide more practice with expository writing.

One sub-field of ESL teaching that extends in interesting ways across all grade levels of ESL instruction is the issue of ESL teacher training. Over the past 10 years, there has been considerable discussion on the issue of teacher training and teacher education (Crandall 2000a; Freeman & Johnson 1998; Johnson 2000). Greater emphasis is being given to reflective teaching practices, teacher inquiry, the importance of experiential knowledge, the role of teacher cognition and teacher decision making, the importance of assessment in language teacher education, and the role of the non-native language teacher. These issues will continue to be major topics of discussion for the coming decade.

Foreign language teaching. In North American contexts, foreign language teaching has a more limited role than in other parts of the world. Even in traditional teaching contexts with standard university requirements and secondary school requirements, more schools and universities are waiving these requirements or making foreign language study optional. Nonetheless, in high schools and university settings, there are still a high percentage of students taking courses in various foreign languages. Foreign language study in elementary schools and early secondary school settings is more common in Canada than in the U.S., though there are many K-12 schools in the U.S. where foreign languages are taught and some where foreign language learning is emphasized (McGroarty 2003; Met 2003; Phillips 2003).

Foreign language classes at the university level experienced deceasing enrollments during the 1970s and 1980s. By 2000, however, the enrollments were again at the 1970 level (at about 1.1 million students enrolled in university foreign language courses in the U.S.; see Klee 2000). While traditional languages such as French, German, and Russian have declined in enrollments and graduating majors, Spanish majors and majors in less-common language have increased considerably. Another indicator of the ambivalence of U.S. students toward foreign languages is the 1/3 decline in majors graduating from foreign languages departments between 1970 and 1996 (Klee 2000). An interesting area of university level foreign language instruction has been the effort to develop content-based curricula for students and language across the curriculum. The goal is to move away from a more structural curriculum and toward a curriculum with will actively engage students and lead to real uses of the foreign language for learning purposes beyond the foreign language classroom (Fichera & Straight 1997; Krueger & Ryan 1993; Stryker & Leaver 1997).

K-12 foreign language instruction is most commonly reserved for the last three years of secondary education. There are, however, numerous elementary school programs that introduce children to another language. For example, there are dual language schools and many FLES (foreign language in elementary schools) programs in the U.S. (Met 1993; Met & Lorenz 1997; Rosenbusch 1995). A large but separate aspect of language instruction in the K-12 educational system of the U.S. and Canada centers on bilingual education. This topic, however, is generally seen as distinct from foreign language education except in some cases of heritage language instruction, which may or may not be a part of bilingual education. In heritage language instruction, language minority students learn their first language. In many cases, this instruction is seen as part of a bilingual education program, but heritage language instruction is not always fully integrated with the larger content curriculum of the school (a situation often found with less-common languages and with Native American languages). (See Peyton et al. 2001, for a discussion of the full range of heritage language issues.)

Bilingual education. Bilingual education in both Canada and the U.S. has been an area in Applied Linguistics (and outside Applied Linguistics as well) that has generated considerable discussion and debate. In Canada, the various programs for French immersion and heritage language development have been a regular source of research in SLA, language teaching, and curriculum design (Bialystok 2001; Genesee 2001; Swain 2000b; Wesche 2000). In Canada, there is considerable governmental and community support for bilingualism and bilingual education. The situation is far more complex and less supportive for bilingualism in the U.S., where bilingual education is clearly on the defensive.

Approximately one tenth of the U.S. population is foreign born (approximately 30 million today; see Ignash 2000) and more than 15% of all K-12 students come from homes where a language other than English is spoken (Crandall 2000b). Over the past 20 years, the majority of these immigrants have come from South and Central America, Mexico, and Asia. One would expect that such cultural and linguistic diversity in the U.S. society would lead to an educational emphasis on, or at least support for, bilingual education. For a number of reasons, however, there is relatively little support for bilingual education from government and educational institutions across the U.S. Why this is the case would require a major article in itself, though there are several excellent resource books and articles on the current situation in U.S. bilingual education (Crawford 2000, 2003; Cummins 2000; Francis & Reyhner 2002; Ricento 1998; Valdez 2001).

The status and effectiveness of bilingual education in the U.S. is explored carefully in Cummins (2000) and Valdez (2001). Both authors examine the prior research on the effectiveness of bilingual education and the theoretical positions taken by various proponents and opponents of bilingual education. Cummins argues that much research has lost focus, and claims made by research reviews and meta-analyses do not provide clear guidelines for policy decisions. He argues that research on bilingual education needs to be conducted carefully and, only after extensive converging findings from well-controlled studies are established, can effective policies for education be advanced. Valdez provides a detailed description of the situation of bilingual instruction in many U.S. schools. The poor outcomes often noted with bilingual education emerge from a combination of weak institutional support in schools, a lack of appropriate funding for programs, inadequate instruction, low student motivation, and larger societal disregard for the needs of language minority students. These issues are also succinctly described in Baker (2003).

L2 instructional approaches. In Canada and the U.S., there are still two dominant orientations to second language instruction: communicative language teaching (CLT) and language skills instruction. CLT is the dominant orientation to ESL instruction in pre-academic settings. In pre-university and university ESL programs, language skills instruction, in which course are designed to focus on specific language skills, is still a dominant curricular orientation, as much for administrative convenience as for instructional effectiveness. In K-12 bilingual education, ESL versions of whole-language instruction are also common. More recent changes in teaching approaches involve language learning strategy instruction, task-based instruction, and content-based instruction.

Strategy instruction is seen as a very important aspect of language learning. Communicative language teaching focuses more on learning strategies and communicative strategies important for oral interaction, while English for Academic Purposes focuses more on learning strategies and comprehension strategies important for learners in more advanced academic settings (Chamot 2001; Chamot & O'Malley 1994; Cohen 1998; Oxford 1996, 2001). Cohen (1998) argues that strategies can be divided in terms of language learning strategies and language using strategies. He further argues that language learning curricula can be usefully developed around a strategies-based approach (SBI) to language learning. Kern (2000) addresses strategy learning and strategy instruction in foreign language contexts for literacy learning and proposes a number of effective practical ideas for strategy-based instruction.

Two other curricular approaches that have gained popularity in North America are content-based instruction (CBI) and task-based instruction (TBI). Content-based approaches go back to efforts in the early 1980s to create content-specific learning environments for university courses in Canada and extended content and language learning settings for K-12 contexts (Brinton, Snow & Wesche 1989; Crandall 1987; Mohan 1986). CBI has also drawn heavily on elementary (K-6) thematic instruction and secondary-level reading in the content areas. At present, CBI is gaining wider acceptance in foreign language instruction in university contexts and in secondary school settings as sheltered instruction. It is also being used increasingly in academic ESL programs (see Stoller 2004).

Task-based instruction also has its current roots in the 1980s with specific task-based curricula in EFL settings. Overall, it is not used as widely in practice as CBI, but it is a preferred approach in much SLA research and it is easily adaptable within a CLT curriculum. It responds both to the goal of maintaining a semantic focus during language instruction, but also allowing attention to language form to varying degrees depending on types of tasks used. TBI also provides effective ways to distinguish learning that focuses on accuracy, fluency, and complexity (Wesche & Skehan 2002). One danger of TBI is that it can easily fragment into discrete task exercises much like any structural curriculum, though such an outcome is not inevitable for TBI. TBI and CBI can also be seen as two general and complementary orientations that provide extended content and language practice, both of which focus on meaning and have the potential to engage students in meaningful project work while learning language.

Language and culture

The field of language and culture stands at the intersection of language learning, language teaching, stylistics, literature, and language standards. As such, it engages a territory that is as large as Applied Linguistics itself. It is not a well-developed field in North American Applied Linguistics, but for teachers and scholars working in modern language departments, this field is a central one to their interests and concerns. It also is a field that extend beyond Applied Linguistics altogether. To the extent that it is a part of the mosaic of Applied Linguistics, it addresses issues of how culture and learning intersect, how culture influences learning, and how cultural issues can be used to teach language more effectively. The leading research being done in this area in the US is Kramsch (1993, 2000). While there are many other modern language scholars interested in the relation between culture, literature, and language teaching, few would identify themselves as applied linguists.

More recently, Kramsch (2002) has argued that language learning limited to CLT ignores some of the most important cultural aspects of language learning. In university foreign language contexts, at least, studying language is also an ideal way to expose students to cultural standards and more literate uses of language beyond practice in interactional communication. Exposing students to cultural and language standards should be a valid goal for language learning in academic settings and should not be ignored.

Corpus linguistics

Corpus linguistics has emerged over the past 15 years as an important area of applied linguistics research and application. While some corpus linguistics research is associated with historical linguistics and language varieties (e.g., Meyer 1992), a major direction in corpus linguistics has been associated with the development of applied discourse analysis, lexicography, grammars, and language teaching resources (e.g., Biber, et al. 1998). In the U.S., corpus research, with strong applied linguistics uses, have been developed notably by Biber and his colleagues (Biber, Conrad & Reppen 1998; Conrad 2002; Conrad & Biber 2001) and by Swales and his colleagues (Simpson & Swales 2001).

Corpus linguistics has been used for various applied linguistics purposes. It has been used to explore many aspects of discourse analysis and language use, examining the uses of discourse markers, the writing development of students, textbook language, authentic language for materials writing, realistic grammar points for instruction, lexical variety and range in text materials, discourse and text segments for assessment uses, and possible instructional applications of corpus analysis directly with students. In some cases, corpus linguistics may involve very large corpora and extensive use of automated analyses by computer. In other cases, corpus analysis may involve smaller collections of texts and less dramatic applications of computational resources, but still produce important results (e.g., Hinkel 2002).

Corpus linguistics also raises concerns from critics that corpus analysis is sometimes put forward, and sometimes exuberantly, as the new and primary direction for discourse analysis and language teaching applications. Widdowson (2000, 2003)[3] has argued most strongly for a cautious position on corpus linguistics applications, pointing out that "externalized language" data should not always be privileged as the language most appropriate for language learning and language teaching situations. In the coming years, both the increasing applications of corpus linguistics, and the debates concerning the appropriate uses of corpus analyses will continue.

Critical perspectives on applied linguistics
An issue that has gained much attention in recent discussions in Applied Linguistics is the role of critical theories such as critical discourse analysis (CDA), critical pedagogy, and critical language assessment. Critical perspectives have their origins in social theories that gained popularity in the 1970s and entered into applied linguistics discussions in the mid 1980s (Luke 2002). Most of the work on CDA in the 1980s and early 1990s was developed by European scholars. However, by the early 1990s, two areas of CDA merged with critical social theory and literary post-modernist theory in the U.S., and emerged in L2 writing theory and immigrant ESL/EAP instruction. L2 writing researchers have drawn on post-modernist views to assert the rights of students to their own goals in educational institutions, moving away from needs analysis of a pragmatic nature to students rights and a critical-pragmatic view of teaching and learning writing (Benesch 1999; 2001; Canagarajah 1999, 2002).

Kumaravadivelu (1999, 2001) is one of the few North American applied linguists who have sought to translate CDA (as opposed to more general post-modernist theories) into ESL instruction. In his earlier article, Kumaravadivelu (1999) adapts CDA to critical classroom discourse analysis, a natural extension of CDA methods, examining patterns of interaction and negotiation in classroom contexts. In a later article (2001), he argues that teachers need to develop their own critical stances to instruction and interaction in the classroom, leading to a call for a distinct type of teacher education model.

One of the valid and on-going criticisms of CDA and critical pedagogy is that it often refuses to be critically reflexive with respect to its own positionings (see, e.g., Widdowson 1998). Critical theorists tend to speak with remarkable assurance about the machinations and ulterior motives of others and the ignorance of groups swayed by institutional power and assumed natural rights. CDA also has been accused of playing theoretical games when people in the real world need real-world solutions to their problems or their future goals (see Johnston 1999, for a balanced critique). A further argument is that little work in CDA, or more general theorizing about critical pedagogy, addresses the practical world of teaching and learning in ways that demonstrate effective instructional practices or better learning outcomes in contexts that are applicable to large L2 student populations.

Nonetheless, there are some critical theorists who have made real contributions in demonstrating how critical pedagogy can be an effective way to build sustained language and content instruction. Benesch (2001) provides a number of contexts in which critical pedagogy can be seen as creating engaging and challenging course curricula for specific groups of L2 students (see also Canagarajah 2002). Norton (2000, 2001) reports on studies which similarly argue for the need for teachers to be more aware of their students' lives and their own role in the educational process, and then use that knowledge to develop more responsive curricula. This perspective on promoting critical and reflexive practices by teachers is also developed outside critical pedagogy in sociocultural approaches to instruction (Duff & Uchida 1997) and in more reflexive practices in EAP (Johns 1997), without the additional requirement of direct political activism.

Language assessment

Language assessment issues and practices have gained increasing attention among applied linguists and this trend holds true for Applied Linguistics in North America. Among the issues that have been actively discussed in recent years are test validity, fairness in testing, performance assessment, evidence-centered design, language-skills constructs, and technology in language assessment. In addition, the TOEFL program at Educational Testing Service is now moving to a redesigned TOEFL (named New TOEFL at the moment) after seven years of discussion, consulting, and directed research.

Validity issues in language assessment took a major turn with Messick's (1989) article on validity in testing. In this article, the construct of validity was defined as including construct validity (including reliability), appropriateness (accounting for the values of test takers and test makers), usability, and social consequences of testing. Taking this model as a starting point, Bachman and Palmer (1996) reviewed existing testing practices and argued for ways to apply Messick's approach to a range of practical and standardized language testing situation. Chapelle (1999) and Kunnan (1998) both provide accessible and succinct explanations of Messick's approach to validity. At present, Messick's views on validity continue to strongly influence language testing practices and test development. Closely related to the concept of validity is an increasing emphasis given to fairness in testing. A number of recent publications have raised this issue, either under the concept of fairness (Kunnan 1999) or as a matter of ethical testing practices (Bachman 2000).

Performance assessment has also captured the interests of testing researchers worldwide, including in North America. Performance assessment has been around for a long time outside of language testing (e.g., workplace performance and professional licensing tests), and within language testing; essay writing is a standard language performance task. The application of performance assessment also complements well many efforts to develop task-based curricula since the best way to assess outcomes is by demonstrating successful performance on various language tasks. A major effort to develop language assessment along these lines can be seen in a set of recent publications from the University of Hawaii (Brown et al. 2002; Norris 2001; Norris et al. 1998; cf. Bachman 2002).

A further development that has emerged strongly in the past five to ten years in language assessment is the move to evidence-centered design for developing language tests. In principle, the concept is straightforward. Tests are developed on the basis of research evidence that supports the underlying construct and the claims to be inferred from test results. Test scores only allow a person to *infer* one or more language abilities. The claims about these abilities, that a test is supposed to represent, should be supported with as much research evidence as possible to support the inference from a score. This design principle is a foundation for Messick's validity construct, and it has been a major goal of a number of recent test development projects, including new TOEFL (see Mislevy, Stenberg & Almond 1998, 2002, for discussion of evidence-centered design).

Over the past 10 years, language assessment practices, particularly high stakes assessment, have moved back to testing specific language skills. Partly, this trend has grown from the recognition that integrative tests do not provide a profile of specific component skills underlying language proficiency; partly, this trend has grown from the on-going need to assess more specific language abilities; and partly, it has emerged from efforts to describe more precisely just what test scores mean, including possible diagnostic profiles. Evidence for this trend can be seen in the series of language assessment volumes in the past 5 years from Cambridge University Press that cover reading, writing, listening, vocabulary, LSP (series editors Charles Alderson and Lyle Bachman). Further evidence is seen in the research supporting the development of New TOEFL (TOEFL Research Monograph series, 25 reports to date).

A final major trend that has gained considerable momentum in North America is the move to incorporate technology into language assessment practices. More high-stakes tests are being offered via computer (along with tasks that make better use of the human-computer interface — highlighting, deleting, using click and drag, etc.). Computer adaptive testing (CAT) has also been an approach that has been used recently for a number of language tests (Chalhoub-Deville 1999; Chalhoub-Deville & Deville 1999). Finally, in the technology area, many computer applications provide means for changing test delivery and test scoring. Latent Semantic Analysis (Landauer, Foltz & Laham 1998) has provided a reliable way to machine score certain types of writing tests (Foltz, Kintsch & Landauer 1998). E-Rater is a new tool for analyzing a wide range of essay types with reasonable reliability (Burstein & Chodorow 2002; Powers et al. 2002). Phone Pass (Ordinate.com) uses a very powerful speech recognition processing program to score test takers who speak into a phone for ten minutes. Expanded bandwidth over the internet has allowed for speech capture at remote testing sites and immediate transmission to host computers for storage and later scoring.

The largest language testing project in North America for the past eight years has been the research effort by ETS to develop New TOEFL. The project began with a core team developing a framework for building a new test from the bottom up, beginning from research on the constructs to be tested, then moving to specific claims about language abilities and tasks that will provide evidence about the claims, to scoring and scaling issues, and to test delivery issues. The test will assess all four language skills and also include tasks that integrate multiple language skills. Many testing consultants from around the world have been involved in the project at various points, and the test itself is slated to become operational worldwide in Fall 2005.

Language policy and planning
The field of language policy and planning has been strongly represented by North American research over the past five to ten years. North American scholars have analyzed in great detail many of the issues surrounding bilingual education, the English-only movement, governmental language policies in Canada, language maintenance and language revitalization, and language spread and shift. Language policy and planning can be done at many levels: national, regional, local, institutional, and individual. Sometime language policies are planned, but many times policies emerge in unplanned ways that have a significant impact on groups of language users and language learners (Eggington 2002). (The choice of foreign languages offered in secondary schools is usually a good case of unplanned policy making in many school districts in the U.S.)

Planned language policies and their implementation have clear organizational models that suggest ways to engage in these types of activities (Kaplan & Baldauf 1997). Canada has official language policies regarding the language communities of the country and efforts at various governmental levels have provided some support for minority languages (see Beaujot 1998; Edwards 1998). However, many issues that are covered under language policy and planning usually do not arise from a well-planned approach. Often specific events or political issues lead to partially planned policies (and often failures in implementation). The Ebonics debate in the U.S. is a good case of events preceding any planning and the many competing voices then making any rational policy almost impossible to develop, no less implement. Various versions of English-only amendments passed by specific states in the U.S. also illustrate the many unforeseen consequences of politicized and adversarial language policies (Crawford 2000; Ricento 1998).

The spread of English throughout all other language communities in North America is an issue that has grown increasingly in importance, discussed primarily in terms of language shift and language maintenance. In North American contexts, at least, it is very difficult to reverse language shift once it has begun to take hold within a minority community. The U.S. provides many examples of language shift, from Hispanic populations in California, to Puerto Rican populations in New York, to indigenous populations across the western U.S. (Crawford 2000; Fishman 1991, 2001; House 2002; McCarty 2002; Rivera-Mills 2001).

In the face of extreme pressures from English in North America, several authors have argued for the increasing need for language maintenance and language revitalization, particularly following the appearance of Fishman's (1991) book *Reversing Language shift*. While this book explored issues of language maintenance and renewal in many language contexts world-wide, it also addressed a number of contexts specifically in the U. S. Since that time, discussions of maintaining immigrant and indigenous languages in North America have been reported in multiple publications (Edwards 1998; Fishman 2001; Francis & Reyhner 2002; M. Garcia 2003; Hinton 2003: Hinton & Hale 2001). In most cases in North America, language shift among immigrant and indigenous language groups has proven to be very hard to reverse in the long run.

The topic of Language planning and policy also represents one way to locate research on world Englishes, championed by Kachru (1992 1997) and developed over 20 years by the journal, *World Englishes* (Kachru & Smith 1985–2004). While world Englishes is a topic that is discussed more consistently outside North America than within, this review would be remiss in not recognizing the groundbreaking work of Kachru in this field.

Language use in professional contexts
A major area of Applied Linguistics that has generated a growing volume of important research is language use (and abuse) in professional and academic settings. On balance, much more of this research is being carried out in Europe, Australia, and Asia than in North America, though important contributions have been made in the areas of language and the law, bilingual interpretation, language and medicine, and language and science (McGroarty 2002).

In the area of language and the law, work by Shuy (1993, 1997, 1998), Berk-Seligson (1990, 1999, 2000), and Conley and O'Barr (1990, 1998) highlight a consistent investigation of a) the language practices in court settings, b) evidence collection and interrogations, and c) bilingual interpreting. Shuy explores a wide range of legal issues in his publications, including how language provides evidence for legal uses; what uses of language constitute such crimes as bribery, threats, agreements to illegal activity, promising, and perjury; and how language works in interrogations and confessions. Conley and O'Barr (1990, 1998) have focused on how legal discourse works, how different people understand legal language in different ways, and how persons can be disadvantaged by not understanding language use in legal settings. In addition, Solan (1993) examines the language of judges and how such language use impacts the outcomes of legal proceedings. Dumas (2000) examines the comprehensibility of legal texts, jury instructions, and the difficulties that jurors have with legal language. Finally there are a number of studies and support articles that examine the role and effectiveness of legal interpretation — when it is done appropriately and when it is done inappropriately (Berk-Seligson 1990, 2000; Gonzalez, Vasquez, & Mikkelson 1991).

Bilingual interpretation in legal, community, conference, and other settings has been an area of applied linguistics work in the U. S., though not to the extent as in other regions of the world. Berk-Seligson (see above) is the primary source for legal interpreting. Interpreting in community settings, at least in the U. S., is commonly viewed as inadequate because appropriate funding to pay for skilled interpreters is often not available. More general work on the bilingual and translation processing skills of interpreters is discussed in Valdez and Angelelli (2003) and Schweda Nicholson (1995, 1999, 2002).

The role of language in medical and therapy contexts is also being seen as increasingly important, particularly for appropriate services for L2 and second-dialect patients and clients. In medical settings, there are great divides between the care provider and the patient in terms of power, knowledge, and often gender. Hyden and Mishler (1999) examine the various ways doctor-patient interactions unfold and point out ways in which patients may not be understood appropriately or may not get the treatment they need. McGroarty (2002) provides a useful review of issues involved in language use in medical contexts: the realizations of power and resistance, including the role of gender (Todd & Fisher 1993), the language used to train medical practitioners (Cicourel 1992), and the differing language uses by different types of providers (Fisher 1995). An important outcome of many studies in this field is the role that narrative plays in medical interactions of various types. Medical language can often be seen as interpretive, involving narratives that explain a patient's situation, a doctor's interpretation, or a patient's new identity (Frank 1995; Hunter 1991; Kleinman 1988).

Language in science has evolved along two lines over the past decade in Applied Linguistics: the linguistic analysis of science writing and scientific genres (e.g., Swales 1990, 1998) and the rhetorical analyses of scientific writing, including historical analyses (Atkinson 1999a, 1999b; Bazerman 1994, 2001). Atkinson (1999a) reviews several studies that identify specific linguistic features of scientific writing (e.g., passives, hedges, grammatical subjects). Swales' development of the CARS model for analyzing introduction sections to research articles has led to many subsequent studies and the analyses of many other genre types. This approach has also led to many suggestions for advanced writing instruction in various disciplinary genres. Rhetorical analyses of scientific writing approaches are exemplified by Bazerman's (1991, 1994, 1999) studies of the writing of scientists such as Lewontin & Gould, Priestley, and Edison. The goal of these analyses is to demonstrate how knowledge is constructed not only empirically but also rhetorically. A final area of research has involved the development of science writing over longer periods of historical time (Atkinson 1999b).

Technology in applied linguistics
In this last sub-section of current directions in Applied Linguistics, I will not signpost specific studies and reviews that are available, partly because it is very challenging to keep up with all areas of technology applications, partly because technology uses have been incorporated into discussions in other sections of this review, and partly because many of the technology opportunities are still in the realm of potential rather than established successful outcomes.

Technology is permeating many areas of applied linguistics research, from corpus linguistics, to new statistical options for research, to natural language processing applications in assessment, and to on-line processing experiments and modeling of learning behavior. In these areas, the promise of technology is fairly well established if still only in early stages of applications. In future years, all well-trained practicing applied linguists will need to be comfortable with various aspects of computer uses as well as other innovative technologies for research

Technology applications in language learning are still located somewhere between the realm of potential, on the one hand, and widespread use and acceptance, on the other. CALL approaches and techniques have developed considerably from being one step removed from book versions. The uses of local area networks, the internet, and e-mail have led to major changes in opportunities for task-based and content-based instruction (Egbert & Hanson-Smith 1999). These changes are accelerating with faster computers, expanded memory, and wider bandwidth access to the internet. With computers becoming less expensive every few months, it will soon be possible to expect almost all students to have computers and be skilled in using them (at least in North America). A response that is commonly heard about the growth of technology in language learning and teaching is that technology does not necessarily provide better learning or better teaching. However, this argument misses the point that the technologies will some day be a part of students' knowledge and students' expectations, regardless of its demonstrated effectiveness. Most students do not want to feel that they are learning in an environment that is "behind the times".

One of the most obvious problems that arises out of such an educational scenario is how to train teachers to use new technologies, no less to keep up with their students. This is a serious problem now and it is likely to become a major issue in teacher training within a decade. At issue is not how to train teachers to learn any specific technology but how teachers will learn 'how to learn about technologies' on a continual basis. How such teacher training will be carried out is an open question, but one that will become more and more pressing with each passing year. It is also a site that is ideal for innovation-process research.

A final issue with respect to technology is the problem of fair and equal access to technologies and resources, both within classes and schools and across differing educational systems. With the increasing uses of technologies in schools, and subsequent expectations for skills that can be applied to disciplinary training and work skills, those students who do not have access to expected technologies will be in double jeopardy; they will have less access to technologies while learning language, and they will have fewer technology skills that will be expected by others following language training. How this problem will be addressed by differing institutions and educational systems is also an open question, but this issue will need to be addressed at some point in the future if there is to be greater fairness in language learning opportunities. Of course, there will always be new technologies coming along, and how new technologies will impact language teaching and language research is beyond anyone's crystal ball gazing at this time.

Applied linguistics and problem solving

Applied linguists are problem solvers and they try to solve language problems. The research areas reported on above represent such efforts to solve problems in areas of language knowledge, language learning, language uses, language assessment, and language policies. Which applied linguistics themes will increase in importance as major issues is a topic that certainly is speculative, but one that is nonetheless worth attempting. In reflecting on the current state of Applied Linguistics in North America, it is evident that some issues will continue as major enterprises, such as SLA, language assessment, language policy and planning, and bilingualism/bilingual education. Other issues that will grow in prominence include the following (as a brave guess).

Technology uses and the consequences of technology applications will only become more important, as I argued above. When technology will change from a site of interesting applications to a fundamental problem of access for all language learners is a good question. (I do not have an answer, but having applied linguists address this issue as a research topic would be welcome.) A second area that will grow in importance is the role of descriptive linguistics as a foundation for applied linguistic work. As much as practicing applied linguists may be fascinated by formal linguistic theories (of many stripes), the wasted effort that comes from collecting theory-internal data and the lack of application of these theories to real world problems will make formal theories more of a luxury for applied linguists than a necessity. (This view does not mean that all applied linguists can afford to ignore formal linguistic theory, but formal research in the name of Applied Linguistics needs to be well justified at the level of realistic problem-solving activity.) A third area will involve increasing emphasis on new approaches to research and a wider recognition that quantitative versus qualitative debates are pointless. Both research approaches are sometimes done well and sometimes done badly. They are complementary approaches that serve complementary purposes, and when done well, each has an important role to play (Duff 2002).

A fourth area that will be a growing focus of interest is studies of expertise and its development, and its translation into learning expertise, teaching expertise, and expertise in the various ways that language is used professionally and socially (see, e.g., Ferrari 2002). Because expertise research represents the upper end of research on individual differences, expertise research should be easily adaptable to applied linguistics contexts. A fifth area that will gain increasing attention will be research on innovation itself. Innovation research is already well established in many fields. With the growing speed of change in all areas of Applied Linguistics and an increasing need to adapt quickly, research on innovation processes will become an important tool for applied linguists (Fullan 1993, 2000; Markee 1997). Sixth, increasing attention will be given to issues of fairness, access, and ethics in all areas where applied linguists carry out research and engage in applied linguistic practices. Seventh and finally, an area of growing importance will center on how to train applied linguistics students to engage in language-based problems and issues in a rapidly changing world. Increasing informational resources, increasing technical demands on researchers, increasingly complex issues and research approaches, and new questions that arise, make the training of future applied linguists a challenging undertaking. How various applied linguistics programs do this, and do this well, will represent an interesting challenge.

Conclusion

One of the difficulties of writing an extended overview of Applied Linguistics is that the survey demands are overly broad, and even then, many issues and researchers do not receive a deserved mention. In touching upon so many areas, and doing one's best to understand the full scope of issues under consideration, it is easy to become a collector of many ideas but a master of none. In this article, I have decided that I would try to map out a territory, that being Applied Linguistics in North America, rather than address three or four topics in some detail primarily because I personally have some connections and interests in these issues. Providing a map means that key issues and references are only signposted and noted for their importance, though I am aware that such signposting can sometimes devolve into dull reading. So I make my apology here. This article would need to be a full book if each area in this review included descriptions of specific studies; instead, the interested reader will need to do the detailed exploration on his or her own.

Now that I have offered an apology, I will also say that there is a necessary place for broad overviews. There are times when one needs to step back and try to see the forest that we reside in rather than grow a few new trees. If there are not any specific trees grown in this overview, I hope that the forest at least seems to be an appealing place to do one's work.

Notes

* I would like to thank my colleagues Bill Crawford, Mary McGroarty, and Fredricka Stoller for feedback on various aspects of this review.

1. This review is indeed a personal perspective, and all the limitations one might expect from a singular perspective readily apply. One can only cover so much territory, and the scope of this review inevitably reveals many gaps in my personal knowledge of the field. I am sure that I have inadvertently overlooked much important work by North American Applied Linguists and I apologize for this beforehand. I also do not cover applied linguistics research in Mexico except peripherally. There is a strong applied linguistics tradition in Mexico, but I do not read Spanish and most publications of their work are in Spanish and published in Mexico.

2. I intentionally refer to AAAL as a North American applied linguistics organization. While many would see it as a US organization, it has had two Canadian Presidents since 1998, and three other Canadians have served on the Executive Committee since that time. AAAL is also recognized by many Applied Linguists in Canada as their major organization and conference. AAAL held its annual conference in 2000 in Canada and currently intends to hold its 2006 conference in Canada. The statement endorsed by AAAL on applied linguistic activity in North America was originally used to request recognition of Applied Linguistics as a research discipline by the National Research Council of the US government. However, in drafting the document, one member of the committee was Canadian, and this person provided important input into the document. Interested readers should contact AAAL to request a copy of the statement.

3. While I have tried hard to limit my references to North American scholars, I must transport Henry Widdowson temporarily, with apologies, to refer to his critical discussions of corpus linguistics. His commentary on corpus linguistics and its applications is unique in its analyses of corpora as resources for language learning and language teaching.

References

Alvermann, D. and A. J. Eakle. (2003). Comprehension instruction: Adolescents and their multiple literacies. In A. Sweet and C. Snow (eds), *Rethinking reading comprehension*, pp. 12–29. New York: Guilford.

Atkinson, D. (1999a). Language and science. *Annual Review of Applied Linguistics* 19: 193–214.

Atkinson, D. (1999b). *Scientific discourse in sociohistorical context*. Mahwah, NJ: Lawrence Erlbaum.

Bachman, L. (2000). Modern language testing at the turn of the century: Assuring that what get counted counts. *Language Testing* 17: 1–42.

Bachman, L. (2002). Some reflections on task-based language performance assessment. *Language Testing* 19: 453–476.

Bachman, L. and A. Palmer (1996). *Language testing in practice*. Oxford: Oxford University Press.

Bailey, K. (1996). The best laid plans: Teachers' in-class decisions to depart from their lesson plans. In K. Bailey and D. Nunan (eds), *Voices from the language classroom*, pp. 15–40. Cambridge: Cambridge University Press.

Bailey, K. (2001). Action research, teacher research, and classroom research in language teaching. In M. Celce-Murcia (ed.), *Teaching English as a second or foreign language* (3rd ed.), pp. 489–498. Boston: Heinle & Heinle.

Baker, C. (2003). Education as a site of language contact. *Annual Review of Applied Linguistics* 23: 95–112.

Bardovi-Harlig, K. (1999). The interlanguage of interlanguage pragmatics: A research agenda for acquisitional pragmatics. *Language Learning* 49: 677–713.

Bardovi-Harlig, K. (2002). Pragmatics and second language acquisition. In R. B. Kaplan (ed.), *The Oxford handbook of applied linguistics*, pp. 182–192. Oxford: Oxford University Press.

Bayley, R. and D. Preston. (eds) (1996). *Second language acquisition and linguistic variation*. Amsterdam: John Benjamins.

Bazerman, C. (1991). How natural philosophers can cooperate: The literary technology of coordinated investigation in Joseph Priestly's *History and present state of electricity (1767)*. In C. Bazerman and J. Paradis (eds), *Textual dynamics of the profession*, pp. 13–44. Madison: University of Wisconsin Press.

Bazerman, C. (1994). *Constructing experience*. Carbondale: Southern Illinois University Press.

Bazerman, C. (1999). *The language of Edison's light*. Cambridge, MA: MIT Press.

Bazerman, C. (2001). Nuclear information: One rhetorical moment in the construction of the information age. *Written Communication* 18: 259–295.

Beaujot, R. (1998). Demographic considerations in Canadian language policy. In T. Ricento and B. Burnaby (eds), *Language and politics in the United States and Canada*, pp. 71–83. Mahwah, NJ: Lawrence Erlbaum.

Belcher, D. and A. Hirvela (eds) (2001). *Linking literacies: Perspectives on L2 reading-writing connections*. Ann Arbor, MI: University of Michigan Press.

Benesch, S. (1999). Thinking critically, thinking dialogically. *TESOL Quarterly* 33: 573–580.

Benesch, S. (2001). *Critical English for academic purposes: Theory, politics, and practice*. Mahwah, NJ: Lawrence Erlbaum.

Berk-Seligson, S. (1990). *The bilingual courtroom: Court interpreters in the judicial process*. Chicago: University of Chicago Press.

Berk-Seligson, S. (1999). The impact of court interpreting on the coerciveness of leading questions. *Forensic Linguistics* 6: 30–56.

Berk-Seligson, S. (2000). Interpreting for the police: Issues in pre-trial phases of the judicial process. *Forensic Linguistics* 7: 212–237.

Bernhardt, E. (2000). Second-langauge reading as a case study of reading scholarship in the 20th century. In M. Kamil, P. Mosenthal, P. D. Pearson and R. Barr (eds), *Handbook of reading research* (Vol 3), pp. 791–811. Mahwah, NJ: Lawrence Erlbaum.

Bernhardt, E. (2003). Challenges to reading research from a multilingual world. *Reading Research Quarterly* 38: 112–117.

Bialystok, E. (2001). *Bilingualism in development: Language, literacy & Cognition*. Cambridge: Cambridge University Press.

Biber, D., S. Conrad and R. Reppen. (1998). *Corpus linguistics: Investigating language structure and use*. Cambridge: Cambridge University Press.

Biber, D., S. Johansson, S., Conrad and E. Finegan. (1998). *Longman grammar of spoken and written English*. London: Longman.

Boxer, D. (2002). Discourse issues in cross-cultural pragmatics. *Annual Review of Applied Linguistics* 22: 150–167.

Brinton, D., A. Snow and M. Wesche. (1989). *Content-based second language instruction*. Rowley, MA: Newbury House.

Brown, J. D., T. Hudson, J. Norris and W. Bonk. (2002). *An investigation of second language task-based performance assessment*. Honolulu, HI: University of Hawaii, Second Language Teaching and Curriculum Center.

Brown, H. D. (2000). *Principles of language learning and teaching* (4th ed.). White Plains, NY: Longman.

Burstein, J. and M. Chodorow. (2002). Directions in automated essay scoring. In R. B. Kaplan (ed.), *The Oxford handbook of applied linguistics*, pp. 487–497. Oxford: Oxford University Press.

Canagarajah, A. S. (1999). *Resisting linguistic imperialism in English teaching*. Oxford: Oxford University Press.

Canagarajah, A. S. (2002). *Critical academic writing and multilingual students*. Ann Arbor, MI: University of Michigan Press.

Carrell, P. and W. Grabe. (2002). Reading. In N. Schmitt (ed.), *An introduction to applied linguistics*. London: Arnold.

Casanave, C. (2004). *Controversies in second language writing*. Ann Arbor, MI: University of Michigan Press.

Celce-Murcia, M. (ed.) (2001). *Teaching English as a second or foreign language* (3rd ed.). Boston: Heinle & Heinle.

Chalhoub-Deville, M. (ed.) (1999). *Issues in computer-adaptive testing of reading proficiency*. Cambridge: Cambridge University Press.

Chalhoub-Deville, M. and C. Deville. (1999). Computer adaptive testing in second language contexts. *Annual Review of Applied Linguistics* 19: 273–299.

Chamot, A. U. (2001). The role of learning strategies in second language acquisition. In M. Breen (ed.), *Learner contributions to language learning*, pp. 25–43. London: Longman.

Chamot, A. U. and M. O'Malley. (1994). *The CALLA handbook*. New York: Addison-Wesley Longman.

Chapelle, C. (1999). Validity in language assessment. *Annual Review of Applied Linguistics* 19: 254–272.

Chapelle, C. (2002). Computer-assisted language learning. In R. B. Kaplan (ed.), *The Oxford handbook of applied linguistics*, pp. 498–505. Oxford: Oxford University Press.

Cicourel, A. (1992). The interpenetration of communicative contexts: Examples from medical encounters. In A. Duranti and C. Goodwin (eds), *Rethinking context: Language as an interactive phenomenon*, pp. 291–310. Cambridge: Cambridge University Press.

Cohen, A. (1998). *Strategies in learning and using a second language*. London: Longman.

Conley, J. and W. O'Barr. (1990). *Rules and relationships: The ethnography of legal discourse*. Chicago: University of Chicago Press.

Conley, J. and W. O'Barr. (1998). *Just words: Law, language and power*. Chicago: University of Chicago Press.

Conrad, S. (2002). Corpus linguistics approach for discourse analysis. *Annual Review of Applied Linguistics* 22: 75–95.

Conrad, S. and D. Biber (eds) (2001). *Variation in English: Multi-dimensional studies*. Harlow, Essex: Longman.

Cook, G. (2003). *Applied linguistics*. Oxford: Oxford University Press.

Crandall, J. (ed.) (1987). *ESL through content area instruction: Mathematics, science, social science*. Englewood Cliffs, NJ: Prentice Hall Regents/Center for Applied Linguistics.

Crandall, J. (2000a). Language teacher education. *Annual Review of Applied Linguistics* 20: 34–55.

Crandall, J. (2000b). The role of the university in preparing teachers for a linguistically diverse society. In J. Rosenthal (ed.), *Handbook of undergraduate second language education*, pp. 279–299. Mahwah, NJ: Lawrence Erlbaum.

Crawford, J. (2000). *At war with diversity: U. S. language policy in an age of anxiety*. Clevedon: Multilingual Matters.

Crawford, J. (2003). James Crawford's language policy website. Available: http://ourworld.compuserve.com/homepages/JWCRAWFORD/. [Retrieved 2003, December 1].

Cummins, J. (2000). *Language, power and pedagogy: Bilingual children in the crossfire*. Clevedon: Multilingual Matters.

de Bot, K. (2000). Psycholinguistics in applied linguistics: Trends and perspectives. *Annual Review of Applied Linguistics* 20: 224–237.

Dörnyei, Z. and R. Schmidt (eds) (2001). *Motivation and second language acquisition* (Technical report #23). Honolulu, HI: University of Hawaii, Second Language Teaching and Curriculum Center.

Doughty, C. and J. Williams (eds) (1998). *Focus on form in classroom second language acquisition*. Cambridge: Cambridge University Press.

Duff, P. (2002). Research approaches in applied linguistics. In R. B. Kaplan (ed.), *The Oxford handbook of applied linguistics*, pp. 13–23. Oxford: Oxford University Press.

Duff, P. and Y. Uchida. (1997). The negotiation of teachers' scoiocultural identities and practices in post-secondary EFL classrooms. *TESOL Quarterly 31*: 451–486.

Dumas, B. (2000). U. S. pattern jury instructions: Problems and proposals. *Forensic Linguistics 7*: 49–71.

Edwards, J. (ed.) (1998). *Language in Canada*. Cambridge: Cambridge University Press.

Egbert, J. and E. Hanson-Smith (eds.) (1999). *CALL environments: Research, practice, and critical issues.* Alexandria, VA: TESOL.

Eggington, W. (2002). Unplanned language planning. In R.B. Kaplan (ed.), *The Oxford handbook of applied linguistics*, pp. 404–415. Oxford: Oxford University Press.

Ellis, N. and R. Schmidt. (1997). Morphology and longer distance dependencies: Laboratory research illuminating the A in SLA. *Studies in Second Language Acquisition* 19: 145–171.

Eubank, L. and A. Juffs. (2000). Recent research on the acquisition of L2 competence: Morphosyntax and argument structure. In L. Cheng and R. Sybesma (eds), *The first GLOT international state-of-the-art book: The latest in linguistics*, pp. 131–170. Berlin: Mouton de Gruyter.

Faltis, C. and P. Wolfe (eds) (1999). *So much to say: Adolescents, bilingualism, and ESL in the secondary school.* New York: Teacher's College Press.

Ferrari, M. (ed.) (2002). *The pursuit of excellence through education.* Mahwah, NJ: Lawrence Erlbaum.

Ferris, D. and J. Hedgcock. (1998). *Teaching ESL composition.* Mahwah, NJ: Lawrence Erlbaum.

Fichera, V. and H.S. Straight (eds) (1997). *Using language across the curriculum.* Binghamton, NY: SUNY Binghamton, Center for Research in Translation.

Fisher, S. (1995). *Nursing wounds: Nurse practitioners, doctors, women patients and the negotiation of meaning.* New Brunswick, NJ: Rutgers University Press.

Fishman, J. (1991). *Reversing language shift: Theoretical and empirical foundations of assistance to threatened languages.* Clevedon: Multilingual Matters.

Fishman, J. (2001). Why is it so hard to save a threatened language? In J. Fishman (ed.), *Can threatened languages be saved?*, pp. 1–22. Clevedon: Multilingual Matters.

Fitzgerald, J. (2003). Multilingual reading theory. *Reading Research Quarterly* 38: 118–122.

Flege, J., M. Munro and I. MacKay. (1995). Factors affecting degree of perceived foreign accent in a second language. *Journal of the Acoustical Society of America* 97: 3125–3134.

Foltz, P., W. Kintsch and T. Landauer. (1998). The measurement of textual coherence with latent semantic analysis. *Discourse Processes* 25: 285–307.

Francis, N. and J. Reyhner. (2002). *Language and literacy teaching for indigenous education.* Clevedon: Multilingual Matters.

Frank, A. (1995). *The wounded storyteller: Body, illness, and ethics.* Chicago: University of Chicago Press.

Frawley, W. and J. Lantolf. (1985). Second language discourse: A Vygotskean perspective. *Applied Linguistics* 6: 19–44.

Freeman, D. and K. Johnson. (1998). Reconceptualizing the knowledge base of language teacher education. *TESOL Quarterly* 32: 397–417.

Fullan, M. (1993). *Change forces: Probing the depth of educational reform.* London: Falmer.

Fullan, M. (2000). The return of large-scale reform. *Journal of Educational Change* 1: 1–23.

Garcia, G. (2000). Bilingual children's reading. In M. Kamil, P. Mosenthal, P.D. Pearson and R. Barr (eds), *Handbook of reading research* (Vol 3), pp. 813–834. Mahwah, NJ: Lawrence Erlbaum.

Garcia, G. (2003). The reading comprehension development and instruction of English-language learners. In A. Sweet and C. Snow (eds), *Rethinking reading comprehension*, pp. 30–50. New York: Guilford.

Garcia, M. (2003). Recent research on language maintenance. *Annual Review of Applied Linguistic* 23: 3–21.

Gardner, R. (2000). Correlation, causation, motivation and second language acquisition. *Canadian Psychology* 41: 10–24.

Gardner, R. (2002). Social psychological perspective on second language acquisition. In R.B. Kaplan (ed.), *The Oxford handbook of applied linguistics*, pp. 160–169. Oxford: Oxford University Press.

Gass, S. (2000). Fundamentals of second language acquisition. In J. Rosenthal (ed.), *Handbook of undergraduate second language education*, pp. 29–46. Mahwah, NJ: Lawrence Erlbaum.

Gass, S. (2002). An interactionist perspective on second language acquisition. In R.B. Kaplan (ed.), *The Oxford handbook of applied linguistics*, pp. 170–181. Oxford: Oxford University Press.

Gass, S., A. Mackey and T. Pica. (1998). The role of input and interaction in second language acquisition: Introduction to the special issue. *Modern Language Journal* 82: 299–307.

Genesee, F. (2001). Bilingual first language acquisition. *Annual Review of Applied Linguistics* 21: 153–168.

Geva, E. and L. Siegal. (2000). Orthographic and cognitive factors in the concurrent development of basic reading skills in two languages. *Reading and Writing: An Interdisciplinary Journal* 12: 1–30.

Gonzalez, R., V. Vasquez and H. Mikkelson. (1991). *Fundamentals of court interpretation.* Durham: Carolina Academic Press.

Grabe, W. (2002). Applied linguistics: An emerging discipline for the twenty-first century. In R.B. Kaplan (ed.), *The Oxford handbook of applied linguistics*, pp. 3–12. Oxford: Oxford University Press.

Grabe, W. and F. Stoller. (2002). *Teaching and researching reading.* London: Longman.

Hall, J.K., (1993). The role of oral practices in the accomplishment of our everyday lives: The sociocultural dimension of interaction with implications for the learning of another language. *Applied Linguistics* 14: 145–166.

Hall, J.K. and L. Verplaeste (eds) (2000). *Second and foreign language learning through classroom instruction.* Mahwah, NJ: Lawrence Erlbaum.

Hall, J.K. and M. Walsh. (2002). Teacher-student interaction and language learning. *Annual Review of Applied Linguistics* 22: 186–203.

Harklau, L. (2002). The role of writing in classroom second language acquisition. *Journal of Second Language Writing* 11: 329–350.

Harrington, M. (2002). Cognitive perspectives on second language acquisition. In R.B. Kaplan (ed.), *The Oxford handbook of applied linguistics*, pp. 124–140. Oxford: Oxford University Press.

Hawkins, R. (2001). The theoretical significance of Universal Grammar in second language acquisition. *Second Language Research* 21: 345–367.

Hinkel, E. (2002). *Second language writers' text.* Mahwah, NJ: Lawrence Erlbaum.

Hinton, L. (2003). Language revitalization. *Annual Review of Applied Linguistics* 23: 44–57.

Hinton, L. and K. Hale (eds) (2001). *The green book of language revitalization in practice.* San Diego: Academic Press.

Horwitz, E. (2001). Language anxiety and achievement. *Annual Review of Applied Linguistics* 21: 112–126.

House, D. (2002). *Language shift among the Navajos.* Tucson, AZ: University of Arizona Press.

Hunter, M. (1991). *Doctor's stories: The narrative structure of medical knowledge.* Princeton: Princeton University Press.

Hyden, L. and E. Mishler. (1999). Language and medicine. *Annual Review of Applied Linguistics* 19: 174–192.

Ignash, J. (2000). Linguistic diversity, immigration, and today's undergraduates: Demographics. In J. Rosenthal (ed.), *Handbook of undergraduate second language education*, pp. 3–27. Mahwah, NJ: Lawrence Erlbaum.

Jiang, N. (2002). Form-meaning mapping in vocabulary acquisition in a second language. *Studies in Second Language Acquisition* 24: 617–637.

Jimenez, R. (2003). Literacy and Latino students in the United States: Some considerations, questions, and new directions. *Reading Research Quarterly* 38: 122–128.

Johns, A. (1997). *Text, role, and context.* Cambridge: Cambridge University Press.

Johns, A. (ed.) (2001). *Genre in the classroom.* Mahwah, NJ: Lawrence Erlbaum.

Johnson, K. (ed.) (2000) *Teacher education.* Alexandria, VA: TESOL.

Johnston, B. (1999). Putting critical pedagogy in its place: A personal account. *TESOL Quarterly* 33: 557–565.

Juffs, A. (2002). Formal linguistics perspectives on second language acquisition. In R.B. Kaplan (ed.), *The Oxford handbook of applied linguistics*, pp. 87–103. Oxford: Oxford University Press.

Juffs, A. (2004). Representation, processing and working memory in a second language. *The Transactions of the Philological Society.* In press.

Kachru, B.B. (ed.) (1992). *The other tongue — English across cultures* (2nd ed.) Urbana, IL: University of Illinois Press.

Kachru, B.B. (1997). World Englishes and English-using communities. *Annual Review of Applied Linguistics: Multilingualism* 17: 66–87.

Kachru, B.B. and L E. Smith (eds) (1982–2004). *World Englishes.*

Kandil, M. and N. Jiang. (2003, October). *Language switching costs: Role of scripts.* Paper presented at the 26th annual Second Language Research Forum. University of Arizona, Tucson, AZ.

Kaplan, R.B. (ed.) (2002). *The Oxford handbook of applied linguistics.* Oxford: Oxford University Press.

Kaplan, R.B. and R. Baldauf. (1997). *Language planning: From practice to theory.* Clevedon: Multilingual Matters.

Kasper, G. and K. Rose (eds) (2002). *Pragmatic development in a second language. Language Learning* 52, Supplement 1.

Kern, R. (2000). *Literacy and language teaching*. Oxford: Oxford University Press.

Klee, C. (2000). Foreign language instruction. In J. Rosenthal (ed.), *Handbook of undergraduate second language education*, pp. 49–72. Mahwah, NJ: Lawrence Erlbaum.

Kleinman, A. 1988. *The illness narratives: Suffering, healing, and the human condition*. New York: Basic Books.

Koda, K. (2004). *Insight into second language reading*. Cambridge: Cambridge University Press.

Kramsch, C. (1993). *Context and culture in language teaching*. Oxford: Oxford University Press.

Kramsch, C. (2000). Second language acquisition, applied linguistics, and the teaching of foreign languages. *Modern Language Journal* 84: 311–326.

Kramsch, C. (2002). Standard, norm, and variability in language learning. In S. Gass, K. Bardovi-Harlig, S. Magnan and J. Walz (eds), *Pedagogical norms for second and foreign language learning and teaching*, pp. 59–79. Clevedon: Multilingual Matters.

Kroll, J., E. Michael, N. Tokowicz and R. Dufour. (2002). The development of lexical fluency in a second language. *Second Language Research* 18: 137–171.

Kroll, B. (ed.) (2003). *Exploring the dynamics of second language writing*. Cambridge: Cambridge University Press.

Krueger, M. and F. Ryan (eds) (1993). *Language and content: Discipline-based approaches to language study*. Lexington, MA: Heath.

Kumaravadivelu, B. (1999). Critical classroom discourse analysis. *TESOL Quarterly* 33: 453–484.

Kumaravadivelu, B. (2001). Toward a postmethod pedagogy. *TESOL Quarterly* 35: 537–560.

Kunnan, A. (1998). Approaches to validation in language assessment. In A. Kunnan (ed.), *Validation in language assessment*, pp. 1–16. Mahwah, NJ: Lawrence Erlbaum.

Kunnan, A. (ed.) (1999). *Fairness and validation in language assessment*. Cambridge: Cambridge University Press.

Landauer, T., P. Foltz and D. Laham. (1998). An introduction to latent semantic analysis. *Discourse Processes* 25: 259–284.

Lantolf, J. (ed.) (2000). *Sociocultural theory and second language learning*. Oxford: Oxford University Press.

Lantolf, J. (2002). Sociocultural theory and second language acquisition. In R. B. Kaplan (ed.), *The Oxford handbook of applied linguistics*, pp. 104–114. Oxford: Oxford University Press.

Lantolf, J. and G. Appel (eds) (1994). *Vygotskean approaches to second language research*. Norwood, NJ: Ablex.

Larsen-Freeman, D. (2000). Second language acquisition and applied linguistics. *Annual Review of Applied Linguistics* 20: 165–181.

Larsen-Freeman, D. (2001). Individual cognitive/affective learner contributions and differential success in second language acquisition. In M. Breen (ed.), *Learner contributions to language learning*, pp. 12–24. London: Longman.

Lightbown, P. (1998). The importance of timing in focus on form. In C. Doughty and J. Williams (eds), *Focus on form in classroom second language acquisition*, pp. 177–196. Cambridge: Cambridge University Press.

Lightbown, P. and N. Spada. (1999). *How languages are learned* (2nd ed.). Oxford: Oxford University Press.

Long, M. (1996). The role of linguistic environment in second language acquisition. In W. Ritchie and T. Bhatia (eds), *Handbook of second language acquisition*, pp. 413–468. San Diego: Academic Press.

Luke, A. (2002). Beyond science and ideology critique: Developments in critical discourse analysis. *Annual Review of Applied Linguistics* 22: 96–110.

Mackey, A. (1999). Input, interaction, and second language development. *Studies in Second Language Acquisition* 21: 557–587.

MacWhinney, B. (1997). Second language acquisition and the competition model. In A. de Groot and J. Kroll (eds), *Tutorials in bilingualism*, pp. 113–142. Mahwah, NJ: Lawrence Erlbaum.

Major, R. (2001). *Foreign accent: The ontogeny and phylogeny of second language phonology*. Mahwah, NJ: Lawrence Erlbaum.

Markee, N. (1997). *Managing curricular innovation*. Cambridge: Cambridge University Press.

Masgoret, A.-M. and R. Gardner. (2003). Attitudes, motivation, and second language learning: A meta-analysis of studies conducted by Gardner and associates. *Language Learning* 53: 123–163.

McCafferty, S. (1992). The use of private speech by adult second language learners: A cross-cultural study. *Modern Language Journal* 76: 179–189.

McCarthy, M. (2001). *Issues in applied linguistics*. Cambridge: Cambridge University Press.

McCarty, T. (2002). *A place to be Navajo: Rough Rock and the struggle for self-determination in indigenous schooling.* Mahwah, NJ: Lawrence Erlbaum.

McGroarty, M. (2002). Language uses in professional contexts. In R. B. Kaplan (ed.), *The Oxford handbook of applied linguistics*, pp. 262–274. Oxford: Oxford University Press.

McGroarty, M. (2003). Half full, half empty, or not the half of it? *Modern Language Journal* 87: 586–588.

Merino, B. and L. Hammond. (2002). Writing to learn: Science in the upper-elementary bilingual classroom. In M. Schleppegrell and M. C. Colombi (eds), *Developing advanced literacy in first and second languages*, pp. 227–243. Mahwah, NJ: Lawrence Erlbaum.

Messick, S. (1989). Validity. In R. Linn (ed.), *Educational measurement*, pp. 13–103. New York: Macmillan.

Met, M. (1993). Second language learning in magnet school contexts. *Annual Review of Applied Linguistics* 13: 71–85.

Met, M. (2003). Developing language education policies for our schools. *Modern Language Journal* 87: 589–592.

Met, M. and E. Lorenz. (1997). Lessons from U. S. immersion programs: Two decades of experience. In R. K. Johnson and M. Swain (eds), *Immersion education: International perspectives*, pp. 243–264. Cambridge: Cambridge University Press.

Meyer, C. (1992). *Apposition in contemporary American English.* Cambridge: Cambridge University Press.

Mislevy, R., L. Steinberg and R. Almond. (1998, November). *On the roles of task model variables in assessment design.* Paper presented at conference on generating items for cognitive texts: Theory and practice. Princeton, NJ: Educational Testing Service.

Mislevy, R., L. Steinberg and R. Almond. (2002). Design and analysis in task-based language assessment. *Language Testing* 19: 477–496.

Mohan, B. (1986). *Language and content.* Reading, MA: Addison-Wesley.

Moll, L. (ed.) (1990). *Vygotsky and education: Instructional implications and applications of sociohistorical psychology.* Cambridge: Cambridge University Press.

Norris, J. (2001). Identifying rating criteria for task-based EAP assessment. In T. Hudson and J. D. Brown (eds), *A focus on language test development: Expanding the language proficiency construct across a variety of texts*, pp. 163–204. Honolulu, HI: University of Hawaii, Second Language Teaching and Curriculum Center.

Norris, J., J. D. Brown, T. Hudson, and J. Yoshioka. (1998). *Designing second language performance assessments.* Honolulu, HI: University of Hawaii, Second language Teaching and Curriculum Center.

Norris, J. and L. Ortega. (2000). Effectiveness of L2 instruction: A research synthesis and quantitative meta-analysis. *Language Learning* 50: 417–528.

Norton, B. (2000). *Identity and language learning: Gender, ethnicity and educational change.* London: Longman.

Norton, B. (2001). Non-participation, imagined communities and the language classroom. In M. Breen (ed.), *Learner contributions to language learning*, pp. 159–182. London: Longman.

Norton, B. and K. Toohey. (2002). Identity and language learning. In R. B. Kaplan (ed.), *The Oxford handbook of applied linguistics*, pp. 115–123. Oxford: Oxford University Press.

Odlin, T. (2003).Cross-linguistic influence. In C. Doughty and M. Long (eds), *Handbook of second language acquisition*, pp. 436–486. Malden, MA: Blackwell.

Oxford, R. (1996). *Language learning strategies around the world: Cross-cultural perspectives.* Honolulu, HI: University of Hawaii, Second Language Teaching and Curriculum Center.

Oxford, R. (2000). ESL/EFL learning strategies: Synthesis of research. In R. Carter and D. Nunan (eds), *English language teaching handbook*, pp. 166–172. Cambridge: Cambridge University Press.

Oxford, R. (2002). Sources of variation in language learning. In R. B. Kaplan (ed.), *The Oxford handbook of applied linguistics*, pp. 245–252. Oxford: Oxford University Press.

Perfetti, C., J. Van Dyke and L. Hart. (2001). The psycholinguistics of basic literacy. *Annual Review of Applied Linguistics* 21: 127–149.

Peyton, J. K., S. McGinnis and D. Ranard (eds) (2001). *Heritage languages in America.* McHenry, IL: Delta Systems/Center for Applied Linguistics.

Phillips, J. K. (2003). Implications of language education policies for language study in schools and universities. *Modern Language Journal* 87: 579–586.

Poole, D. (2002). Discourse analysis and applied linguistics. In R. B. Kaplan (ed.), *The Oxford handbook of applied linguistics*, pp. 73–84. Oxford: Oxford University Press.

Powers, D., J. Burstein, M. Chodorow, M. Fowles, K. Kukich. (2002). Stumping *e-rater*: Challenging the validity of automated essay scoring. *Computers in Human Behavior* 18: 103–134.

Preston, D. (2002). A variationist perspective on second language acquisition: Psycholinguistics concerns. In R. B. Kaplan (ed.), *The Oxford handbook of applied linguistics*, pp. 141–159. Oxford: Oxford University Press.

Ricento, T. (1998). National language policy in the United States. In T. Ricento and B. Burnaby (eds), *Language and politics in the United States and Canada*, pp. 85–112. Mahwah, NJ: Lawrence Erlbaum.

Rivera-Mills, S. (2001). Acculturation and communicative need: Language shift in an ethnically diverse Hispanic community. *Southwest Journal of Linguistics* 20: 211–221.

Robinson, P. (ed.) (2001). *Cognition and second language instruction*. Cambridge: Cambridge University Press.

Robinson, P. (ed.) (2002). *Individual differences and instructed language learning*. Philadelphia, PA: John Benjamins.

Rosenbusch, M. (1995). Language learners in the elementary school: Investing in the future. In R. Donato and R. Terry (eds), *Foreign language learning: The journey of a lifetime*, pp. 1–36. Lincolnwood, IL: National Textbook Company.

Scarcella, R. (2002). Some key factors affecting English learners' development of advanced literacy. In M. Schleppegrell and M. C. Colombi (ed.), *Literacy in first and second languages: Meaning with power*, pp. 209–226. Mahwah, NJ: Lawrence Erlbaum.

Schinke-Llano, L. (1993). On the value of a Vygotskean framework for SLA theory and research. *Language Learning* 43: 121–129.

Schmitt, N. (ed.) (2002). *An introduction to applied linguistics*. London: Arnold.

Schumann, J. (1997). *The neurobiology of affect in language*. Boston: Blackwell.

Schumann, J. (2001). Appraisal psychology, neurobiology and language. *Annual Review of Applied Linguistics* 21: 23–42.

Schumann, J., S. Crowell, N. Jones, N. Lee, S. Schuchert and L. Wood. (2004). *The Neurobiology of learning*. Mahwah, NJ: Lawrence Erlbaum.

Schwartz, B. (1999). Let's make up your mind: "Special nativist" perspectives on language, modularity of mind and nonnative language acquisition. *Studies in Second Language Acquisition* 21: 635–655.

Schwartz, B. and R. Sprouse. (2000). When syntactic theories evolve: Consequences for L2 acquisition research. In J. Archibald (ed.), *Second language acquisition and syntactic theory*, pp. 156–186. Oxford: Blackwell.

Schweda-Nicholson, N. (1995). Translation and interpretation. *Annual Review of Applied Linguistics* 15: 42–62.

Schweda-Nicholson, N. (1999). Language policy development for interpreter services at the Executive Office for Immigration Review. *Language Problems & Language Planning* 23: 37–63.

Schweda-Nicholson, N. (2002). Interpretation. In R. B. Kaplan (ed.), *The Oxford handbook of applied linguistics*, pp. 443–456. Oxford: Oxford University Press.

Scovel, T. (2000). A critical review of the critical period research. *Annual Review of Applied Linguistics* 20: 213–223.

Segalowitz, N. (2001). On the evolving connections between psychology and linguistics. *Annual Review of Applied Linguistics* 21: 3–22.

Segalowitz, N. and J. Hulstijn. (In press). Automaticity in bilingualism and second language learning. In J. F. Kroll and A. M. B. De Groot (eds), *Handbook of bilingualism: Psycholinguistic approaches*. Malden, MA: Blackwell.

Segalowitz, N. and P. Lightbown. (1999). Psycholinguistic approaches to SLA. *Annual Review of Applied Linguistics* 19: 43–63.

Seidlhofer, B. (2003). *Controversies in applied linguistics*. Oxford: Oxford University Press.

Shuy, R. (1993). *Language Crimes: The use and abuse of language evidence in the courtroom*. Cambridge, MA: Blackwell.

Shuy, R. (1997). Ten unanswered language questions about Miranda. *Forensic Linguistics* 4: 175–196.

Shuy, R. (1998). *The language of confession, interrogation and deception*. Thousand Oaks, CA: Sage.

Silva, T. and P. Matsuda. (eds) (2001). *On second language writing*. Mahwah, NJ: Lawrence Erlbaum.

Simpson, R. and J. Swales. (eds) (2001). *Corpus linguistics in North America: Selections from the 1999 symposium.* Ann Arbor, MI: University of Michigan Press.

Singleton, D. (2001). Age and second language acquisition. *Annual Review of Applied Linguistics* 21: 77–89.

Solan, L. (1993). *The language of judges.* Chicago: University of Chicago Press.

Spada, N. (1997). Form-focused instruction and second language acquisition: A review of classroom an laboratory research. *Language Teaching* 30: 73–87.

Sparks, D. and L. Ganschow (2001). Aptitude for learning a foreign language. *Annual Review of Applied Linguistics* 21: 90–111.

Stoller, F. (2004). Content-based instruction: Perspectives on curriculum planning. *Annual Review of Applied Linguistics* 24.

Stryker, S. and B. Leaver (eds) (1997). *Content-based instruction in the foreign language classroom.* Washington, DC: Georgetown University Press.

Swain (2000a). The output hypothesis and beyond: Mediating acquisition through collaborative dialogue. In J. Lantolf (ed.), *Sociocultural theory and second language learning*, pp. 97–114. Oxford: Oxford University Press.

Swain, M. (2000b). French immersion research in Canada: Recent contributions to SLA and applied linguistics. *Annual Review of Applied Linguistics* 20: 199–212.

Swain, M., L. Brooks and A. Tocalli-Beller. (2002). Peer-peer dialogue as a means of second language learning. *Annual Review of Applied Linguistics* 22: 171–185.

Swales, J. (1990). *Genre analysis.* Cambridge: Cambridge University Press.

Swales, J. (1998). *Other floors, other voices: A textography of a small university building.* Mahwah, NJ: Lawrence Erlbaum.

Swales, J. (2000). Languages for specific purposes. *Annual Review of Applied Linguistics* 20: 59–76.

Tarone, E. (2000). Still wrestling with 'context' in interlanguage theory. *Annual Review of Applied Linguistics* 20: 182–198.

Tarone, E. and G-Q. Liu. (1995). Situational context, variation and second language acquisition theory. In G. Cook and B. Seidlhofer (eds), *Principle and practice in applied linguistics: Studies in honour of H. G. Widdowson*, pp. 107–124. Oxford: Oxford University Press.

Todd, A. and S. Fisher (eds) (1993). *The social organization of doctor-patient communication* (2nd ed.) Norwood, NJ: Ablex.

Tucker, G. R. (2000). Concluding thoughts: Applied linguistics at the juncture of millennia. *Annual Review of Applied Linguistics* 20: 241–249.

Tucker, G. R. (2003). Language contact and change: Summary observations. *Annual Review of Applied Linguistics* 23: 243–249.

Valdez, G. (2001). *Learning and not learning English: Latino students in American schools.* New York: Teacher's College Press.

Valdes, G. and C. Angelelli. (2003). Interpreters, interpreting and the study of biolingualism. *Annual Review of Applied Linguistics* 23: 58–78.

van Lier, L. (1996). *Interaction in the language classroom.* London: Longman.

VanPatten, B. (ed.) (2003). *Processing instruction.* Mahwah, NJ: Lawrence Erlbaum.

Wells, G. (1999). *Dialogic inquiry: Toward a sociocultural practice and theory of education.* Cambridge: Cambridge University Press.

Wesche, M. B. (2000). A Canadian perspective: Second language teaching and learning in the university. In J. Rosenthal (ed.), *Handbook of undergraduate second language education*, pp. 187–208. Mahwah, NJ: Lawrence Erlbaum.

Wesche, M. B. and P. Skehan. (2002). Communicative, task-based and content-based language instruction. In R. B. Kaplan (ed.), *The Oxford handbook of applied linguistics*, pp. 207–228. Oxford: Oxford University Press.

White, L. (2000). Second language acquisition: From initial state to final state. In J. Archibald (ed.), *Second language acquisition and linguistic theory*, pp. 130–155. Oxford: Blackwell.

Widdowson, H. (1998). The theory and practice of critical discourse analysis: Review article. *Applied Linguistics* 19: 136–151.

Widdowson, H. (2000). Object language and the language subject: on the mediating role of applied linguistics. *Annual Review of Applied Linguistics* 20: 21–33.

Widdowson, H. (2003). *Defining issues in English language teaching*. Oxford: Oxford University Press.

Young, R. (1999). Sociolinguistic approaches to SLA. *Annual Review of Applied Linguistics* 19: 105–132.

Zuengler, J. and J. Mori. (2002). Microanalysis of classroom discourse: A critical consideration of method. *Applied Linguistics* 23: 283–288.

Résumé

Cette vue d'ensemble se concentre principalement sur le travail de la Linguistique Appliquée en Amérique du Nord, et met aussi l'accent sur les publications des six dernières années. Après une courte partie explicative sur la nature et le statut de la Linguistique Appliquée, l'article passe en revue un nombre important de champs de recherche en Linguistique Appliquée. Ceux-ci incluent l'acquisition d'une seconde langue (et ces sous-domaines variés), la recherche sur la lecture et l'écriture d'une seconde langue, l'enseignement et l'apprentissage des langues, la culture et les langues, la linguistique de corpus, les perspectives critiques, l'évaluation des langues, la politique et plannification linguistiques, les usages langagiés dans des contextes professionnels, et la technologie en Linguistique Appliquée. Cette vue d'ensemble se termine par des commentaires sur sept champs possibles concernant le développement de la Linguistique Appliquée, en plus des champs dominants mentionnés ci-dessus.

DISCUSSION

Applied linguistics in 2004

Unity in diversity?

Christopher Brumfit
University of Southampton

This collection of papers offers a fascinating insight into the variety of concerns that characterise applied linguistics at the beginning of the twenty-first century. Although no compilation such as this can expect to be comprehensive in coverage of applied linguistic research, nor even to represent all the major currents of opinion that affect the discipline, the coverage is truly impressive, with political, historical, and social issues appearing just as important as technical and linguistic ones. What may seem, at first sight, to be a surprising concern for non-scientific issues in several papers has to be recognised as one sign of a mature discipline, that is to say, one which has developed its own social infrastructures that provide a solid, but contestable presence in the debates of scholars in many parts of the world.

A brief characterisation of the main concerns of these papers will illustrate the point I am making, for the authors take markedly different views of their task. Two writers, Cavalcanti (Brazil) and de Bot (Europe), take a broadly historical approach, though the latter concentrates more on the ways in which major external historical events have influenced approaches to language-related problems. Kleinsasser (Australia and New Zealand), while he retains some historical dimension, is more concerned with a survey of present practice, particularly through the contents and structure of Masters' courses in applied linguistics. Pakir (Asia) and Makoni & Meinhof (Africa) concentrate more on the relationship between what many applied linguists no doubt think of as the 'centre' (work in the United States, or perhaps in English-language contexts), and the 'periphery' (work outside the major [sometimes ex-] imperial countries, or work on languages other than English). Both papers are concerned to make a political and ideological point, as well as points about natural justice and the well-being of our professional understanding of language, and Makoni & Meinhof particularly show in some detail how 'western' conceptualisations of language impose inappropriate categorisations on language practices observable in Africa.

In contrast, both Bygate (UK) and Grabe (North America) concern themselves with issues internal to the discipline, though still extremely important ones. Bygate raises, for example, issues about the relationship between applied linguistics researchers and the practitioners whom in some sense they must serve, or about the relationship between the researchers' unavoidably subjective interpretations and their 'objective' data. Grabe, in a long and fascinating paper, surveys work in the most active areas of applied linguistics (although, as Pakir would certainly remind us, 'active' among English-using researchers). It is noteworthy, however, that many of those whose work he cites are not themselves of north American origin, may not even have worked for significant periods in north America, but nonetheless present regularly in north American conferences, and publish work that is widely marketed there.

In earlier papers (see Brumfit, 2001, Chapter 14) I have characterised stages through which applied linguistics developed as mediation of linguistics (Corder, 1973), as interdisciplinary interaction (Strevens, 1980), as a technology (Kaplan & Widdowson, 1992), as a methodology (Crystal, 1981), and as an autonomous theoretical and practical discipline (Widdowson, 1979). More recently, the notion of autonomy for any discipline has been challenged, and Pennycook (for example) has argued (1994:303):

AILA Review 17 (2004), 133–136.
ISSN 1461–0213 / E-ISSN 1570–5595 © John Benjamins Publishing Company

> With the gradual consolidation of applied linguistics… there has been a constant move towards educational expertise being defined as in the hands of the predominantly male Western applied linguistics academy, rather than in the hands of the largely female teaching practitioners.

Several points are interesting about this ten-year-old statement when it is set against the papers in this issue of *AILA Review*. First, it seems now to be widely accepted that applied linguistics, even with its origins (as several writers note in this volume) in language teaching, is far wider than language teaching in its scope. Second, the strongest calls for independence are not so much on behalf of practitioners like teachers (though Bygate explores the question of how we integrate practitioner expertise into our research) as on behalf of local, and particularly non-English-speaking, linguists and applied linguists. Furthermore, the reason for this marks something of a return to a central concern with language and, perhaps, a retreat from the frequent cross-disciplinary perspectives of work in the 1980s and 90s — though SLA remained a noteworthy exception to the cross-disciplinary shift. Pakir and Makoni & Meinhoff are most concerned about the concentration on language models with English as default language of reference, monolingualism as the assumed norm, and national identity presumed to be centred on a single powerful state language. Both papers suggest that listening to work with other languages, whether those of powerful states, like Chinese and Japanese, with large non-national speaker populations, like Hindi or Igbo, or for local use mainly with small populations, like Ateso. Yet even in making this statement, we are falling into a trap set for us by Makoni & Meinhof, for we are reifying language continua into particular languages with names, and thus distorting patterns of user behaviour which are not, as we appear to be, constrained by terminology.

There are unavoidably major gaps in this sequence of 'snapshots', as Gass and Makoni describe these papers in their introduction. Since so many papers have accepted the 'social turn' in scholarship, and acknowledge the interplay of history, ideology, economics and politics on any international discipline, it is appropriate to draw attention to the most significant of these gaps. de Bot refers to the absence of Spanish in European deliberations, and nothing here from the Spanish-speaking world is only partly compensated for by the Latin-American experience reported by Cavalcanti from Brazil. de Bot also comments on the decline of Russian-learning numbers in eastern Europe; there are strong traditions of applied linguistic research to draw upon that were centred on Russian-language publications. Perhaps it is too early to understand the complexities of developing scholarship in the post-Soviet Russian-speaking world. But both the relationship between Russian and western European languages after the changes in the EU, and the whole spectrum of linguistic practices in central Asia is a rich area for local research that needs wider international publication.

But Russia is in a new position not just because of the implosion of the Soviet Union, but also because of its significant cultural and political role in a post 9/11 world. And the greatest absentee from this feast of applied linguistic work is Islamic and/or Arabic-using scholarship. The calls that have come strongly from Africa and Asia for a greater voice in international applied linguistic work apply equally to Arabic work. Since the first major increase in oil prices there has been massive investment in education, English-teaching and advanced training for Arabic-speaking students. It is difficult to gather information about activity across such a large, and politically diverse part of the world, but it is clear that there are thoughtful discussions about (for example) the role of English in Islamic countries, the positions that teachers need to adopt for local needs, and language and identity. Major works on such topics (e.g., Suleiman, 2003) are readily available to international scholarship, but a strong sense of local work is absent, and can only be obtained from websites which come and go.

It is clear, though, and perhaps surprising, that the diversity does not reflect a discipline falling apart. From the strongly language-centred work on SLA to work on language policy, both described in Grabe's and Kleinsasser's papers, from the calls for a reworking of our conceptions of language by Pakir and Makoni & Meinhoff, and from the descriptions of dilemmas for researchers explored by Bygate, the discipline is recognisably an exploration of language practices and of real-world problems in which language is central. Although there have been striking changes since the work of the early-modern period (as we might characterise it now) of the 1960s, we appear to have developed a striking international shared agenda. In some parts of the world it centres more on language teaching issues than in others, and everywhere it is subject to market-forces, funding constraints and constraints imposed by political concerns, but none of the issues raised (with strong links to events in European history) by de Bot would be alien to researchers in other parts of the world, though priorities and specific social conditions will vary. Even the insider-outsider tension attacked by Pakir is recognisably a struggle over access to the same broad agenda, albeit one which will inevitably shift in response to greater equalisation of access.

To a considerable extent, Pakir and Makoni & Meinhof are complaining about power relations in the world, and describe a situation shared with other social sciences, and with scholarship generally. Many Europeans too will respond to some of the senses of exclusion that they describe, and Grabe is able to take for granted the presence of many non-American scholars within his North American overview precisely because of the economic strength of research and scholarship in the USA and Canada. To a lesser extent, UK, Australia and New Zealand are all implicated in this easy internationalisation also, for they benefit from a substantial educational trade that supports courses in applied linguistics and is greatly fuelled by the English language.

But there are a number of features shared by these papers that reflect less on power relations than on our own practices within the profession. There is a lack of cross-geographical perspective in the papers, no doubt partly an inevitable result of the regional remit that was given. Yet many, perhaps all, of the problems are shared by some people in all the regions (for example practitioners being ignored or marginalised), and by many people in some other regions (for example centre versus periphery concerns). Again, it is striking that the very concrete empirical work with which the academic journals are filled is little discussed in relation to the larger ideological issues that are raised. Yet, because of detailed analysis, we are far more aware now than we were thirty years ago of the relationships between language variation, identity, power, ideology, learning, and literacy, for example. Most if not all the issues we have studied in context are more complex than they were thought to be. But teachers still have to teach, administrators to make decisions, politicians to allocate resources, planners to distinguish efficient from less efficient policies. In between the data-scholars in the journals, and the macro-commentators in AILA is a whole layer of people trying to make useful generalisations from complex evidence for particular law-courts and hospitals, schools and publishing houses, funding agencies and ministries. Their work is often reported locally or not at all, but they represent the interface between scholarship and practice, and the transfer of perceived good practice from one place to another can only be helpful.

So what could AILA do to improve the situation? My tone will already have conveyed that I do not think that we alone can redress the balance between the wealthy university-and-researcher-rich countries and those less privileged. We can work for greater equality politically and economically, but that is a long project and our colleagues will not primarily be applied linguists. But applied linguists can do a number of useful things. We can, for example, ensure that there is regular reporting of major scholarship in languages that do not have widespread currency. Pakir draws attention several times to 'mainstream' journals not reviewing major applied linguistic work in (for example) Japanese. The Cambridge abstracting journal *Language Teaching* has recently started publishing survey articles of work in languages other than English. Could not this practice be made more frequent and more widespread? Perhaps we have to acknowledge that most scholars will be working through English, rather than constantly exhorting them to multilingualism, and adjust our mediation practices accordingly. Can we also perhaps have regular bibliographies *quality-controlled by local scholars* of the two or three most interesting works in any one year from as many countries as possible published through Newsletters, or even in the *AILA Review*? Outsiders do not want a mass of material, but they will find insider-selected outstanding work immensely helpful in expanding their range of knowledge. We are now in a position where in all language groups there are scholars with near-native-speaker English who can act as intellectual go-betweens, so there is no excuse why every applied linguist in the world should not have at least second-hand access to non-English work through indirect contacts with English-speaking local scholars.

This is not a long way from what AILA has always tried to facilitate of course: a wealth of local, contextualised activity regularly in touch with practitioners of similar work elsewhere. But the knowledge explosion means that we are all, every one of us, unable to keep up with everything that is going on, even in our own fields. Consequently, carefully selected examples of important work from sources that do not have an easy outlet (whether because of language, or geographical and political situation) need to be provided to ensure that all applied linguists have a two-way connection with work that — by definition — must challenge the assumptions of the complacent.

References

Brumfit, C J 2001, *Individual Freedom in Language Teaching*. Oxford: Oxford University Press

Corder, S P 1973, *Introducing Applied Linguistics*. Harmondsworth: Penguin

Crystal, D 1981, *Directions in Applied Linguistics*. London: Academic Press

Kaplan, R B & Widdowson, H G 1992, 'Applied linguistics' in W Bright (ed.) *International Encyclopedia of Linguistics*, Vol.1. New York: Oxford University Press: 76

Pennycook, A 1994, *The Cultural Politics of English as an International Language*. Harlow: Longman

Suleiman, Yasir 2003, *The Arabic Language and National Identity*. Edinburgh: Edinburgh University Press

Widdowson, H G 1979, *Explorations in Applied Linguistics*. Oxford: Oxford University Press

Author's address

Christopher Brumfit
Applied Language Research Centre
School of Humanities
University of Southampton, UK

New and Recent Paperbacks

The Acquisition of Spanish

Morphosyntactic development in monolingual and bilingual L1 acquisition and adult L2 acquisition

Silvina A. Montrul

[Language Acquisition and Language Disorders, 37] 2004. xv, 400 pp. + index

Hb 90 272 5296 3 EUR 125.00 1 58811 604 2 USD 150.00

Pb 90 272 5297 1 EUR 42.00 1 58811 605 0 USD 49.95

Expected Winter 04-05

"This is well written and is generally well informed, compendious, comprehensive and well referenced and, for this reason alone, worth publishing as a useful account of generative research done into the acquisition of Spanish."

Andrew Radford, *University of Essex*

Examination copy upon request

How to Use Corpora in Language Teaching

Edited by John McH. Sinclair

This book is intensely practical, written mainly by a new generation of language teachers who are acknowledged experts in central aspects of the discipline. It offers advice on what to do in the classroom, how to cope with teachers' queries about language, what corpora to use including learner corpora and spoken corpora and how to handle the variability of language.

Contributions by: Michael Barlow; Silvia Bernardini; Susan Conrad; Pernilla Danielsson; Anna Mauranen; Nadja Nesselhauf; Luísa Alice Santos Pereira; Pascual Pérez-Paredes; Ute Römer; John McH. Sinclair; Gyula Tankó; Amy B.M. Tsui.

[Studies in Corpus Linguistics, 12] 2004. viii, 308 pp.

Hb 90 272 2282 7 EUR 95.00 1 58811 490 2 USD 114.00

Pb 90 272 2283 5 EUR 36.00 1 58811 491 0 USD 42.95

Examination copy upon request

Multiple Voices in the Translation Classroom

Activities, tasks and projects

Maria González Davies

Provides teaching ideas that can be adapted to different learning environments and that can be used with different language combinations. This volume will be of interest to translation teachers, to foreign language teachers who wish to include translation in their classes, to graduates and professional translators interested in becoming teachers, and also to administrators exploring the possibility of starting a new translation programme.

[Benjamins Translation Library, 54] 2004. x, 262 pp.

Hb 90 272 1660 6 EUR 125.00 1 58811 527 5 USD 150.00

Pb 90 272 1661 4 EUR 36.00 1 58811 547 X USD 42.95

Examination copy upon request

For full title information see **www.benjamins.com/jbp**

Theory Construction in Second Language Acquisition

Geoff Jordan

[Language Learning & Language Teaching, 8] 2004. xviii, 295 pp.
Hb 90 272 1705 X EUR 98.00 / 1 58811 481 3 USD 118.00
Pb 90 272 1706 8 EUR 36.00 / 1 58811 482 1 USD 42.95

"Overall, Jordan offers a very knowledgeable and well-written account of theory construction in general and theorising in the field of second language research in particular, which should be of interest to virtually everyone in the diverse SLA community, from postgraduate students to senior scholars. "
Karen Roehr, *Lancaster University* on Linguist List 15.1864, 2004

Formulaic Sequences

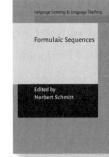

Acquisition, processing and use
Edited by Norbert Schmitt

This volume opens new directions in FS research, concentrating on how FS are acquired and processed by the mind, both in the L1 and L2. The studies use a wide range of methodologies, many of them innovative, and thus the volume serves as a model for future research in the area.

[Language Learning & Language Teaching, 9] 2004. x, 304 pp.
Hb 90 272 1707 6 EUR 98.00 / 1 58811 499 6 USD 118.00
Pb 90 272 1708 4 EUR 36.00 / 1 58811 500 3 USD 42.95

Vocabulary in a Second Language

Selection, acquisition, and testing
Edited by Paul Bogaards and Batia Laufer

This book is intended as an up-to-date overview of the important domain of the lexicon for researchers in the field of second language acquisition, teacher trainers and professional teachers of second or foreign languages.

[Language Learning & Language Teaching, 10] 2004. xiv, 234 pp.
Hb 90 272 1709 2 EUR 105.00 / 1 58811 540 2 USD 126.00
Pb 90 272 1710 6 EUR 36.00 / 1 58811 541 0 USD 42.95

Pedagogical Norms for Second and Foreign Language Learning and Teaching

Edited by **Susan M. Gass, Kathleen Bardovi-Harlig, Sally Sieloff Magnan and Joel Walz**

Language Learning & Language Teaching, 5] 2002. vi, 305 pp.
Hb 90 272 1699 1 EUR 90.00 / 1 58811 261 6 USD 108.00
Pb 90 272 1700 9 EUR 33.00 / 1 58811 262 4 USD 39.95

"The present volume is a valuable contribution to our understanding of one of the major concepts in language pedagogy and will no doubt become an indispensable reference tool for researchers and practitioners in the fields of applied and educational linguistics."
Svetlana **Kurtes**, *University of Cambridge*, on Linguist List 14.66, 2003

Computer Learner Corpora, Second Language Acquisition and Foreign Language Teaching

Edited by **Sylviane Granger, Joseph Hung and Stephanie Petch-Tyson**

This book takes stock of current research into computer learner corpora conducted both by ELT and SLA specialists and aims to give practical insight to researchers who may be considering compiling a corpus of learner data or embarking on learner corpus research.

Language Learning & Language Teaching, 6] 2002. x, 246 pp.
Hb 90 272 1701 7 EUR 80.00 / 1 58811 293 4 USD 96.00
Pb 90 272 1702 5 EUR 36.00 / 1 58811 294 2 USD 42.95

English Language Learning and Technology

Carol A. Chapelle
Iowa State University

Language Learning & Language Teaching, 7] 2003. xvi, 213 pp.
Hb 90 272 1703 3 EUR 95.00 / 1 58811 447 3 USD 114.00
Pb 90 272 1704 1 EUR 33.00 / 1 58811 448 1 USD 39.95

The text is invaluable as a literature review, research guide, and source of discussion."
Jonathon **Reinhardt**, *Penn State University* on Linguist List 15.1971, 2004

New edition

Introduction to Discourse Studies

Jan Renkema

Introduction to Discourse Studies follows on Jan Renkema's
successful *Discourse Studies: An Introductory Textbook* (1993),
published in four languages. This new book deals with even
more key concepts in discourse studies and approaches major
issues in this field from the Anglo-American and European as
well as the Australian traditions. It provides a 'scientific toolkit'
for future courses on discourse studies and serves as a stepping
stone to the independent study of professional literature.

2004. x, 363 pp.
Hb   90 272 2610 5   EUR 115.00 / 1 58811 529 1   USD 138.00
Pb   90 272 3221 0   EUR 36.00 / 1 58811 530 5   USD 42.95

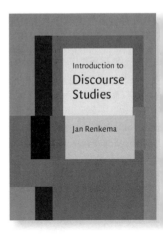

Table of contents

"This is the book we have all
been waiting for: an excellent
and comprehensive, very well
written, theoretically innovative overview of and introduction to Discourse Studies,
much needed in Linguistics,
Cultural Studies and in the
Social Sciences. It appeals to
students as well as to scholars
in many disciplines. For any-
body concerned with the analysis of texts and discourses,
this book is a 'must-read'."
Ruth Wodak, Prof. of Discourse
Studies (Vienna/Lancaster)

Access to on-line full-text subscriptions

John Benjamins Publishing Company's journals are available in on-line full-text format to regular subscribers as of each volume starting from the year 2000. Some of our journals have additional (non-print) information available through this medium that is referred to in the articles.

Registration with *ingentaJournals* is included in your regular subscription. If you do not subscribe, we offer a pay-per-view service per article.

Full text is provided in PDF. In order to read these documents you will need Adobe Acrobat Reader which is freely available from
http://www.adobe.com/products/acrobat/readermain.html

How to register

www.ingenta.com/isis/register/ChooseRegistration/ingenta

To register, *Ingenta* will ask for your subscription or client number. This number appears on your invoice and on the address label on your printed copy.

Institutional subscribers can take advantage of Direct Access allowing your users to log in from a registered location without having to register username and password each time.

Subscriptions through your agent: If your agent provides Benjamins with your address data, you can register as described above with your Benjamins client number. When your registration has been processed, you can access *Ingenta* directly or via your agent's gateway.

Private subscribers have access to the on-line service and will be provided with an individual username and password by *Ingenta* when registering with their client number.

Ingenta offers a full range of electronic journal services such as direct links to your subscribed journals and new-publication alerts.

Further information is available on

www.ingenta.com and
www.benjamins.com/jbp/journals/e_instruct.html